RACING POST
ANNUAL 2026

Racing Post Floor 7, The Podium, South Bank Tower Estate, 30 Stamford Street, London, SE1 9LS. 0203 034 8900

Editor Nick Pulford
Art editor David Dew
Cover design Duncan Olner
Chief photographers Edward Whitaker, Patrick McCann
Other photography Mark Cranham, Getty, John Grossick, Caroline Norris
Picture artworking Stefan Searle
Feature writers Scott Burton, Andrew Dietz, Richard Forristal, Jack Haynes, David Jennings, Catherine Macrae, James Milton, Lee Mottershead, Lewis Porteous, Nick Pulford, John Randall, Peter Thomas
Reporters David Carr, Steve Dennis, Conor Fennelly, Jonathan Harding, Sam Hendry, Rodney Masters, David Milnes, Julian Muscat, Justin O'Hanlon, Tom Peacock, Maddy Playle, Matt Rennie

Dialogue Content Marketing Ltd
Advertising Sales
Gary Millone, 07775 037559, gary.millone@dialogue.agency

1st floor, Fuel studios, Kiln House Pottergate, Norwich NR2 1DX
dialogue.agency

Distribution/availability
01933 304858 help@racingpost.com

Published by Pitch Publishing on behalf of Racing Post, 9 Donnington Park, 85 Birdham Road, Chichester, West Sussex, PO20 7AJ

© 2025, Pitch Publishing and Racing Post

A CIP catalogue record is available for this book from the British Library.
ISBN 978-1801509701

Printed in Great Britain by Short Run Press.

racingpost.com/shop

ONCE again it is a pleasure and a privilege to Annual, now in its 15th year. We really hop these 208 pages.

It is endlessly interesting to see those pages to a vivid portrait of the racing year, coloured in week after week by incredible feats on the track. Each year provides more than enough stories of brilliance, drama, happiness and heartache to project the most positive image of what a great sport horseracing is.

For brilliance you could read about Inothewayurthinkin, the new king of steeplechasing, or the sensational exploits of middle-distance Flat champion Calandagan. Or about any of the new stars who came out to captivate us, from Ombudsman to Haiti Couleurs and many more.

For drama it would be hard to beat Golden Ace's 25-1 upset in the Champion Hurdle or pacemaker Qirat's stealing of the Sussex Stakes at 150-1.

For happiness there was the raw emotion of Nick Rockett's Grand National triumph for the father-and-son team of Willie and Patrick Mullins. Put aside that the result emphasised their Closutton stable's overwhelming strength, this was really all about family.

For heartache exhibit A might be Minnie Hauk's gallant defeat by Daryz in the Prix de l'Arc de Triomphe. She almost had Paris, but not quite.

Tragically, this racing year also brought heartbreak of the very worst kind. Michael O'Sullivan's death, at the age of 24, following a fall at Thurles in February was a stark reminder of the risks that our heroes in the saddle take in pursuit of the sport that they, and we, love so much.

★★★★

THE stories of the year are strikingly told by our excellent team of writers, accompanied by a stunning selection of photographs taken principally by Edward Whitaker and Patrick McCann.

Ireland editor Richard Forristal delves deep into what Aintree glory meant to the Mullins family, France correspondent Scott Burton charts Daryz's remarkable journey to Arc glory and David Jennings takes us back to the poignancy of Marine Nationale's Queen Mother Champion Chase.

There is much more besides. The retirement of Rachael Blackmore after one last blast at Cheltenham, the positivity of National Racehorse Week and great interviews with Hayley Turner and Derek Thompson.

We know that this is a much-loved book and we are appreciative of that. But it is only the book it is because of this much-loved sport. We should all be appreciative of that.

Nick Pulford

Nick Pulford Editor

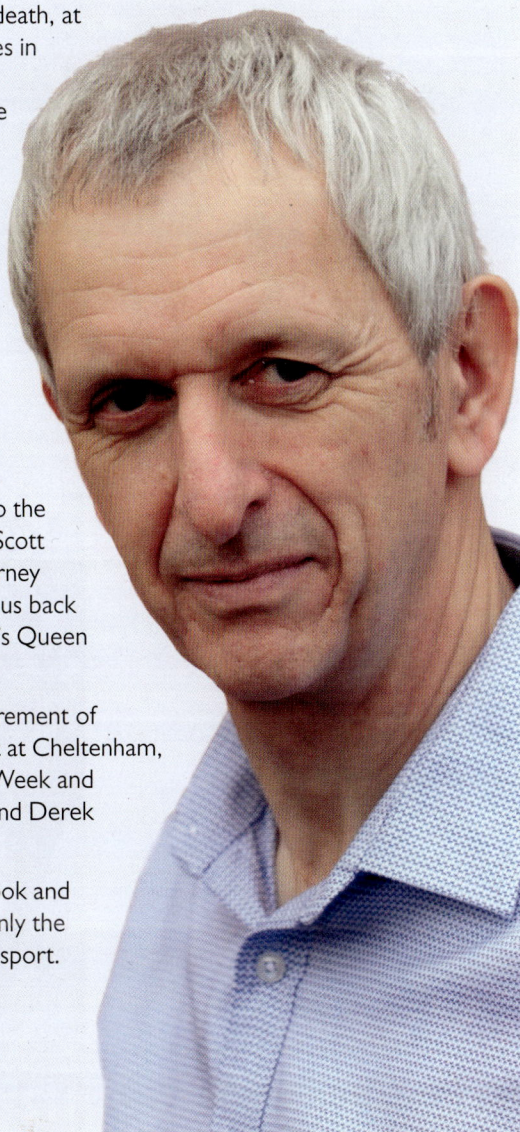

CONTENTS

BIG STORIES

106

182

76

86

128

146

ROCKETT POWER

▼Pure emotion: Patrick and Willie Mullins celebrate their Grand National triumph with Nick Rockett, pictured right jumping the water at the end of the first circuit

Willie Mullins landed another Grand National, and an unprecedented 1-2-3 to boot, but this was all about family and overwhelming emotion as son Patrick triumphed on Nick Rockett

By Richard Forristal
Ireland editor

THE 2025 Grand National in many ways reaffirmed the extent to which the race and the game have changed. Viewed through that prism, it was easy to see how the latest edition might have validated critics' fears that jump racing's marquee event was condemned to lose its distinctive lustre.

Less of a challenge for the horses and more focused on quality, they might say. It was a second victory in a row for Willie Mullins, the sport's single most dominant trainer in an era of superpowers, and a third in four years for his family. The preserve of the elite, the critics could lament.

This time, Nick Rockett thwarted the returning hero I Am Maximus and Grangeclare West to yield an unprecedented 1-2-3 for the Closutton wizard, who ended up with five of the first seven home, having been responsible for each of the first five as the field crossed the final fence.

Eight of the first nine were Irish-trained and Nick Rockett was the highest-rated winner since at least 1988. The first three were all among the top four in the weights and there were fewer than a handful of fallers once again as the now familiar sight of a barrage of horses swung for home across the Anchor Bridge crossing on the Melling Road with the dream still alive to some extent or another.

Predictable? Sterile? Lacking in anything that might resemble a fairytale narrative or be a catalyst for the sort of overwhelming emotion that rendered the great race such a romantic phenomenon? The cynics might have had a field day.

Alas, that would be to reckon without the inscrutable, chimerical and enduring magic of Aintree. No matter how much the race has changed, it still means everything.

Mullins has done it all at least once but at his core he is a horseman and a family man, and he had never shared with his son such a powerfully poignant moment as winning the Grand National. Patrick Mullins has

▶ Continues page 6

PRINCESS ROYAL STAND

ridden the wave of his father's success to become the most decorated amateur rider in history, yet uniting to scale the one peak that still resonates far beyond racing's own confines mattered more than either of them imagined.

That raw, unadulterated outpouring of elation made the 2025 National like no other. Even the most hardened, tired malcontents were touched by the extent to which the triumph of Nick Rockett reduced Willie Mullins to an emotional wreck.

Here was a man who had built an empire on the foundations of ruthless pragmatism, transforming perceptions of National Hunt racing as a woolly sporting pursuit to aggressively pursue a more commercial growth model that culminated in an all-conquering enterprise that has smashed records at will. The CEO of a supremely well-oiled franchise, Mullins has never been too susceptible to public displays of affection. But family matters.

It was writ large all over the front page of the Racing Post the day after the National, same as it was on so many other newspapers and websites. Mullins and his wife Jackie, united with their only child in the elation of the moment, having recently become grandparents for the first time, were powerless to resist the onslaught of such homegrown euphoria.

"To win the National is one thing, but to be able to leg your son up and for him to ride the winner is off the charts," Mullins said, 20 years after Ruby Walsh caressed Hedgehunter around Aintree to become the stable's first National winner. "It's incredible, and, for me . . ." he continued, before struggling to get the words out, which he eventually did in hushed tones. ". . . it brings back memories. My mother wasn't here this year . . .

"I don't think anything can be better than this. It's huge. Now I know how Ted Walsh felt when Ruby won it for him. To win it as a trainer is wonderful but what a special day for Patrick. I just can't comprehend it or take it in."

★★★★

FOR PATRICK, this was a glorious realisation of his wildest dreams. In the weeks preceding the Grand National, Nick Rockett was the one he had pinned his hopes on partnering. Paul Townend was always going to be drawn to I Am Maximus, Brian Hayes had a relationship with Grangeclare West, as did Danny Mullins with both Minella Cocooner and Meetingofthewaters, electing to go with the latter in the end.

The case for Nick Rockett was strong. He was an experienced staying chaser who had been third in the previous season's bet365 Gold Cup and had seized two of the proven National trials in the new year. He dominated the Thyestes Chase at Gowran Park when the choice of Townend and sent off joint-favourite off a handicap rating of 152. Then, after being allocated a National mark of 163 for 11st 8lb, he thwarted the reigning Irish Grand National winner Intense Raffles in the Bobbyjo at Fairyhouse.

What was not to like? Well, at

▲ Home run: Nick Rockett leads the 1-2-3 ahead of I Am Maximus and Grangeclare West (red); below, Patrick Mullins celebrates with groom Katie Walton and with his father

Aintree he was 15lb worse off with Intense Raffles, he had a hefty enough weight for a horse described as small by his rider and he wasn't going to get the very soft ground he relished. Maybe there was also a sense that he had already had his couple of big days, albeit that wasn't the feeling inside the camp.

For them, Nick Rockett was every inch a contender, yet the market didn't want to know him come the day and his price drifted to a 33-1 SP. None of the five other Closutton runners started bigger.

Patrick Mullins certainly didn't ride him like a rank outsider and he never looked like one once the

tapes went up. They had a wobble at Becher's first time but Mullins brought him wider second time around, and the only other moment of concern was at the fence before that on the final lap. Otherwise, the eight-year-old tanked along behind the leading group under a cool and measured ride from an assiduous man who had given an opportunity like this plenty of thought.

They joined issue with Minella Cocooner, Grangeclare West and Bravemansgame as they crossed the second-last, with Townend also trying to get I Am Maximus into the conversation around the outside. Mullins, though, was visibly travelling best of all.

He held on to Nick Rockett down to the final fence and they led I Am Maximus over the last by a whisker. At that stage, he had to press go, and from there, beyond the Elbow and all the way to immortality, his game mount was holding the returning champ. I Am Maximus emerged with immense credit to be denied by just two and a half lengths under 11st 12lb, with Grangeclare West half a length further behind.

★★★★

IT WAS the defining moment of a wonderful career for the winning rider, who was able to eloquently put into words the sentiments with which his father had struggled. For a man drowning in ecstasy, he cut a pretty composed figure.

"It's everything I dreamed of since I was a kid and it's all downhill from here," said the 35-year-old rider, who was the second amateur to win the race in four runnings following Sam Waley-Cohen's triumph on Mullins' cousin Emmet's Noble Yeats in 2022.

"When I was five I used to read books about the race and Red Rum. To put my name there is incredibly special. He's a brilliant horse, not very big, but so brave. I always thought I had a great chance."

Elaborating on the run, he said: "We got too good a start and we were too handy. He was jumping brilliantly but I was taking him back everywhere. At the Canal Turn second time I was wondering if I'd dropped back too far but then once I asked him to make up ground he got there easily and I was going to get there too soon. I had that in mind when we got to the last, so I was bopping around until we got to the Elbow and then I said to myself 'I'm going to go, I'm going to enjoy this'."

On the intensity of the aftermath, he added: "My father has given me so much, and we wouldn't be the type of father and son who would say it to one another, but obviously I owe him everything, so I hope he and my mother got as big of a kick out of it as I did."

Asked about the way in which the triumph had affected his father, Mullins said: "That caught me by surprise as much as anyone else. Seeing him like that made me emotional as well."

▶Continues page 8

'Winning this one has been tougher. The feeling is relief'

WILLIE MULLINS' domination of the Grand National propelled him to a second British jump trainers' championship in a row in another phenomenal season for his all-conquering Closutton stable.

Seven days after Nick Rockett's triumph, Mullins took the Scottish Grand National with Captain Cody (and had runner-up Klarc Kent) – it was his second consecutive double in the Aintree and Ayr marathons. Dan Skelton had been 1-10 to take the title going into Aintree; Mullins was 1-6 coming out of Ayr just over a week later.

Skelton still led going into the final day of the season at Sandown on April 26 but Mullins powered past his British rival to win by £193,867, helped hugely by Il Etait Temps's victory in the Celebration Chase and by saddling the second, third, fourth and fifth in the bet365 Gold Cup. Mullins, who took the lead for the very first time in the season just after 3pm on the final day, amassed total prize-money of £3,570,991 – an increase of almost £250,000 from his previous win.

"The feeling is relief," said Mullins after lifting the trophy. "It was tough work the last few weeks and I feel sorry for Dan, who was leading the whole way. We had a fantastic last few months and, when it became a possibility, we went for it. They had to run out of their skins for us to win. Probably the first time you win is sweeter but this has been tougher."

Seven days after Sandown, Mullins was crowned Irish champion for an incredible 19th time with another dominant win by more than €2m. "It was a lot less stressful today than last Saturday anyway," he said on the final day at Punchestown.

Stable jockey Paul Townend took his seventh Irish championship and Patrick Mullins was champion amateur for the 17th time. Townend's sister Jody was champion lady rider for the fifth year in a row.

Mullins was leading trainer at the Cheltenham Festival for the seventh year in a row, equalling the record of ten winners he set in 2022. It was his 12th leading trainer award in all and his total of festival winners now stands at 113.

He also dominated the Irish Racing Festival with seven winners and the Punchestown festival with 15 winners.

In the end-of-season Anglo-Irish Jumps Classifications, Mullins had the top-rated chaser and hurdler again with the same duo of Galopin Des Champs (although he was joint-champion this time with Inothewayurthinkin) and State Man. Ryanair Chase winner Fact To File was the clear winner in the middle-distance chase division and Majborough was the leading novice chaser.

★★★★

MULLINS snr was entitled to be overcome by such a heart-rending affair, and his candid response might also have been infused by the background context. Nick Rockett came into his orbit following a chance encounter with Sadie Andrew, an old friend with whom he had made his first holy communion many years earlier.

Sadie moved to the UK and married Stewart Andrew, whose colours had previously been carried to big-race glory by Ever Blessed in the 1999 Hennessy Gold Cup. Mullins sourced Nick Rockett out of Pat Doyle's yard, but Sadie saw him race just once, when he finished fourth in a Fairyhouse bumper in December 2022. Five days later she died, mere weeks after being diagnosed with terminal cancer.

The horse, and a bond formed with Mullins in the wake of her death, would prove a source of tremendous solace for Stewart. Mullins invited him to Australia to watch Absurde and Vauban run in the Melbourne Cup, and it was there the plan was hatched over a cheap bottle of wine.

"We ended up in a restaurant at 2am in Melbourne," said Stewart. "We knew it was a classy joint because the wine list had the choice of red or white. Willie said the plan was to win the Thyestes, the Bobbyjo and then we'll go to Aintree. What can you say about him, he's a gentleman.

"Nick Rockett was my wife's horse – she wanted to have one in training with Willie. Everybody seemed to have written him off in the National. He drifted in the betting and they all told me why he couldn't win but he won the best two trials in Ireland easily, including the Thyestes, which he won by a distance giving weight away. This is a class horse with the heart of a lion."

★★★★

FOR Mullins, the victory, rinsed with such deep meaning, knocked him sideways.

It also meant he was back in contention for the trainers' title. From an even more hopeless position than had been the case the previous season, the defence of his championship was again launched in a whirlwind on the Thursday of Aintree. At that point he had been £1.3 million behind, but taking £860,000 out of the National's £1m purse helped to reduce Dan Skelton's pre-Aintree lead to just £122,026 by the Saturday evening.

A prospect that many saw as wholly improbable on Thursday morning was almost inevitable three days later. Skelton would improve his total haul by nearly £400,000, beating Mullins' winning tally from 2023-24 by more than £50,000, but it still wasn't enough to withstand the onslaught.

"To sire the winning rider, to train the winner and to have Jackie here," Mullins mused. "We planned this with Stewart Andrew over A$10 bottles of wine in Australia. All great plans come together. I went to school with Sadie years ago. I met her years later at the sales and we went for a cup of tea. I said I'd buy a horse for her and here we are.

"I just couldn't believe it," he added. "I thought somewhere around the second-last that this could happen, but then I saw Paul coming alive [on I Am Maximus]. Then I just kept breathing, hoping he wouldn't make a mistake at the last. Then I thought coming up to the Elbow that maybe Paul was going to outstay him. Then next, I couldn't believe it."

That sense of incredulity echoed far and wide. Jackie, who managed to maintain her trademark elegant composure, captured the essence of it all for the Mullins clan.

"It's such an amazing day," she said. "Patrick always wanted to win a Grade 1 in England against the professionals and he did that [on Gaelic Warrior] on Thursday, and now for him to win the National as well . . . amazing."

'Don't take it away from me'

Patrick Mullins gives the inside view of the start and finish of the greatest race of his life

"IT DOESN'T get any better than this," I say to Katie Walton as we turn out of the parade ring with Nick Rockett for the Grand National. We head out under the stands. It's loud. It's hot. It's claustrophobic.

Bravemansgame plants himself. We're stuck. The horse won't go out. He swings left, he swings right. The bottleneck grows behind us and Nick Rockett is starting to get anxious at the wait. I tell Katie to let go and I squeeze on by. Running into trouble before the start even.

I canter down and look at the first, head back and get my girth checked. Turn and look for the field. Most people are already there. I want to be somewhere in the middle but it looks packed tight. I wait until the line starts the turn and needle in beside Brian Hayes on Grangeclare West. He gives me a nod.

The starter is calling us in. We're walking. We're jig-jogging. One or two break into a canter but get back. The line bulges. It goes taut. We're on the tape. "Away you go!"

Nick Rockett is like a cork out of a bottle. I've got daylight all around me. The outside of the line is slightly ahead and coming in. I don't want to go down to the first with no company or no lead, so I sit slightly against the reins and the daylight gets filled by horses without being eclipsed.

We rush toward the first. At this speed you have to go forward. We meet it long and take it well. Breathe.

★★★★

I TAKE a fresh hold of the reins and keep our powder dry. Let them come to us. Green and gold appear on my outside. The last fence stretches all across my vision. Give me a stride, give me a stride. It appears, safe rather than dicey. Squeeze with my legs, hold with my hands. Nick barely breaks stride over it. The horse on my outer has disappeared again.

"Sit up" flashes across my mind but I dismiss it. My mother always told me, there's a time to go. A time when checking the momentum breaks it. I bop away, asking without demanding. There's nothing but a green field ahead of us. No rail or fence to guide us. I fixate on the Elbow. I feel Nick start to idle. The dream starts to shimmer.

The horse on my outer appears again. Green and gold, McManus silks. Nick picks up with him. The shimmer solidifies. We've still got a chance.

I try to keep straight and tight to the Elbow, not to let something up my inside. I hear ". . . Meetingofthewaters . . ." from the commentator but I think it's I Am Maximus beside me. He's level with us again but he hasn't passed us. He hasn't passed us. The shimmer is still there.

Finally, we're at the Elbow. I pull my stick. Head down, I push, I squeeze, I growl, I will. One. Two. Three. I look up for the line. It's not close. My breaths are getting shorter and faster; ". . . on the wide outside . . ." breaks through my hearing. I hate the run-in like a drowning man hates the sea. Four. Five. Six. I look up again. Closer. Closer.

I'm looking for a shadow, and I'm waiting for Nemesis to arrive and it doesn't. Seven. No more bullets to fire. Don't take it away from me. Not now. Push. Squeeze. Pant. Will. We cross the line in front and . . . and . . . And I smile. I might never stop.

These are edited excerpts from an article that appeared in the Racing Post on April 9

RACING RUNS IN US

Horse racing is embedded in culture and communities all over Ireland.
Even if we don't realise it, we're all connected to it.

HORSE
RACING
IRELAND

▶Victory salute: Mark Walsh passes the post on Inothewayurthinkin in the Cheltenham Gold Cup; right, groom Caoimhe O'Brien joins the celebrations with the new king of chasing

KNOCKOUT BLOW

Inothewayurthinkin proved himself the new force in chasing's heavyweight division with his Cheltenham Gold Cup victory over the reigning champ

By Richard Forristal

THE saying goes that history is written by the winners but oftentimes the vanquished do far more than might be credited for embellishing a particular legacy.

That much is surely true of the 2025 Cheltenham Gold Cup. A race won by Inothewayurthinkin, it was an epoch-defining event that lived up to its billing as a spectacle if not the pre-ordained script surrounding it.

Galopin Des Champs arrived in the Cotswolds on the cusp of something truly special. He was a dual Gold Cup winner whose body of work was simply irrefutable. A three-time Cheltenham Festival victor, a ten-time Grade 1 winner over fences and already a three-time Irish Gold Cup hero.

Willie Mullins' dark destroyer had been given every opportunity to stake a claim to be spoken of in the pantheon of chasing greats, and he did all that. Mullins had been here just four years earlier but Al

▶Continues page 12

Boum Photo will never be revered in nearly the same fashion. He was trained to peak once a year in March.

In the context of a modern staying chaser, Galopin Des Champs has been campaigned with abandon and demonstrated a steadfast resolution to match his redolent class, a trait that reveals itself in his high cruising speed and cat-like jumping.

Greg and Audrey Turley's son of Timos has his vulnerabilities, as was evidenced by four successive defeats at Punchestown, but his capacity to bounce back speaks volumes of his constitution.

Beaten once more in the John Durkan Memorial Chase on his seasonal return, he duly exacted revenge on stablemate Fact To File in the Savills Chase before returning to Leopardstown for a truly superior demonstration in the Irish Gold Cup.

That filleting was enough for JP McManus to abandon Fact To File's Gold Cup aspirations, yet the beaten challenger nonetheless went on to confirm his enormous talent when demolishing his Ryanair Chase opposition at Cheltenham in March. It looked the most positive of omens ahead of Galopin Des Champs' attempt to carve his image into steeplechasing's equivalent of Mount Rushmore alongside Golden Miller, Cottage Rake, Arkle and Best Mate.

★★★★

McMANUS, though, would have his say yet. It wasn't that he had abandoned all hope of beating Galopin Des Champs by diverting Fact To File, more that he realised he had to try something different. In Gavin Cromwell, he had a willing ally, for both men believed in Inothewayurthinkin's latent ability and between them they conspired to bring him to the most exquisitely well-timed crescendo for

▲Crowning glory: Inothewayurthinkin jumps the final fence in front of reigning champion Galopin Des Champs; inset, winning rider Mark Walsh is congratulated by Paul Townend; below, Walsh cherishes his golden moment

the Friday of the festival.

A brother to their previous year's Mares' Chase winner Limerick Lace, he had hinted at his enormous potential as a novice when he improved dramatically for the step up in trip and soft ground to bolt up in the 2024 Kim Muir Handicap Chase under Derek O'Connor. A handicap mark of 145, achieved over distances short of his optimum, helped on that occasion.

However, he then went to Aintree and thumped some decent horses to dance home under Mark Walsh in the Grade 1 Mildmay Novices' Chase. He looked every inch a Gold Cup candidate at that point, but Fact To File was in the vanguard of McManus's team of precocious second-season chasers when the autumn came around.

Cromwell pitched Inothewayurthinkin into each of the same three Grade 1s in which Fact To File and Galopin Des Champs traded those early blows, but his contender was clearly still learning and screws were still to be tightened. The facts are he was beaten 36 lengths in the John Durkan, 15 and a half lengths in

▶Continues page 14

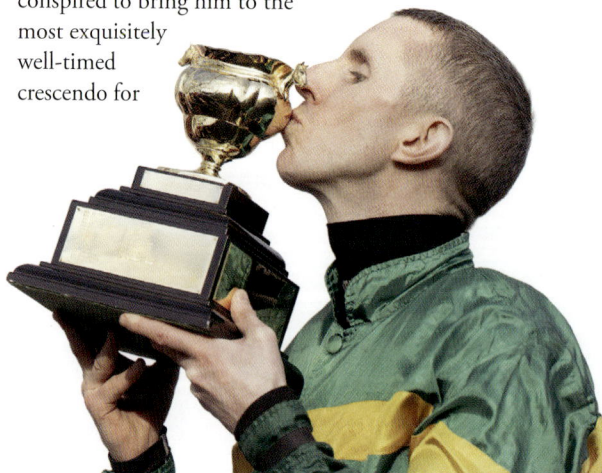

the Savills and an eye-catching seven and a quarter lengths in the Irish Gold Cup. He was getting the hang of things.

Maybe more pertinently, such was the nature of his progress that he hadn't been embroiled in hard races. As Galopin Des Champs and Fact To File softened each other up, Keith Donoghue elected for the kid-glove treatment on Inothewayurthinkin, which is quite the luxury.

Their outing in the Irish Gold Cup was particularly encouraging. Donoghue gave him one slap behind the saddle after turning in but the race had developed in front of them at that stage. Inothewayurthinkin kept finding, though, and weaved his way between horses to be a staying-on fourth.

The seven-year-old had previously been entered in the Gold Cup only to be taken out earlier in the season, but circumstances were starting to overtake him. McManus and Cromwell were of like mind and he was supplemented for the sport's marquee steeplechase at a cost of £25,000.

The long-term ante-post favourite for the Grand National suddenly had his priorities rearranged. "I think he has a chance of winning it," McManus said of the decision in a pre-Cheltenham interview with the Racing Post. "I wouldn't be running him for fun as he's very well handicapped in the National and favourite for the race."

★★★★

IT PROVED to be a thoroughly inspired intervention. Walsh, McManus's first jockey, was back on board in the Gold Cup for the first time since the Mildmay. He settled Inothewayurthinkin on or near the inside from the get-go and, although the 15-2 shot nudged the first fence, for the most part he found a lovely rhythm.

In contrast, on ground better than he might relish, Galopin Des Champs rarely looked to be

travelling or jumping with his usual zest for Paul Townend. The 8-13 favourite reached for the second ditch as they made the sweeping ascent out of the back straight for the first time and he wasn't getting through the air with all of his trademark efficiency.

Then Ahoy Senor crashed out at the ditch down the back for the final time, hampering Monty's Star, who in turn broadsided Galopin Des Champs. Townend quickly got him back on an even keel, but it was hardly ideal. Nevertheless, as Gentlemansgame and The Real Whacker took them along, he had a couple of lengths on Inothewayurthinkin down the inner.

Walsh was keeping a close eye on Townend just outside him and he switched out to track his move as they swung down the hill towards the fourth-last, which Inothewayurthinkin rubbed. He never missed a beat, though, and from there Walsh's main concern was getting the split he needed between Corbetts Cross in the second McManus silks and Monty's Star. He was travelling well enough to bustle his way through, allowing him to continue to mark Townend's every move as the roar cascaded down from an expectant crowd in the grandstand.

Galopin Des Champs took Gentlemansgame as they straightened up for the second-last and for a fleeting moment it looked like immortality beckoned. It wasn't to be.

Walsh squeezed Inothewayurthinkin up alongside on touching down after two out, led over the last and such was his superiority on the day there wasn't ever really a skirmish. From the final fence to the line, the challenger put six lengths between himself and the outgoing champion.

To the runner-up's credit, there was a yawning 12 lengths back to Gentlemansgame in third. Nothing else could still get close

▸Continues page 16

Chaser of the season

INOTHEWAYURTHINKIN made a huge leap in his Cheltenham Gold Cup victory. He went into the race on a Racing Post Rating of 163 and came out the other side rated nearly a stone and a half higher on 182.

That made him the chaser of the season on RPRs, bettering Galopin Des Champs' 181 for his Savills Chase success in December. The two-time Gold Cup winner was an excellent benchmark for Inothewayurthinkin, of course, and ran to an RPR of 175 in his six-length Cheltenham defeat. His peak rating is 184 in the previous season's Savills Chase and he has twice run to 183.

Inothewayurthinkin and Galopin Des Champs were joint-champions in the chase rankings of the Anglo-Irish Jumps Classifications on a mark of 176. It was the third consecutive season at the top for Galopin Des Champs, who had stood alone on 179 in the previous two campaigns. They were the first joint-leaders since Looks Like Trouble and See More Business in 1999-00 – the first season of the Classifications.

Top-rated chasers 2024-25

RPR	Horse
182	Inothewayurthinkin
181	Galopin Des Champs
177	Fact To File
175	Il Etait Temps, Jonbon
173	Marine Nationale
172	Banbridge, Gaelic Warrior, I Am Maximus, Protektorat

▲Different class: Inothewayurthinkin jumps to an RPR of 182 with his Gold Cup victory

to Mullins' star but, on this day, he had no answer for the younger, fresher heavyweight on the up.

★★★★

FOR Cromwell, who, from humble origins as a farrier, has muscled his way into the elite as a top-four trainer in Ireland, it was another piece de resistance. He had already saddled Espoir D'Allen to a famous Champion Hurdle victory for McManus under Walsh in 2019, so this confirmed his prowess as someone who can deliver with the right material.

"All these trainers, they know more about the horses than I do," McManus said in reference to Cromwell afterwards when asked about the decision to supplement. "You have to trust they're doing the right thing and I have every confidence in Gavin. He's a very special man. You don't hear too often from him – if ever! – but he gets the job done."

Acknowledging the context of what they had achieved, McManus added: "Galopin Des Champs has been a great champion. To beat him, we burst a bubble. I don't get any satisfaction out of that but it's so good to win the race."

In a way, Galopin Des Champs was blindsided by a sucker punch. He had raced at the sharp end three times already before March and maybe Inothewayurthinkin brought fresher legs to the Cotswolds, but the runner-up went a long way toward kiboshing that theory when he laid his Punchestown hoodoo to rest in bombastic style a month later.

That could readily be interpreted as the ultimate compliment to Inothewayurthinkin, and there is absolutely no doubt that Cromwell made for Cheltenham as much in hope as expectation. He knew he was getting one cut at the champion and he didn't miss.

"Galopin Des Champs was a dual Gold Cup winner, but we were coming here to try to win the race – we weren't coming to pick up the pieces," he said afterwards in that typically reticent manner of his. "We thought we'd have a good chance if everything was right."

The County Meath-based trainer's trajectory has been quite something. His earnings graph is on a stark upward curve and he nearly doubled his 2023-24 final domestic yield of €1.3 million when totalling more than €2m in 2024-25 to leapfrog Henry de Bromhead and grab third place in the championship for a first time.

He has a broad band of patrons, but McManus's support has underpinned his ascent. "I first got to know Gavin when we bought Jer's Girl," said Frank Berry, McManus's racing manager. "He's improved every single year since then. He has a lovely, easy way of going about things. He never gets too up or too down. He never gets too disappointed or too excited. He's top class."

Of his nurturing of Inothewayurthinkin, he added: "He has a great patience. He has brought this horse along quietly, getting experience into him and what he has done with [him at Cheltenham] is a credit to him. He has had a few hiccups, it hasn't been completely straightforward, but he's brought him along lovely and hasn't been in any rush."

★★★★

WALSH is cut from similarly unassuming cloth. In many ways, he and Cromwell epitomise McManus's oft-quoted maxim that there would be many more fish in the sea if they would only learn to keep their mouths shut. Retained rider in Ireland for the perennial champion owner, Walsh isn't inclined to play the media game but is never less than pleasant and courteous.

▲ Trophy winners: owner JP McManus receives the Cheltenham Gold Cup from Princess Anne after Inothewayurthinkin's victory; the next day's Racing Post front page; below, winning trainer Gavin Cromwell

For many years, he operated in the shadows of AP McCoy and Barry Geraghty, so this was a moment to savour for him, and McManus wasn't ever likely to be tempted to look elsewhere. Without any fanfare or fuss, that is the status Walsh has earned since succeeding Geraghty on the home-based horses in 2020. He delivers when the chips are down.

"It's brilliant," he said after securing McManus a second Gold Cup following Synchronised's 2012 success. "It's something you dream of when you're a kid wanting to be a jockey, winning the Gold Cup and the Grand National and things like that, so it's a dream come true."

At the time, the National was still an option for Inothewayurthinkin, and the modern incarnation of it is very different to the iteration that claimed Synchronised's life on his next start after that triumph at Cheltenham. Still, the decision that came soon after to call a halt to Inothewayurthinkin's season was a surprise to few.

He had done his job, in the process denying a colossus of modern jump racing a seminal slice of history. That is quite a legacy.

Quai De Bethune cools down after his last-gasp win in the Golden Gates Handicap at Royal Ascot. The Andrew Balding-trained 12-1 shot got up by a nose under Oisin Murphy to deny 11-4 favourite Seraph Gabriel

EDWARD WHITAKER (RACINGPOST.COM/PHOTOS)

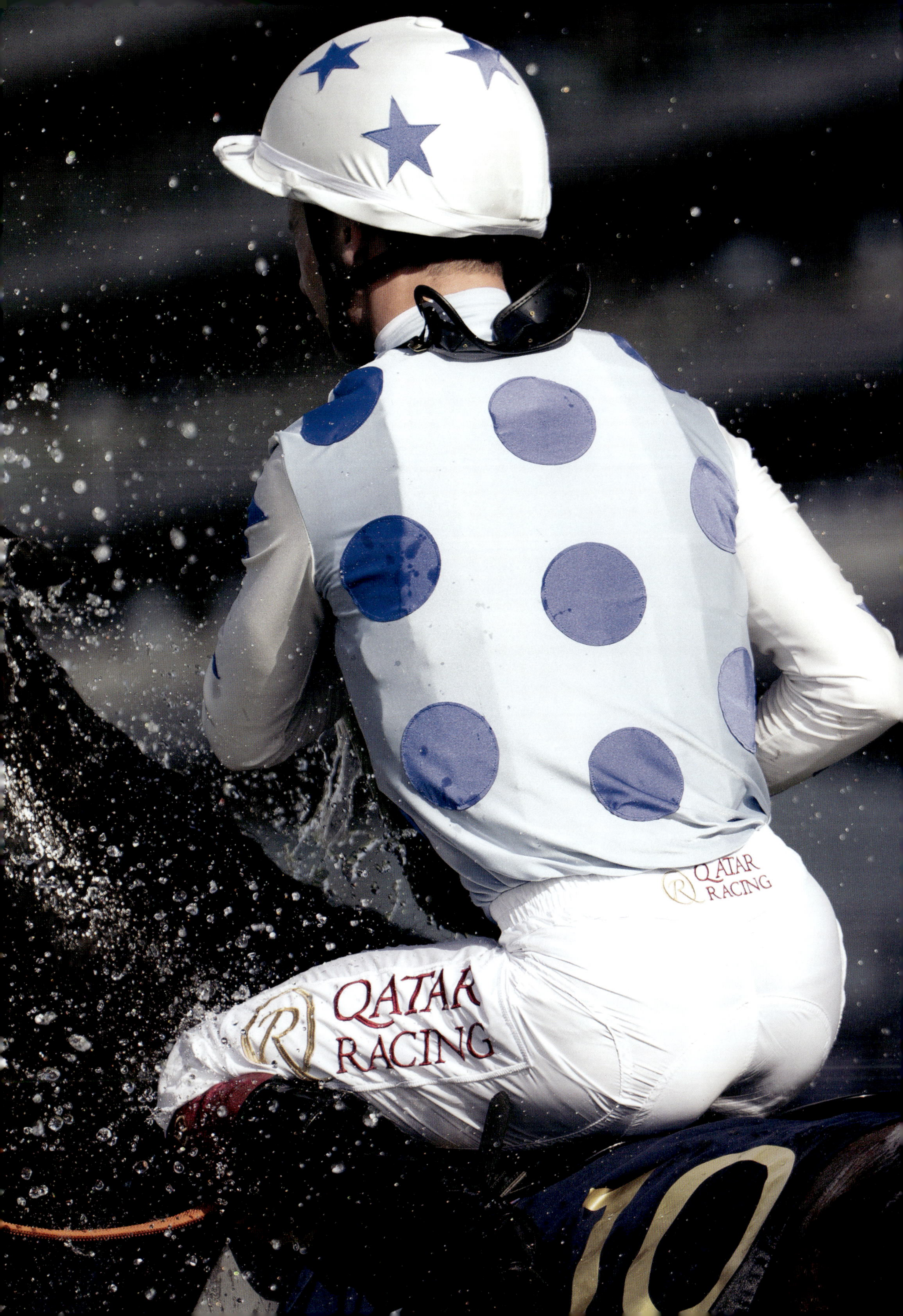
QATAR
RACING
QATAR
RACING

By Lewis Porteous

WHAT happened at the two-furlong pole in the St James's Palace Stakes was one of the most jaw-dropping moments of the 2025 Flat season. It was there that we saw the sort of rare athletic brilliance craved by lovers of the thoroughbred. On Royal Ascot's lavish stage, Field Of Gold delivered a performance that marked him out as a magnificent miler.

He had done something similar in the Irish 2,000 Guineas, yet this was on another level. When Colin Keane asked his mount to quicken, he positively surged out of his hands, settling the race against two fellow European Guineas winners with a sublime burst of acceleration.

Rounding the home turn, the 8-11 favourite appeared short of racing room. Not for long. Keane and his mount muscled through a tight gap between outsiders Rashabar and First Wave, ensuring a clear run up Ascot's short straight. Field Of Gold was four wide as he moved smoothly towards the head of the race. In behind were Ruling Court, who had beaten him in the 2,000 Guineas, and the French Guineas winner Henri Matisse. Their riders were hoping to pounce late. They had no chance.

Everyone else was hard at work as they reached the two-furlong pole, while Field

Electric Field

Of Gold, looking a size bigger and entirely at ease, waltzed on by. The afterburners went on and he shot clear in a flash. Race over.

"That was absolutely wonderful to behold," said joint-trainer John Gosden as he followed Field Of Gold back along the walkway to the winner's enclosure. Passionate racing fans recognised immediately that this had been a display of exceptional quality. Even the more uninitiated in the Royal Ascot crowd would have appreciated that there was something different about Juddmonte's magnificent grey.

"They went a strong pace, he came around them and then he was gone," Gosden added. "I thought for a moment, 'My God, he's gone too soon', but he kept up that gallop to the end. It was a wonderful performance."

★★★★

FIELD OF GOLD'S crowning moment had a sense of deja vu. Eleven years earlier, his Gosden-trained sire Kingman

had finished second in the 2,000 Guineas, bounced back to land the Irish 2,000 and then emphatically reversed form with his Newmarket conqueror – in his case Night Of Thunder – in the St James's Palace. Field Of Gold did likewise with Ruling Court courtesy of an electrifying change of pace that left his fellow Classic winners standing. He came home three and a half lengths clear of Henri Matisse, with Ruling Court another three and three-quarter lengths back in third.

If it looked good, just imagine how it felt to be the one fortunate enough to join him on the ride. It certainly beat a day at Alton Towers for Keane.

"Good horses make it look easy," said the rider who had been recently appointed as the Juddmonte number one. "It was a very good renewal of the

race. I don't know when the last time three Guineas winners clashed was, but Field Of Gold was very good at the Curragh and very good again today. I'm in a very privileged position and I've had nothing compared to this in recent years. It's a very special day."

The visual impression can often misrepresent the true merit of a performance, but even the biggest sceptics could not find fault with this performance. The time was good and initially it was assessed to be the best performance in the St James's Palace in the history of Racing Post Ratings.

A figure in excess of 130 is reserved for greatness and Field Of Gold was given a mark of
▶Continues page 22

131, 2lb above the previous best in the race achieved by his father in 2014.

The strong pace was undoubtedly advantageous to the production of a big figure but, on top of that, Field Of Gold's dazzling turn of foot had carried him more than four lengths clear of the stalking runner-up Henri Matisse, backing up the view that he was value for even more than the winning margin implied.

"He always impressed as a two-year-old, but he was a big boy and outgrew himself," Gosden said, when asked how early he knew the dapple grey was something out of the ordinary. "This year he has been exemplary in everything he's done. He's been a pleasure to train because he's a laid-back character."

★★★★

THE St James's Palace was the highlight for Field Of Gold, but there were low points before and after his signature performance. The 131 he had merited after Royal Ascot came under increasing pressure of revision before the end of the season and ultimately he slipped back to 128 – now 1lb below his sire's career high from the 2014 St James's Palace.

The first low point came on 2,000 Guineas day at Newmarket. Having left no doubt that he was a much-improved colt compared with the previous year when making a striking seasonal return in the Craven Stakes, his was the name on everyone's lips come the first Classic of the season.

Sent off the 15-8 favourite to give the Gosden stable a first success in the 2,000 Guineas, he was ridden with plenty of confidence by Kieran Shoemark. However, just as Kingman found in 2014, races on the wide expanse of the Rowley Mile can unfold in all manner of ways.

As in the Craven and the St James's Palace, Field Of Gold travelled like the champion he is but his instant turn of foot deserted him when Shoemark

first asked. While the favourite was finishing fastest of all, Ruling Court had begun his charge for home earlier and from a more prominent position, resulting in Field Of Gold going down by half a length.

"The race wasn't probably run in the fractions of the Craven Stakes and we were sat some way back," said Gosden after the race. "The winner has kicked and gone and we ran out of racetrack. Given another 25 yards it would have been ours.

"When this track gets fast like this it can ride slick with a cross-tailwind and they can get away from you. It just got away from us, I'm afraid, as we came into the Dip, from where he was clawing the ground back. I could see it was lost going into the Dip as we were just too far back and the winner got first run."

The race, the ride and the wider tactics were scrutinised to the nth degree in the aftermath and the Guineas turned out to be the last time Shoemark would ride Field Of Gold. Having

▶Continues page 24

'He did something pretty unusual at Ascot. He's a rare talent'

JOHN GOSDEN has had countless big-race winners around the globe in his long and illustrious career but for his son Thady – joint-trainer at Clarehaven since 2021 – there is still a rarity value in having one as good as Field Of Gold.

"He did something pretty unusual at Ascot when he took three lengths out of them in about three strides," he said in a Racing Post interview in July. "I haven't been watching racing for the past 50 years, but in the time I have been I haven't seen a horse do something like that with the speed he showed. He's a rare talent.

"He goes about his business in a very cool and professional manner, although in his faster work, when he's asked, you can see there's something there. But he waits until he's in the zone at the track to really turn it on. He's very composed, but he's got an endless amount of raw speed."

Field Of Gold hogged most of the headlines but there were other stars for Gosden to appreciate in a resurgent year for the yard. Not least their other two Group 1 heroes at Royal Ascot – Godolphin duo Ombudsman in the Prince of Wales's Stakes and Trawlerman in the Gold Cup.

"Royal Ascot was fantastic for the whole yard and each performance stands out for different reasons," Gosden said.

"We liked Ombudsman as a yearling, but he was quite immature early on and was never rushed at any stage – he was allowed to develop in his own time. He came up through the grades well as a three-year-old, but going into the Prince of Wales's there was a bit of a question mark on his first time in a proper Group 1 field. But he showed the class he has."

On Trawlerman, he said: "He's an incredibly kind and genuine horse. He's particularly endearing to a lot of people and for him to win a first Gold Cup in the fashion he did was special."

▲Stable star: Thady Gosden at Clarehaven with Field Of Gold, fresh from his Royal Ascot tour de force

6 Group 1 winners in 2024

Calif
Grosser Dallmayr-Preis, Gr.1, Munich

Tamfana
Sun Chariot Stakes, Gr.1, Newmarket

Gaelic Warrior
Arkle Chase, Gr.1, Cheltenham

Assistent
Grosser Preis von Bayern, Gr.1, Munich

Fantastic Moon
Grosser Preis von Baden, Gr.1, Baden-Baden

Palladium
Deutsches Derby, Gr.1, Hamburg

Spring HIT Sale with Breeze Up: 5th June 2026

Premier Yearling Sale: 4th September 2026

October Mixed Sales: 16th and 17th October 2026

BBAG www.bbag-sales.de BBAG

started the season as first-choice jockey for John and Thady Gosden, he soon lost that position. Off the back of the Newmarket defeat, the announcement came that the stable would adopt a "best available" policy when it came to riding arrangements. "There's no fallout, but it's the ramifications of what happened over the weekend," said Gosden snr a few days after the Guineas.

Keane, the Irish champion jockey, was called up for the Irish 2,000 Guineas on his home ground at the Curragh. Field Of Gold was a hotter favourite at even-money and this time there was no problem. Reminiscent of his sire, who gained compensation for an unlucky defeat at Newmarket with an easy win in Ireland, he cantered down the outside of the field, led at the furlong marker and opened up his cylinders to win by three and three-quarter lengths.

Gosden snr was in no doubt of the winner's merit. "That ability to be laid-back at home, half asleep and then when you press the button, they can turn it on, is a great thing," he said. "Some Kingmans can be flighty but this is a very relaxed horse. He's right up there and I think he's as good as his father."

★ ★ ★ ★

FIELD OF GOLD arguably looked even better than Kingman on his next start at Royal Ascot but then things went awry again. Off a six-week break, he followed the same path as his sire to the Sussex Stakes at Goodwood. He was the 1-3 favourite and many believed the outcome was a formality. Glorious confirmation of his status as a great miler seemed assured.

Keane was sidelined through suspension and William Buick got the call-up. An even more significant replacement, as it turned out, was Qirat for Windlord as Field Of Gold's pacemaker. Windlord had done the job in the Irish 2,000 and the St James's Palace, keeping the

pace honest up front before dropping away to finish second-last in both races. Qirat didn't drop away.

Nor did Buick get to feel the same explosiveness as Keane from the hot favourite. In a race that was almost impossible to fathom, Qirat stole a march on the field and never came back to them, although an injury rather than the tactics was ultimately blamed after Field Of Gold trailed home fourth behind the 150-1 pacemaker.

Having made everything look so easy at the Curragh and Royal Ascot, Field Of Gold just never seemed comfortable at Goodwood. He had plenty of ground to make up from his early position and was plugging on rather than flying at the finish. "The engine wasn't there, simple as that," said Gosden snr, who later revealed the star miler had suffered a "significant joint injury".

By mid-August, Field Of Gold was back cantering in Newmarket and had a new target: the Queen Elizabeth II Stakes on Champions Day at Ascot. "He's had a freshen-up since Goodwood and has been training very well," said Thady Gosden before the race. "The sound surface and straight mile should suit him well and he runs well fresh."

Unfortunately, the 13-8 favourite ran nowhere near as well as he had on his June visit to Ascot. A lacklustre fifth behind 100-1 winner Cicero's Gift was put down to a lack of race sharpness.

'He gave everyone a fantastic day at Newmarket'

RULING COURT, the 2,000 Guineas conqueror of Field Of Gold, had to be put down in August owing to complications arising from the hoof disease laminitis.

Trainer Charlie Appleby said: "Everyone at Godolphin is deeply saddened by the loss of Ruling Court. He gave everyone a fantastic day at Newmarket in May and he will be sorely missed. I would like to thank all of the team, who did everything they could to save him."

Bought for €2.3 million at the Arqana breeze-up sales in May 2024, Ruling Court became the third 2,000 Guineas winner in four years for Godolphin and Appleby following the victories of Coroebus (2022) and Notable Speech (2024).

William Buick's mount got first run on Field Of Gold in the Dip at Newmarket and stayed on strongly for a half-length win. "It's very special," Buick said. "These races are what it's about. He's shown just how good he is."

Always regarded as a Derby horse, the son of Justify was a strong fancy to follow up at Epsom but was withdrawn on raceday due to the rain-softened ground. He went on to finish third to Field Of Gold in the St James's Palace Stakes and then to Delacroix in the Eclipse on what proved to be his final run.

▶Ruling Court and William Buick after their 2,000 Guineas victory

"Coming down to the two pole it felt like he was picking up to be competitive but lack of a run cost us," said Keane, resuming the partnership that had started in grand style. "He's run a massive race after being off for so long."

The second half of the season turned out to be a damp squib for Field Of Gold. The fireworks show he put on before that, however, was something to behold.

▲All change: Field Of Gold (fourth right, pink cap) finishes only fifth to Cicero's Gift at Ascot in October, back at the track where he had done so well a few months earlier in the St James's Palace Stakes (above)

Field Of Gold's shock defeat by his huge-priced pacemaker Qirat in the

DAY THREE OF GLORIOUS GOODWOOD LIVE ON ITV

RACING POST

Thursday, July 31, 2025 Issue No. 13,441

£5.20

GET READY FOR A WHIRLWIND

Ballydoyle star **Whirl** set to whip up a storm in the Nassau Stakes – but it won't be a breeze with top-class older filly See The Fire leading the opposition

Previews, pages 2-9

Pricewise and Paul Kealy, pages 22-25

EDWARD WHITAKER

150-1 Sussex stunner

Qirat becomes Britain's biggest-priced Group 1 winner after flooring Field Of Gold

All the stories from yesterday, pages 14-20

THE REPORT

By Lewis Porteous

IT HAS happened before and it will happen again, but watching Qirat go from pacesetting front-runner for favourite Field Of Gold to 150-1 winner of the Sussex Stakes left the whole of Goodwood in a state of shock.

Who, what and how were the questions being asked by a crowd who came to see the anointing of the best miler of his generation but instead witnessed the longest-priced winner of a Group 1 in Britain [editor's note: until it was eclipsed in October by 200-1 Powerful Glory in the British Champions Sprint].

Beaten by 26 of his 29 rivals in the Hunt Cup at Royal Ascot on his previous start, Qirat was rated 24lb inferior to Field Of Gold and was still available at 20-1 for the Clipper Handicap at next month's Ebor meeting moments before the race.

He did, however, boast a two-from-two record at Goodwood and, more pertinently, was allowed to open up a sizeable lead over the protagonists through the first half of the race.

At one point Qirat even had his own pacemaker in the shape of Ballydoyle's Serengeti, who took him as far as the entrance to the final furlong before passing the baton.

Rosallion did his utmost to close him down from there, but Qirat had enough in reserve to pull off what will be remembered as one of the greatest giantkilling performances of all time.

"He's always threatened to be a good horse, I've just never managed to get it out of him until today," said winning trainer Ralph Beckett. "He was here to set the pace and go 12-second furlongs from the front. That's what he was here to do and the longer he lasted, the better it was for everyone concerned with him. That was the idea.

"Having watched the clock, I think he achieved that, and the last thing I said to Richard Kingscote before he got on him was, 'Keep going on this fellow. He isn't going to stop

Sussex Stakes was captured in the Racing Post's coverage from Goodwood

▼Shock result: The Juddmonte colours are in the winner's enclosure after the Sussex Stakes but the horse is 150-1 shot Qirat, not 1-3 favourite Field Of Gold

and he could run really well here'."

Kingscote, soon to leave Britain to continue his riding career in Hong Kong, said he felt like a thief after the race, but there was no fluke about his mastery from the front.

"I feel like a villain, but when I saw it wasn't a grey nose coming towards me I kept going," said the winning rider. "Ultimately, we were there as a helping hand to go an even gallop and we were somewhat ignored early, then took a lead off Wayne Lordan.

"Towards the cutaway I was thinking he was going well, but you always expect the horses rated 20lb higher to be coming through. I could see Rosallion coming, but my horse kept pulling out.

"I think Ralph was happy to have me on as I like being in front, like my fractions, and it worked out okay. It's a bit surreal but great to be going to Hong Kong on a positive note."

Field Of Gold trailed home in fourth under William Buick. Barry Mahon, European racing manager to Juddmonte, owners of both the beaten favourite and Qirat, said: "It's not the Field Of Gold we know. William felt he didn't handle the track and, for whatever reason, said he felt flat.

"Being gelded has helped Qirat, but he's a half-brother to Bluestocking and has an unbelievable pedigree. Aidan O'Brien always says pedigree comes out and today pedigree came out for him."

THE BACKGROUND

By Lee Mottershead

IN normal circumstances Qirat would have lined up at the meeting in the Coral Golden Mile, a fiercely competitive £150,000 contest in which he was set to compete off a BHA rating of 102.

Had Field Of Gold's usual pacemaker Windlord been available to run in Goodwood's
▶*Continues page 28*

greatest race, Qirat would not have been supplemented for the Sussex at a cost of £70,000. The decision to run the Andrew Balding-trained Windlord in the Gordon Stakes must therefore be considered central to the biggest shock ever recorded in a British Group 1.

That said, in the minutes leading up to the Sussex, Beckett was repeatedly telling people Qirat would significantly outrun his 150-1 odds. He could not possibly have been more right.

Afterwards Beckett did not challenge the suggestion he had been targeting the Golden Mile.

"Yes, he would have run in the handicap," said Beckett, chuckling. "Astonishing, isn't it? I would have fancied him in that because he loves it here."

Mindful of Qirat's fondness for the venue, it was Beckett who first proposed the idea of considering the now three-time Goodwood winner for the Sussex two months before the race.

"In fairness, Ralph wanted to put him in this race when the entries closed in May," said Juddmonte's Barry Mahon.

"I told him he was being ridiculous. Then Windlord, who had been doing the pacemaking duties so well, won the Listed race at Sandown, so I thought he should have a shot at a nice prize in his own right.

"Qirat then looked the obvious pacemaker for this race after he let us down a bit in the Hunt Cup. In fairness to Ralph again, he did say to me in the parade ring that this lad would run a big race."

THE VANQUISHED
By Jonathan Harding

FIELD OF GOLD was sent off a 1-3 favourite to land his third Group 1 of the year. However, he never got involved under William Buick and was beaten three and three-quarter lengths by Qirat.

"We got left back a long way, that's life, and the pacemaker goes and wins it," said joint-trainer John Gosden. "He ran on but didn't seem well balanced on the track. He didn't seem comfortable."

The murmurings in the grandstand when Field Of Gold's chance was gone were soon followed by roars from backers of 11-2 shot Rosallion, who rattled home under Sean Levey before just missing out by a neck. It was another agonising defeat for the four-year-old, who was beaten by a nose in the Queen Anne Stakes at Royal Ascot.

"It's pride, not frustration, but what does he have to do to win?" said trainer Richard Hannon. "Sean did the right thing and moved closer to the pacemakers, and he's run a super race but didn't win. It's life, isn't it?"

THE RACEGOERS
By James Milton

THERE'S a collective gulp as the realisation spreads that the race isn't going to plan for Field Of Gold. As Qirat crosses the line, two young lads have their heads in their hands. People are looking around for an explanation.

Amid the stunned crowd, I spot a wide-eyed man, walking around in dazed circles with his arm raised in triumph.

Did he back the winner? "Yes, yes," he says, showing me the settled bet on his phone: a cool £10 win at 150-1. No point playing each-way at those odds.

This seer is extremely publicity shy – "No name in the paper, please!" – but he agrees to share the thought process behind his bet.

"His pedigree was one of the best and he looked very good in the paddock but nobody was backing him," he explains. "I've owned horses, so when I see them live at the races I can tell which one will win."

These are edited versions of articles that appeared in the Racing Post on July 31

▲ Goodwood gobsmacked: from top, Qirat at the winning post in the Sussex Stakes; parading in front of the stunned crowd; Richard Kingscote and the front-running winner are the centre of attention; Field Of Gold trails home in fourth place behind his pacemaker

100-1 GROUP 1 GIFT

WITH two and a half furlongs to run in the Queen Elizabeth II Stakes, most eyes were on Field Of Gold and Rosallion to the right of the leading group. The big two contenders were racing side by side and being stoked up for the run to the line. It looked like the expected battle for supremacy was about to be fought out.

Suddenly, the attention was caught by a fast-moving challenger in pink and beige stripes on the other side of the group. Many would have moved swiftly past those colours when looking down the racecard for a bet. He was one of the 100-1 outsiders in the Group 1 showpiece. His name was Cicero's Gift. He was about to win.

By the furlong pole Rosallion had faded away. Field Of Gold plugged on without finding the electrifying burst of his previous visit to Ascot. Against the rail Cicero's Gift was flying under Jason Watson. There was no stopping him now.

He passed the post a length and a quarter in front of The Lion In Winter, the one-time Derby favourite who might finally have landed a big prize at three if it wasn't for the interloper.

It was another shock result in a season of big-priced Group 1 winners. Less than an hour and a half earlier, 200-1 shot Powerful Glory had landed the British Champions Sprint. "It's mad, isn't it?" said Charlie Hills, trainer of Cicero's Gift. "After there was a 200-1 winner I thought, 'Well, that counts us out'. I'm speechless."

The five-year-old had long been highly regarded at Hills's Faringdon Place stables but had been tried only once before in Group 1 company. "He's talented but he's been a challenge and hasn't been the soundest," Hills said. "He's getting better but he had to have a whole year off earlier in his career and a lot of patience has gone into him."

Cicero's Gift was a welcome big-race winner in a difficult year for the trainer. Barry Hills, the Lambourn legend who passed on Faringdon Place to his son in 2011, died in June. "As a family we've stayed strong and the old man looking down will be so chuffed, I'd say," Hills said. "Mum is here today, so it's really special."

▼In the pink: Cicero's Gift (left) springs a massive shock in the Queen Elizabeth II Stakes; right, an emotional Jason Watson celebrates his victory

Victory also meant a lot to jockey Jason Watson, who was in tears after the race. This was his first Group 1 win since 2019 after a challenging few years since parting ways with the Roger Charlton yard. "Even though I've had big days and big winners since, it's taken a bit of time for me to get the ball rolling again," he said. "I felt like I came here with a point to prove and I've proved it."

Flying to victory in a pink blur at 100-1 in one of the biggest mile races of the season was a hell of a way to do it.

IN THE PICTURE

King and Queen enjoy first official visit to Newmarket

NEWMARKET'S importance as a racing, training and breeding centre was marked in July by a first official visit from King Charles III and Queen Camilla.

The royal couple have visited the town in a private capacity in recent years to view their horses in training with John and Thady Gosden, William Haggas and Sir Mark Prescott, but this was the first official visit by a monarch since Queen Elizabeth II in 2016.

Among the stops were the National Stud and the Jockey Club Rooms, and there was a walkabout in the High Street. Many in the large crowd had queued for more than four hours to get a glimpse of the royal visitors, who waved and chatted as they made their way along the street.

At the National Stud the King and Queen met chairman Lord Grimthorpe and the four resident stallions, including Stradivarius (*right*), whose owner Bjorn Nielsen was among those present.

"As owners we were all introduced individually to the King and Queen and they were very friendly and down to earth," Nielsen said. "They took a keen interest in the horses and the people. It's great for racing and I was very honoured to be part of it."

Nielsen added: "The King went to give Strad some Polos. I just hoped he wouldn't take his fingers off as Strad can have a go at you, but everything was fine."

The King and Queen are joint-patrons of the Jockey Club, which chose the occasion to announce the launch of the Jockey Club Patrons Scholarship, a scheme designed to support pathways into the racing and breeding industries for young people from ethnically diverse backgrounds.

Baroness Dido Harding, the Jockey Club's senior steward, said: "The launch of the scholarship provides a lasting legacy from their visit. It has been our privilege to introduce them to those working in and supporting our sport right in the heartland of British racing.

"They are already extremely knowledgeable about the industry and this provided an opportunity to celebrate its success and pay tribute to its extensive heritage, while also demonstrating the role that the Jockey Club and our industry plays in the town of Newmarket and the local community."

Newmarket mayor Philippa Winter said: "I was pleased they were able to meet key members of our community and enjoy a walkabout that enabled children and residents to enjoy their visit. It's been a good day for Newmarket and a good day for racing."

Reporting: David Milnes and Nick Pulford
Pictures: Darren Staples and Chris Radburn (Getty)

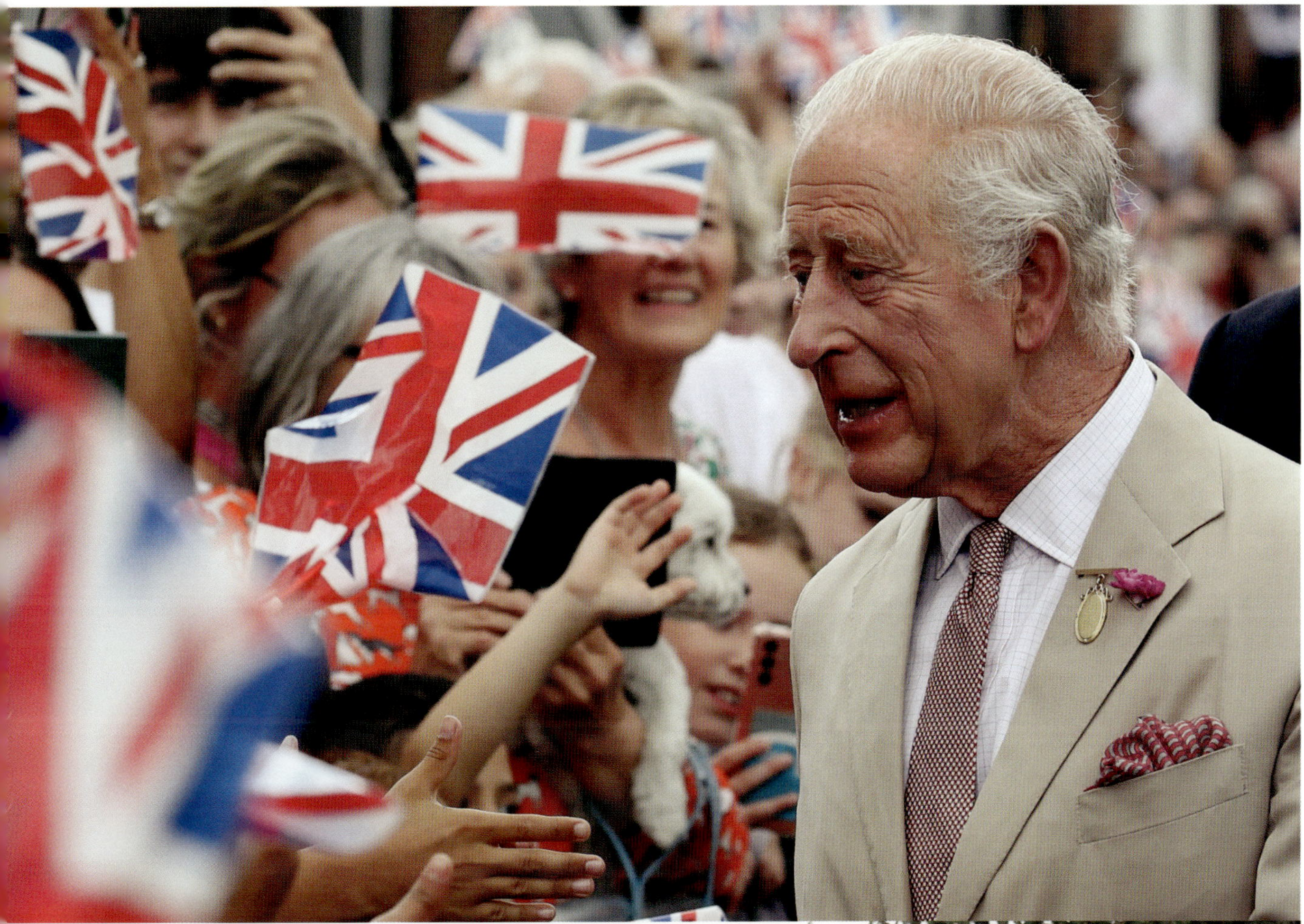

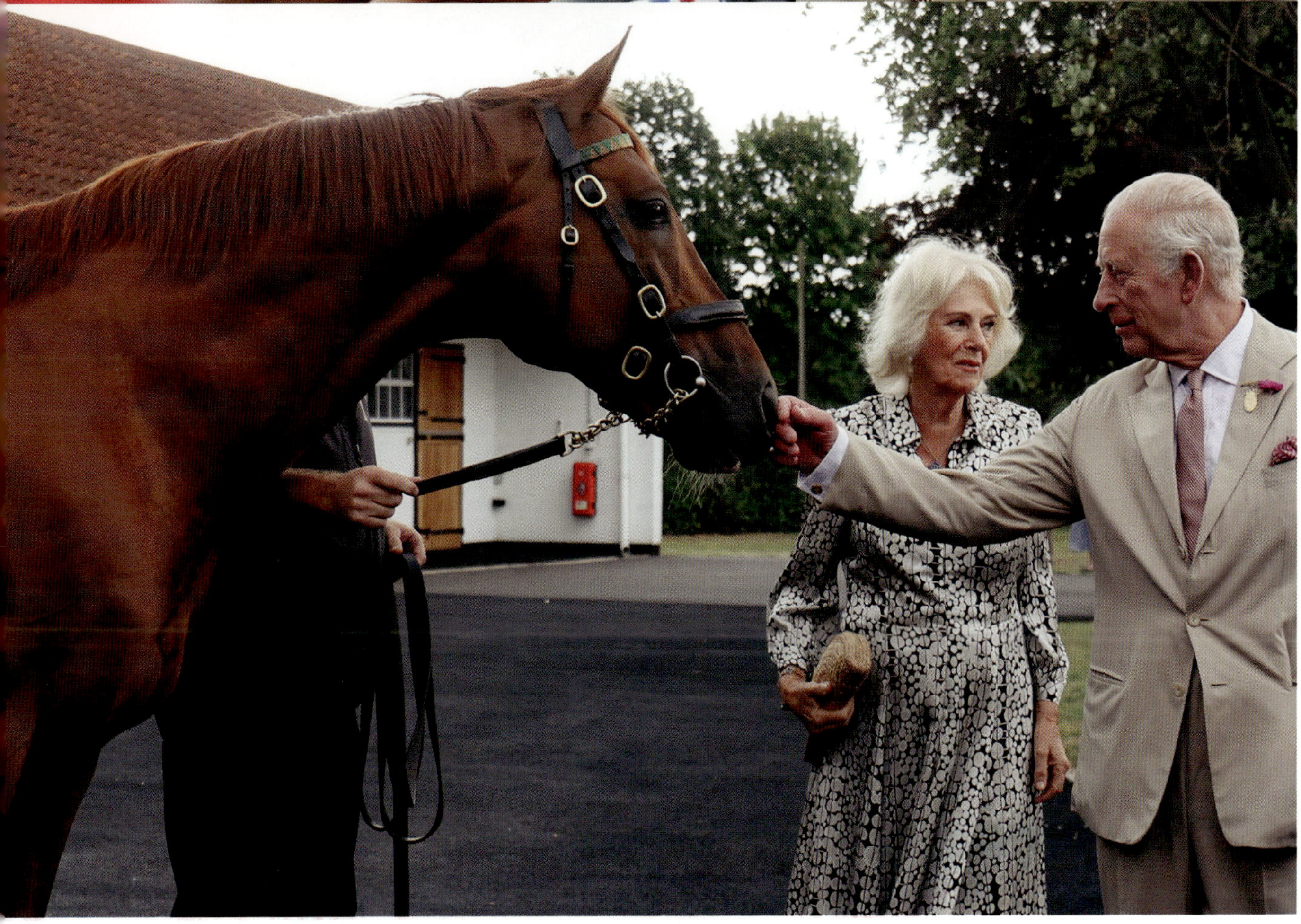

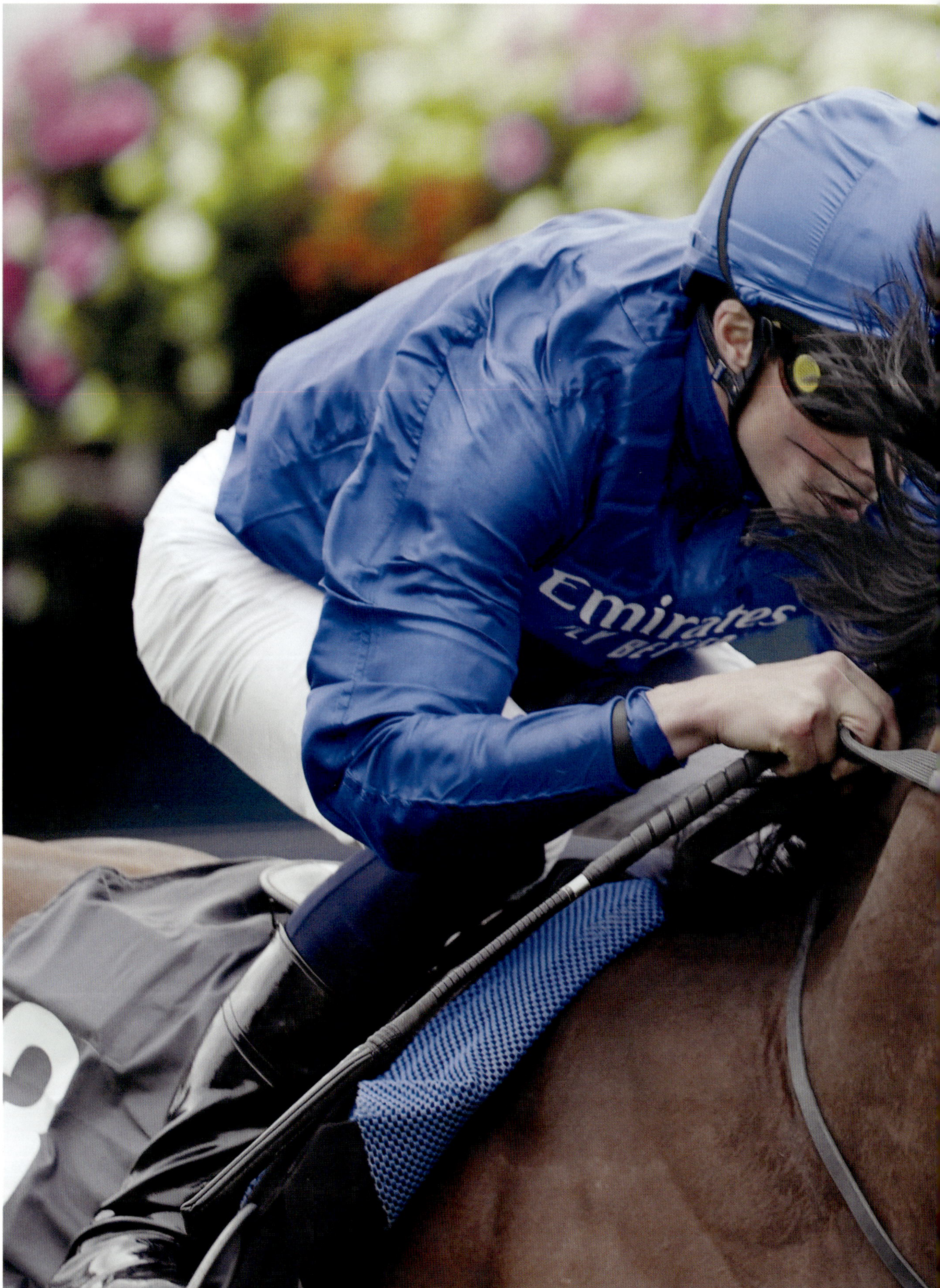
Emirates

MAN OF ACTION

Ombudsman leapt to stardom with extraordinary wins in the Prince of Wales's Stakes at Royal Ascot and the Juddmonte International at York

By Lewis Porteous

W ITH two furlongs to run in the Prince of Wales's Stakes at Royal Ascot, Ombudsman and William Buick were locked behind a wall of five horses racing shoulder to shoulder. Refused entry as he looked for a gap towards the inside, Buick's only choice was to switch around all five of his rivals to the outside. Time was running out and their chance was fading.

As Buick angled to his left, Anmaat, already a Group 1 winner at Ascot, was sent for home. It was a positive move by his rider Jim Crowley and one that would have won most races, but not this one.

With a furlong remaining, Ombudsman finally had daylight in front of him and let rip an almighty turn of foot that catapulted him past the leader with improbable alacrity. Such was his acceleration, Buick's mount didn't just scrape home in front. Instead he had two lengths to spare over Anmaat at the line, turning what had threatened to be an unlucky defeat into a dazzling triumph.

"This horse has an extraordinary turn of foot," declared joint-trainer John Gosden, for whom it was a 70th Royal Ascot winner 35 years after Chicarica – like Ombudsman, owned by Sheikh Mohammed – had become his first.

"We did have him exactly 'au

▶Continues page 36

▲Winning team: Ombudsman and William Buick power to the line in the Juddmonte International at York

point' but I think it's all down to the owner. When we bought him with Anthony Stroud, I said, 'He's immature, give me a chance with him,' and he told me to take as long as you like. He didn't race at two but at three we brought him out. Now he's fully grown and developed, and because Sheikh Mohammed has been patient he's been rewarded."

Patience was also key for Buick on the Godolphin four-year-old, who was making his Group 1 debut on just the sixth start of his career. Drawn in stall one against the rail, Buick was going to be a hostage to fortune with a horse who didn't want to lead and had just one rival behind him turning for home. The pace had been generous throughout, making it even more impressive that Ombudsman was still able to quicken in such emphatic fashion when finally making it into the clear down the wide outside. It was a performance that marked him out as exceptional.

"He'd have been a very unlucky loser, wouldn't he?" said Buick after the race. "They went a hard gallop and we had to ride for a bit of luck. I had to look for a couple of gaps, but he's got such a great turn of foot and picked up when I had to switch his course.

"He was the unknown quantity in the race and I thought he was impressive, very impressive. He's a cool, talented horse and I think that was just a taste of what's to come, for sure."

An unknown quantity no more, Ombudsman had catapulted himself into the upper echelons on Racing Post Ratings. When the dust had settled, he was rated 130. No other Prince of Wales's winner in the last decade had managed to reach that level.

★★★★

THE next stop after Royal Ascot was Sandown for the Eclipse, where Ombudsman was sent off the 6-4 favourite to secure his status as the top mile-and-a-quarter horse in Europe. Next in the betting was Delacroix, dropping back from a mile and a

half in the Derby, and then there was Godolphin's 2,000 Guineas winner Ruling Court. Sosie, fourth in the Arc the previous autumn and a dual Group 1 winner since then, added a French twist to the six-runner line-up. Again the finish was breathtaking, but this time Ombudsman came out on the wrong side.

The way the Eclipse was run would have had Alan Turing scratching his head. The pace was only modest through the early stages, causing the field to bunch and leaving Ombudsman trapped towards the outside of the field. Delacroix had looked the likely pace angle but he was sitting last turning for home as Sosie stacked his rivals up from the front.

Ombudsman again showed a blistering turn of speed in the straight but Buick deployed it almost a furlong earlier than he had at Ascot. The favourite surged to the front but there was still the uphill finish to negotiate. He was in command half a furlong out but Delacroix, galvanised by Ryan Moore, finished in spectacular style to pick Ombudsman's pocket by a neck.

"I did warn people it could be a messy race and I was correct," said John Gosden, not entirely impressed with what he had witnessed. "The French horse sat handy and we thought Delacroix may go forward too, but then it was all the other way round.

"That happens in a small field and it didn't turn out the way we thought, but he's run a wonderful race. He was trapped rather wide and got close to the pace. The others who were up there were out the back and Delacroix has run us down late."

★★★★

ONE of the big talking points after the Eclipse focused on why the Gosdens and Godolphin had left so much to chance regarding the pace. If it was a mistake, they did not repeat it for the Ombudsman-Delacroix rematch in the Juddmonte International at

▼Royal blue: William Buick passes the post in the Prince of Wales's Stakes at Royal Ascot before receiving the trophy; crossing the line in the Juddmonte International at York and the post-race celebrations; the next day's Racing Post front page

York. This time they took matters into their own hands.

"Lending" Birr Castle from Andre Fabre to ensure there was no repeat of the muddling pace in the Eclipse seemed like a sound choice by the Ombudsman camp, although at the halfway point of the International it threatened to backfire spectacularly. For the third race in a row, Ombudsman was embroiled in extraordinary scenes.

Birr Castle, a proven Pattern-race performer in his own right, was allowed to build up a huge lead under Robert Havlin and, with five furlongs to run, he was 20 lengths clear of the other five runners. It was squeaky-bum time for connections and supporters of Ombudsman and Delacroix. Even when Birr Castle's lead began to erode in the home straight, he still held a convincing advantage racing into the final quarter of a mile.

It was now or never for his rivals and, not a moment too soon, Ombudsman darted from the pursuing group to hunt down the pacemaker. It was under totally different circumstances but again Ombudsman was able to show his devastating change of pace as he shot into the lead with a furlong to run. On this occasion Delacroix was unable to replicate his flying finish from Sandown. The distance between the pair at the line was three and a half lengths. Birr Castle held on for third at 150-1, just half a length behind Delacroix.

It was another triumph over adversity. "It was quite extraordinary," said Gosden, who had clearly found the race uncomfortable viewing only a few weeks after seeing Field Of Gold beaten by 150-1 pacemaker Qirat in the Sussex Stakes. "Birr Castle has run a huge race to be third. I thought they'd allowed him to slip the field and at the two-furlong marker I thought they weren't going to catch him. They were playing with fire.

"I said to William if he'd sat

▶Continues page 38

Horseboxes – Uprating and Downplating

Uprating Horseboxes

As you may be aware, the DVSA is paying close attention to the horsebox industry and in particular, to lightweight horseboxes which they suspect may be operating overweight.

We have seen cases of horseboxes being stopped, checked and impounded on the roadside, owing to running overweight. The horses in transit have to be loaded into a different box and taken away, and the resultant fines are ever increasing in size. Yet, there is an alternative.

SvTech is keen to promote its uprating service for lightweight horseboxes (3500kg), whereby the horsebox can gain an extra 200-300kg in payload. This provides vital payload capability when carrying an extra horse and/or tack and offers peace of mind for the owner.

SvTech has carried out extensive work and testing on lightweight models and has covered uprates for most lightweight vehicles.

It is worth noting that some uprates require modifications or changes to the vehicle's braking, tyres and/or suspension, for which SvTech provides a simple

purpose-built suspension assister kit. This will take between 1-2 hours for you to fit. Your horsebox will then go for a formal inspection to bring it into the 'Goods' category, and, depending on the vehicle's age, may also require fitment of a speed limiter, for which there are one or two options. Most importantly, vehicles registered after May 2002 must be fitted with manufacturer's ABS, if going above 3500kg.

If you're unsure, or don't believe that you need to uprate your lightweight horsebox, try taking it to a public weighbridge when you're fully loaded with your horse, tack, passenger, hay, etc. and weigh off each axle individually and the vehicle as a whole. There could be a distinct chance that you've overloaded one of the axles, even if you're within the GVW. If there is a problem, we can help. Call us to discuss your options.

Downplating Horseboxes

Do you own a 10 - 12.5 tonnes horsebox and do you want non-HGV licence holder to drive it? Your horsebox could be downplated to 7.5 tonnes so that any driver with a licence issued prior to 1st Jan 1997 could drive it.

- You are paying too much Vehicle Excise Duty.
- You want to escape the need for a tachograph.

The most important aspect when downplating is to leave yourself suitable payload to carry your goods. The Ministry requires that for horseboxes of 7500kg there is a minimum payload of 2000kg. Hence, when downplating to 7500kg, the unladen weight must not exceed 5500kg. For 3500kg horseboxes, you must ensure that you have a payload of at least 1000kg, thus, when empty it cannot weigh more than 2500kg.

Due to recent changes at DVSA, we are no longer required to make a mechanical change to the vehicle and, once downrated, we will be supplying you with a revised set of Ministry plating certificates, or if exempt, plating and testing, a converter's plate and certificate at the lower weight.

Depending upon vehicle usage, it is at the discretion of DVSA as to whether they will require a formal inspection of your vehicle.

TO DISCOVER YOUR OPTIONS, PLEASE DOWNLOAD, FILL IN AND RETURN OUR ENQUIRY FORM – WWW.SVTECH.CO.UK

SvTech
Special Vehicle Technology

T +44 (0)1772 621800
www.svtech.co.uk/select-your-vehicle-type

four lengths off the pace he might have won by ten lengths. If you divorce yourself from the pacemaker, he only has to be a half-decent horse. You can't give them that ground but when William let Ombudsman go, he absolutely flew. He said he went from second gear to fifth gear just like that. I have to call Andre now and tell him he frightened the living daylights out of us."

Buick was naturally delighted Ombudsman had been able to get the job done, although he couldn't hide the fact that little had gone to plan. "I was thinking, 'This is a bit dangerous'," said the Godolphin number one. "I didn't want to be the person who chased our pacemaker too early but when we came into the straight I had to. When he passed Birr Castle he actually quickened again. To still have that finish at the very end was a monster performance."

★★★★

IT WAS back to Ascot for the final stop on Ombudsman's journey through Britain's top mile-and-a-quarter contests. This was another firecracker.

The Champion Stakes was the final part of the trilogy starring Ombudsman and Delacroix. The Godolphin hero tilted the score 2-1 in his favour but it was not enough to secure victory. Calandagan, the newcomer to the fight, proved strongest of all.

The opening part of the race was important. Buick attempted to track across from stall nine but Mickael Barzalona, drawn two gates inside on Calandagan, held his position. Rather than stay wide the whole way, Buick's only option was to tuck in last of the 11 runners just behind Calandagan.

The pace was strong, set by Devil's Advocate for Godolphin and Mount Kilimanjaro for Coolmore. Coming around the home turn, the big three were all looking to strike from the back up the short straight.

Delacroix could not find an instant response to the

quickening pace. Barzalona passed Christophe Soumillon's mount and went for home. Buick followed him.

Soon the race was between Calandagan and Ombudsman. Barzalona started with a crucial edge and never relinquished it. Having got to his rival's quarters a furlong and a half out, Ombudsman could not sustain the effort in the closing stages. The final margin was two and a quarter lengths.

"We've run a magnificent race in second," Gosden said. "He did get slightly shuffled back and he has tried to come from last. It was

▲Super man: Ombudsman motors to victory at York ahead of Delacroix (right) and the Godolphin pacemaker Birr Castle

a fabulous race against two very good horses. The pacemakers set a proper pace and full marks to the winner. We were coming from behind him and that was tough against a really good horse."

It was another valiant effort from Ombudsman in a demanding season. He never flinched for a moment. On more than one occasion, despite circumstances going against him, he not only managed to get the job done but did it with flair. Just imagine what this rare talent might have delivered had things gone exactly to plan.

Farriers (Registration) Act 1975
PROTECTING EQUINES & THE PUBLIC
FOR 50 YEARS

50

50 years of equine welfare through regulation of farriery

Farriers Registration Council

www.farrier-reg.gov.uk frc@farrier-reg.gov.uk 01733 319911

THE
BIGGER
PICTURE

Team Asia, newcomers to the Shergar Cup
this year, enjoy a champagne celebration of
their victory at Ascot in August. India's Suraj
Narredu, their captain, is flanked by Japanese
pair Ryusei Sakai (left) and Mirai Iwata
EDWARD WHITAKER (RACINGPOST.COM/PHOTOS)

LONGINES

Delacroix made his mark in a stellar mile-and-a-quarter division with sparkling acceleration to win the Eclipse and Irish Champion Stakes

DOUBLE QUICK

By David Jennings
Deputy Ireland editor

NOBODY was really talking about him over the winter but, boy, were we talking about him through the summer. Delacroix was Ballydoyle's MVP in 2025, scoring valuable goals in the Eclipse and Irish Champion Stakes to make himself a rare commodity at stud.

The Lion In Winter was the Ballydoyle buzz horse during the off-season, sitting at

▶ *Continues page 44*

the summit of the market for both the 2,000 Guineas and Derby all winter. When Delacroix reappeared in the Ballysax Stakes at the end of March, however, you got the sense that this dark and handsome son of Dubawi was a pretty big deal.

Delacroix was a decent juvenile. We saw plenty of him at two, running five times and winning the Autumn Stakes at Newmarket before losing out on the bob to Hotazhell in the Group 1 Futurity Trophy at Doncaster on his final start. That proved he was good, but little did we think he would turn out to be as good as he was.

In a Racing Post stable tour at the beginning of April, Aidan O'Brien said this about Delacroix: "He's still babyish but he's growing up. Racing will only help him. We always thought he would stay well and be a middle-distance horse and he's a fine, big, powerful horse. He'll improve plenty fitness-wise."

O'Brien was right. The more we saw of him, the better he got. After breezing through the Ballysax, he rocked on to the Derby Trial at Leopardstown. It was the route High Chaparral took to Epsom when he won the Derby back in 2002. A silky smooth success at 1-3 promoted Delacroix to Derby favourite, helped by the blowout of The Lion In Winter in the Dante.

Not surprisingly he was the chosen one of Ryan Moore out of the Ballydoyle Derby trio at Epsom, eventually going off 2-1, but just about anything that could have gone wrong did go wrong. He was hampered early and was always on the back foot. He never landed a blow and trailed in a well-beaten ninth behind lesser-fancied stablemate Lambourn, who made almost every yard of the running under Wayne Lordan.

It looked as though it might be the end for Delacroix. Well, in terms of him being a top horse, but it was only the beginning. His real story was yet to be written.

★★★★

A MONTH after his Epsom puncture, the wheels were back on for the Eclipse at Sandown. Having been double-digit odds in the weeks leading up to the race, with Moore fully expected to partner Prix du Jockey Club winner Camille Pissarro, Delacroix was hammered all the way into 3-1 before the off. Moore picked him and we soon found out why.

This was no ordinary Eclipse either. The previous year's Arc favourite Sosie was in the six-runner line-up, as well as Camille Pissarro and 2,000 Guineas hero Ruling Court, while the breathtaking Prince of Wales's Stakes winner Ombudsman was sent off 6-4 favourite.

Those on the favourite would have been counting their notes inside the final furlong after William Buick produced Ombudsman to lead. It looked like a race-winning move. But what happened inside the final 100 yards was one of the most

▲On the record: Aidan O'Brien discusses Delacroix's victory in the Irish Champion Stakes (previous pages); below, the next day's front page of the Irish Racing Post

RACING POST
A SENSATIONAL SUNDAY AT THE CURRAGH

DEADLY DELACROIX

extraordinary sights of the whole season. Delacroix couldn't win from where he was. And yet he did.

"He won against the odds at Sandown. Totally," O'Brien said of that ridiculous display, where Delacroix got into all sorts of trouble and traded at an in-running high of 361-1 on Betfair when he had the entire field in front of him with just over a furlong to go. He couldn't win from where he was. And yet he did.

O'Brien summed up that sublime turn of foot by saying: "It was the most extraordinary performance by any horse we've ever had." That is a big claim when you consider all the greats who have been at Ballydoyle.

Explaining such a huge statement, he added: "Because he clipped heels at the two-furlong marker and he still wasn't out. Where he was, the amount of ground he had to make up, you couldn't do it. There's no way you could see him doing it, but he did it. You have to go back and

▶Continues page 46

keep looking at the replay to see if it really did happen. Look where he was two furlongs out and look where the second horse was."

O'Brien was right. The replay needs to be watched over and over again to fully appreciate the magnitude of the achievement. Delacroix was given a Racing Post Rating of 126 for that stellar showing. There was still more to come.

★★★★

THAT enthralling Eclipse showdown with Ombudsman was the beginning of a prolonged and bitter rivalry between the pair. Even O'Brien and John Gosden got involved with a few comments back and forth as the season progressed. It was all harmless fun, but entertaining nonetheless.

O'Brien branded Gosden a bit of a "whinger" on a few occasions, while the master of Clarehaven said he didn't want to take Ombudsman to Leopardstown for the Irish Champion Stakes because he "wouldn't appreciate running against multiple entries from one stable on a track with a short straight".

More about that event soon. That was the day Delacroix defined himself.

The sequel to Delacroix v Ombudsman arrived in the Juddmonte International at York in August. The Gosden camp got their revenge there as the 150-1 pacemaking outsider Birr Castle almost stole the race from the front. He was still clear over a furlong out but Ombudsman quickened up best this time to beat Delacroix by three and a half lengths. Even so, it felt like inconclusive evidence. It was a messy race and the Coolmore colt wasn't seen at his best.

So on to Leopardstown we rolled. No Ombudsman, leaving Delacroix to deliver a career-defining moment. The Irish Champion Stakes is always a classy affair and, despite the Godolphin four-year-old

skipping the bout, we still had Shin Emperor from Japan, 2024 Champion Stakes winner Anmaat and the improving Zahrann, as well as others.

Delacroix blew them all away with an explosive turn of foot on the home turn. Christophe Soumillon was in the saddle this time, with Moore missing most of the autumn with a broken leg.

O'Brien said of that performance: "The unusual thing about Delacroix at Leopardstown was that he was quickening and going sideways at the same time. He wasn't quickening up in a straight line but he was still going by horses, which was extraordinary. That was very strange. You rarely see horses quickening sideways. He has all the things and he's by Dubawi."

That was the day Delacroix's stud career was made. Not only did he have the looks and the size, but he had the speed too. It was instant acceleration on the home turn that put the Leopardstown race to bed and it was so easy on the eye. The

▲Tower of strength: Delacroix in playful mood after exercising with rider Mark Crehan at Ballydoyle; below, winning the Irish Champion Stakes with Christophe Soumillon

experts were understandably impressed. Delacroix was given an RPR of 127, 1lb higher than his Eclipse heroics.

★★★★

THE vibes afterwards were that we wouldn't see Delacroix again. "I can't tell you how important he is," said O'Brien, looking to his future as a stallion. "The lads have been looking for a Dubawi all their life and he's out of a champion. He's a beautiful, big horse with power, strength and everything you want. I'm delighted for the lads that he has won [the Irish Champion]."

So that was that. Or maybe not.

A prolonged spell of dry weather meant we finally had a Champions Day run on good ground at Ascot in mid-October and O'Brien and 'the lads' decided to roll the dice again with Delacroix.

We never expected there to be a third instalment of Delacroix v Ombudsman but that epic trilogy arrived at Ascot. It didn't pan out the way the Coolmore camp had hoped, though.

While the Champion Stakes had been billed as Delacroix v Ombudsman III, French ace Calandagan beat them both, convincingly too. The instant acceleration we saw from Delacroix at Leopardstown just wasn't there at Ascot. It was, of course, the end of a long, hard season. He had a perfectly legitimate excuse.

"He never really travelled like he did last time at Leopardstown, especially when I came into the last turn," Soumillon said after coming home in fourth place. "I tried to take him out a bit to make him sprint but he never really reacted like he did last time. You always want to fight for the win in these types of races but he couldn't do it today."

Delacroix had done it on two other big days when it really mattered. He was one of the main characters in the 2025 Flat season. A sight for sore eyes when in full stride. A delight.

Aidan O'Brien talks to work-riders during first lot at Ballydoyle in March as preparations step up a gear shortly after the start of the Irish Flat turf season

PATRICK McCANN (RACINGPOST.COM/PHOTOS)

DRAMA QUEEN

A Champion Hurdle of twists and turns ended in a 25-1 upset for Jeremy Scott's mare Golden Ace after the shock exits of Constitution Hill and State Man

By Andrew Dietz

WITH more plot twists than a Quentin Tarantino film, the Champion Hurdle encapsulated the glorious unpredictability of jump racing like no other race in 2025.

Not so glorious for the fallen previous winners Constitution Hill and State Man, but spectacularly so for everyone connected with Golden Ace, whose owner Ian Gosden rolled the dice in the biggest two-mile hurdle and hit the mother of all jackpots.

From the chaotic scenes of a scarcely believable spectacle emerged the ultimate victory for the little folk, with 35-horse Somerset trainer Jeremy Scott and Welsh jockey Lorcan Williams the unlikeliest of heroes following Golden Ace's 25-1 championship stunner.

Shock and disbelief reverberated around the stands as the race unfolded in extraordinary fashion. Odds-on favourite Constitution Hill inexplicably came down four out and then State Man dramatically fell at the last with back-to-back wins at his mercy.

Handed the initiative, Golden Ace stayed on up the run-in to seize her moment and become the seventh mare to win the Champion Hurdle. "I think my team at home will be as flabbergasted as I am," said a bewildered Scott. "Amazing, absolutely amazing."

If Scott had got his way, Golden Ace would not have even run in the race. After she had scrambled home in Wincanton's Kingwell Hurdle in February, the sensible option at the festival seemed to be the Mares' Hurdle. She had upset Brighterdaysahead to win the previous year's novice version and looked sure to be competitive against her own sex again. But Gosden had other ideas. He pays the bills, as Scott pointed out, and wanted a shot at the big one.

Going up against a great two-mile hurdler in Constitution Hill might have been viewed as madness. There wasn't just one rival to be scared of either. Brighterdaysahead was pitched into the race rather than the Mares' Hurdle following two impressive Grade 1 wins in Ireland and then there was reigning champion State Man, who after a couple of defeats behind Brighterdaysahead had

won the Irish Champion Hurdle when cashing in on Lossiemouth's fall.

Ultimately, though, the race was billed as a clash between Constitution Hill and Brighterdaysahead.

★★★★

IT HAD been a long road back to a second Champion Hurdle for 2023 winner Constitution Hill, but he was a perfect ten from ten and his adoring public sent him off the well-backed 1-2 favourite. His

▶Continues page 52

previous festival appearances had produced heart-stopping moments. This one would too, but in a different way.

Constitution Hill, who had made a rare mistake at the last when winning his prep in the International Hurdle, was a little keen in the early stages but there did not appear to be any great cause for concern. That all changed at the halfway point. In a flash he was gone. In his exuberant way he took off a long way from the fifth hurdle and this time there was no escape. He nearly brought down Golden Ace, but she just avoided him.

As the great hurdler's unblemished record went up in smoke, groans rang out from the crowd of 55,000. Soon the howls of shock and dismay would grow even louder.

With her main rival gone, Brighterdaysahead hit the front going towards three out but the distress signs were clear and the eye was drawn to State Man travelling powerfully in behind. He led going easily after two out and drew away from his rivals into a five-length lead approaching the last. Then in scenes similar to Annie Power's theatrical demise in the Mares' Hurdle ten years earlier, State Man came down at the last. Absolute pandemonium.

Having gone past Brighterdaysahead, who was weakening when badly hampered by State Man's fall, Golden Ace was left in front. She pressed on up the hill on her own to win by nine lengths from 66-1 shot Burdett Road and 150-1 Winter Fog in third, with Williams afforded the luxury of standing in his irons to start the celebrations before the line.

"She's fantastic and always turns up and runs her race," the jockey said. "When Constitution Hill was out of the race, I thought we might stay on for second, and then when State Man fell at the last, we were there to pick up the pieces, which was the game plan. It's the best day of my life."

Finishing placed, never mind winning, was beyond the wildest of Gosden's dreams with a mare he was advised not to buy before parting with 12,000gns in 2021. "I never even backed her because I thought she's not going to be second," he said. "It's jump racing and you've got to be there at the end. Last year's win at the festival was a dream and this is just absolutely amazing. I can't believe it."

Neither could the trainer. As cries of 'Oh, Jeremy Scott' grew louder and louder from the throng around the winner's enclosure, he struggled to come to terms with what had just happened. "I'm not sure if this is a dream," he said. "It's magic. She's a dear horse and we're so lucky to have her. She's given me the two most memorable days of my life – bar my wedding, of course."

★★★★

FORTUNE had definitely favoured the brave in the most unfathomable of races, in which two Champion Hurdle winners had fallen. State Man was out to retain, Constitution Hill was looking to regain. Thankfully neither was in any undue pain.

Trainer Nicky Henderson and owner Michael Buckley were as shocked as anyone after seeing Constitution Hill fall for the first time in his career. "We have to live with it, but it's cruel," Henderson said. "We waited two years to get back here. He was back and we couldn't have had him any better. State Man had the race won but we didn't get that far to see what would have happened."

Willie Mullins, in a way only the festival's most successful trainer could be, was philosophical about State Man after he was denied back-to-back Champion Hurdle glory in the most crushing manner. "He was just too long at the last and caught the top of it – the same as Annie Power," he said. "It's fantastic for Jeremy to have a win like that with Golden Ace. They

▲ Golden day: from top, Golden Ace comes home at 25-1 in the Champion Hurdle; Lorcan Williams revels in his biggest victory; Jeremy Scott is embraced by the jockey; the trainer is serenaded around the winner's enclosure; below, the next day's Racing Post

were there. They came, they punched, they tried."

The irony that Golden Ace was only in the Champion Hurdle because Gosden was running scared of Mullins' Lossiemouth in the Mares' Hurdle was not lost in the aftermath. Neither was the fact that Lossiemouth only ran in the mares' race, in which she cantered to victory less than three-quarters of an hour earlier, because her connections believed she could not win the Champion.

Lossiemouth did meet Constitution Hill at Aintree but the head-to-head never materialised as Henderson's star fell again – this time two out – and the mare beat the rest easily. A retrieval mission at Punchestown produced even more questions about Constitution Hill when he finished a jaded fifth as State Man got his revenge over Golden Ace by nearly five lengths.

A lot would need to go right for the main protagonists to line up in the next Champion Hurdle and, even if they did, surely it would be impossible to match the drama of 2025.

Acclaimed broadcaster and trainer Ted Walsh summed it up perfectly. "It was the most amazing Champion Hurdle I've ever seen," he said. "It was like something from a Dick Francis novel, pure fiction. If you didn't see it, you wouldn't believe it."

THE
BIGGER PICTURE

Transprint (second left) and Tony Doyle jump the drop fence on their way to winning the Ladies Perpetual Cup cross-country chase at the Punchestown festival in April

PATRICK McCANN (RACINGPOST.COM/PHOTOS)

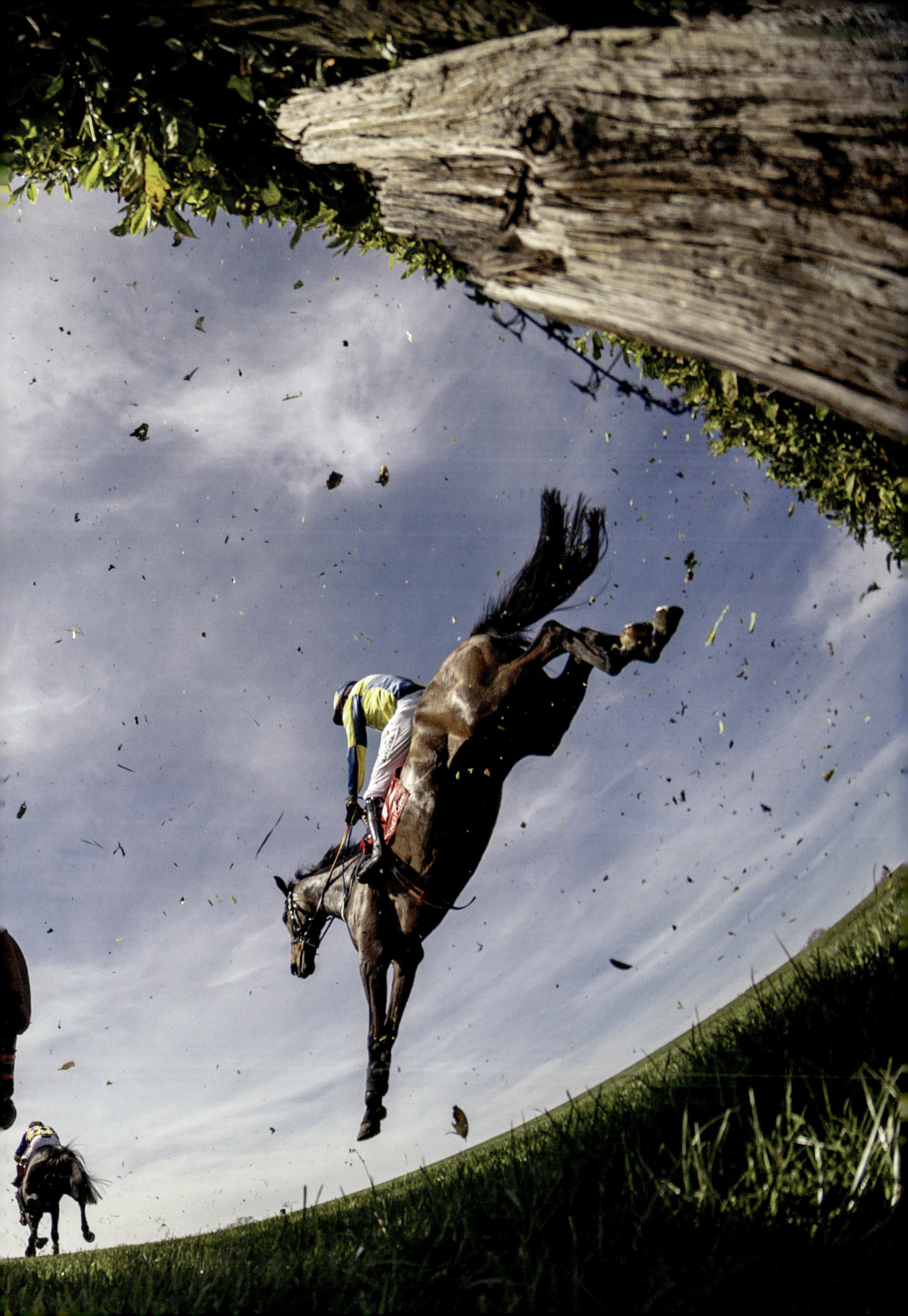

▶Day to remember: Sean Flanagan looks to the heavens after winning the Queen Mother Champion Chase on Marine Nationale

NATIONALE MONUMENT

Marine Nationale landed the Queen Mother Champion Chase just a few weeks after the tragic death of Michael O'Sullivan, the jockey who moulded him

By David Jennings

SEAN FLANAGAN said it better than any of us ever could. "I'm only the man who steered him around today. Michael is the man who made him what he is," were the first words Flanagan uttered to ITV's Alice Plunkett just seconds after Marine Nationale had sprinted up the famous Cheltenham hill to add the Queen Mother Champion Chase to his Supreme success from two years earlier. It was a sensational performance, an 18-length romp in the end, but this was not about the horse. It was about the man who made him.

Back in 2023, it was Michael O'Sullivan on his back. A relative rookie at the time, who had never ridden a festival winner before, he took a pull on Marine Nationale before the final flight and had one go at Facile Vega after the last. Precision timing. It was a masterful piece of riding that announced this confident young Cork jockey to the world. We knew we would be hearing so much more about him. And that we did. But not nearly enough.

On the darkest of days at Thurles in early February, that beautiful young boy suffered what proved to be a fatal fall from Wee Charlie. He was gone. But never forgotten. And in Marine Nationale we all still feel like we have a piece of him around. Something to cling on to. He was the man who made him what he is.

Flanagan gazed up to the sky, shook his head and added: "It's hugely emotional for a lot of reasons. All the jockeys in Ireland and the UK, and in the world, have been under a cloud for the last couple of weeks. Michael will never be forgotten."

O'Sullivan was in the saddle for Marine Nationale's first eight outings, winning the first six of those, and he developed an incredible rapport with the handsome son of French Navy. He lost the ride when opting to step back from his position as Barry Connell's number one in order to explore different avenues, some of which were in France.

Flanagan came in for the ride at Christmas. Marine Nationale continued on a path of gradual progress then and again on his return to Leopardstown for the Dublin Racing Festival. Then he did what Connell told us he would do in the lead-up to the 2025 Champion Chase. He proved to everyone that the Supreme wasn't a flash in the pan. That festival victory with O'Sullivan was only the start of a special journey.

"He probably hasn't been given credit since winning the Supreme," said Connell on this return to the Cheltenham winner's enclosure. "People forget he only had two runs last season, so he was effectively a novice this season and we had to plan a campaign to give him experience.

"He loves this place. He comes alive here. We were very confident but were understated as I was too confident last time and I wasn't going to do that again. That's what he's shown us before. He travels, jumps and is everything you want in a Champion Chase horse. I've been coming here since the 1980s when I was a student, just as a punter, and it's the one race I wanted to win. It's pure, unadulterated, on-the-edge speed.

▸*Continues page 58*

This won't sink in for a long time."

Amid the euphoria, Connell also remembered the man who made him. "The last three or four weeks have been so poignant and raw. It's been horrendous," he said. "Michael and myself went on a journey with Marine Nationale. He rode him during his novice hurdle season. He started as a 7lb claimer and I asked him to turn professional.

"He won three Grade 1s as a claimer, was leading rider on the first day of the festival in 2023 and was then leading conditional. It's a tragedy that he's left us but that's a record he could be proud of. He achieved more than a lot of riders who have been riding for a lot longer ever achieve.

"I'd like to dedicate this win to Michael and his girlfriend Charlotte, who is here with the horse and helped to saddle him. Our hearts go out to her, his family and friends. Racing is a great community and gets behind people when things like this happen and hopefully this is a fitting end."

★★★★

THE Champion Chase itself was a rout. It was supposed to be Jonbon's belated big day in the Cotswolds but it turned into another tale of woe. "We were stood up against the tape and it's gone back and pinged up against his nose. He's just been startled for a second, then they've gone hard," said his rider Nico de Boinville, trying to explain another underwhelming festival effort.

Jonbon has now been runner-up in the Supreme, the Arkle and the Champion Chase. This time he was hammered by a huge margin after a horrendous mistake at the ninth fence halted his momentum and sent him back to the rear of the field. Some said the writing had been on the wall before then and he certainly didn't look to be in his usual slick rhythm. Everything was an effort.

Nicky Henderson was in a philosophical mood after the 5-6

favourite's defeat. He showered the winner with praise rather than wallowing in self-pity. "It's a great result for the winner," he said. "Marine Nationale was the horse we had to fear most, so fair play to them. You've got to grab your opportunities and they did."

And, boy, did Marine Nationale grab that opportunity. He travelled around the place like silk, everything so smooth, and was lightning quick through the air. This was the day he was transformed from a very good horse into potentially a great one.

Flanagan, of course, didn't want to make it about himself. He knew he was only a small cog in the machine but it was still a breakthrough moment for the rider who was once a journeyman going nowhere. His career has turned around in spectacular fashion, despite losing the role as Noel Meade's stable jockey in 2022.

"I'm just lucky I can get on the likes of this lad," Flanagan said. "It's credit to all the people back at Barry's. I'm only drafted in very late to steer him round. The work is already done.

"This is phenomenal. I had a good job and I rode plenty of nice winners on good horses, but that was gone and I was at the point where you either fall off the edge or stumble across a horse like Marine Nationale. It's one horse you're looking for. This is everything to me. Me and my wife have a young family and I never get to spend any time with them, but seeing Daddy doing this will mean it's all worthwhile."

★★★★

IT WAS one of the most emotionally charged Cheltenham Festival afternoons in recent memory. Charlotte Giles, Michael's girlfriend who had lost the love of her life, somehow had the courage to find the right words after Marine Nationale's victory.

"They started their careers together and went on a journey together," she said. "The horse has

▲ Rising to the occasion: from top, Marine Nationale jumps the last in the Queen Mother Champion Chase; Sean Flanagan gives the winner a pat; below, trainer Barry Connell and Charlotte Giles, Michael O'Sullivan's girlfriend, after the race

certainly put his heart and soul into today and it means a lot. At the last jump, I got a bit of a fright, but Michael was with him every step of the way and it was incredible to watch.

"I think the horse has shown what a connection he had with Michael. They understood each other and Michael always rated the horse so highly. In moments like this, we get a great sense that he's here with us."

Michael O'Sullivan was there that day. You could feel him everywhere. He was looking down on one of those unforgettable Cheltenham days when some things are just meant to be. He was the man who made Marine Nationale and the 2025 Champion Chase had his fingerprints all over it.

'Our target is to win three' – Connell

A SECOND Champion Chase triumph at the Punchestown festival confirmed Marine Nationale's arrival in the elite and fuelled dreams of more glory to come.

Having defeated JP McManus's Jonbon at Cheltenham, Barry Connell's star left a favourite in the green and gold trailing again in the Punchestown version. This time it was Fact To File who could not live with him. The runaway Ryanair Chase winner was left well behind in fourth as Marine Nationale powered home by seven lengths from Captain Guinness.

The only three-time winner of Cheltenham's Champion Chase is 1980s hero Badsworth Boy and Connell is aiming to put Marine Nationale alongside him.

"I think this horse has all the attributes to be a multiple Champion Chase winner," the trainer said at Punchestown. "Our target is to win three and equal Badsworth Boy. He's only eight. That was his 12th run – he has no mileage on the clock. He can go back next year at nine, and ten. He grows an extra leg at Cheltenham."

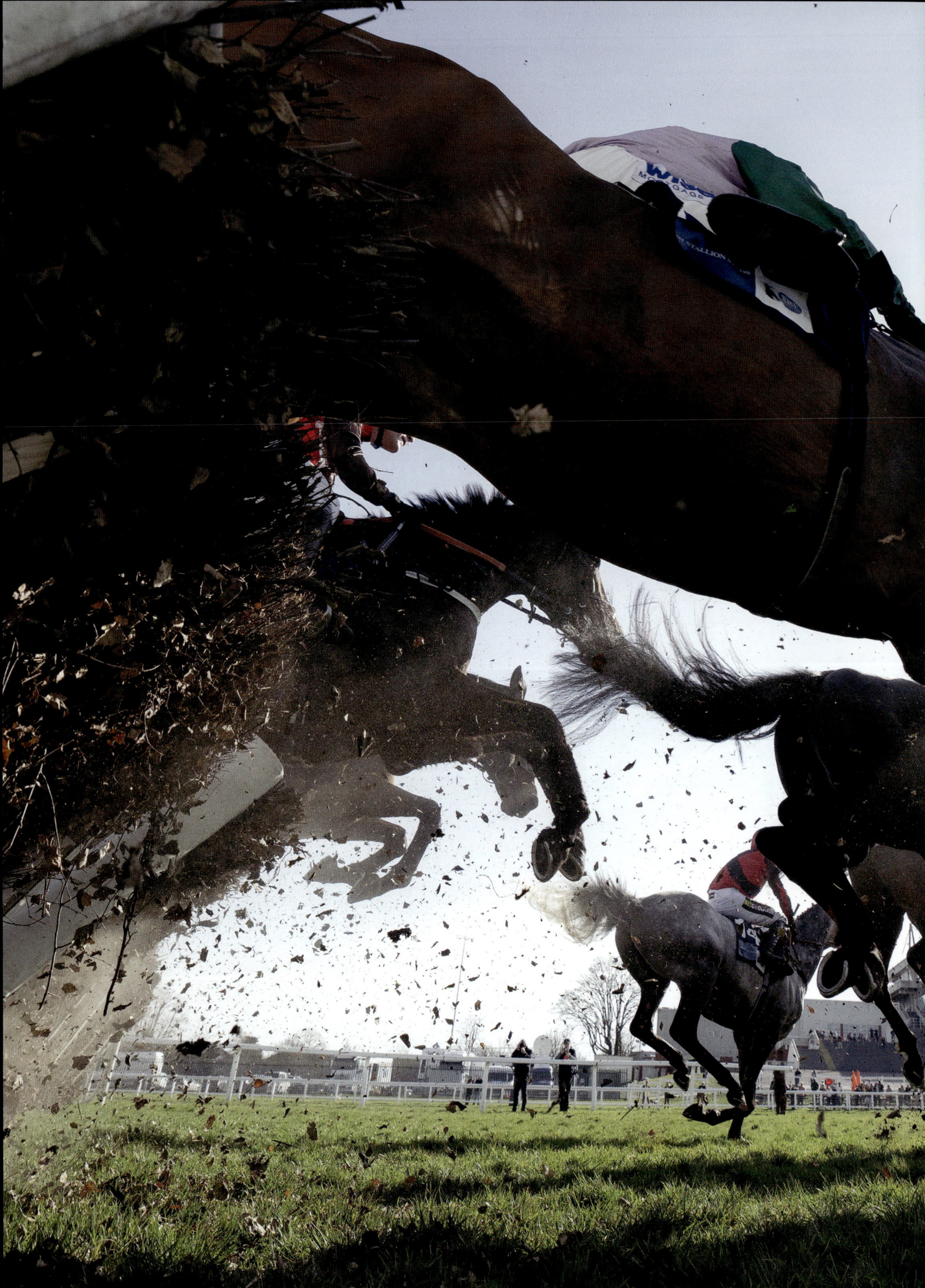

Runners in the thick of the action in the EBF
Novices' Handicap Hurdle Final at Sandown
in March. Victory goes to the Jamie Snowden-
trained 33-1 shot Laurens Bay
EDWARD WHITAKER (RACINGPOST.COM/PHOTOS)

MICHAEL O'SULLIVAN
2000-2025

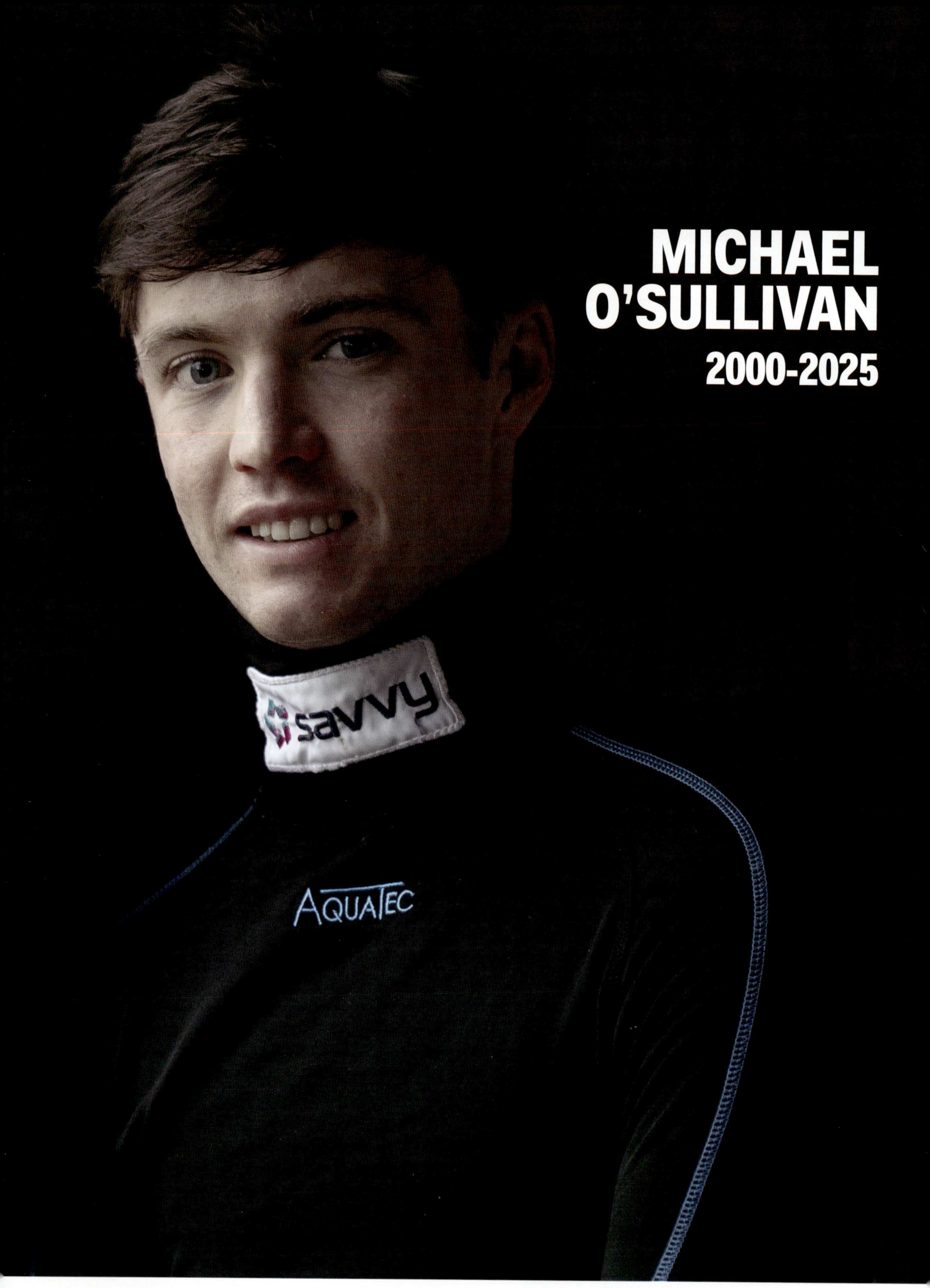

The talented jockey who made his name on Marine Nationale was just 24 when he died in February following a fall at Thurles. He was remembered in these articles from the Racing Post

By Richard Forristal and Justin O'Hanlon

MICHAEL O'SULLIVAN'S family paid tribute to the "extraordinary young man he had become" after the world of racing was plunged into despair when it emerged the Cheltenham Festival-winning jockey had tragically died as a result of the head injuries he sustained in a fall at Thurles on February 6. His death in the early hours of February 16 came just five days shy of his 25th birthday.

O'Sullivan had been in an induced coma in the intensive care unit at Cork University Hospital, having been airlifted after a last-fence fall from Wee Charlie in a handicap chase at the Tipperary track, at which point the remainder of the card was abandoned. He never regained consciousness and died surrounded by his family.

A eulogy published by the family on RIP.ie said: "Michael had accomplished so much in his short life. As a family we are so incredibly proud not only of his achievements in the saddle but of the extraordinary young man he had become. He was full of kindness, integrity, ambition and love, always striving to be the best person he could be.

"Michael will be very sadly missed by Bernie, William, Alan, grandmother 'Granny Mary', aunts, uncles, cousins, Charlotte, his many friends, as well as his weighroom colleagues and the wider racing community."

Announcing the heartbreaking news, Jennifer Pugh, chief medical officer of the Irish Horseracing Regulatory Board, said: "Michael sadly passed away,
▸Continues page 64

▼Crowning moment: Michael O'Sullivan celebrates his win on Marine Nationale in the 2023 Supreme Novices' Hurdle

surrounded by his loving family in Cork University Hospital. We extend our appreciation to the multidisciplinary teams who provided the best of medical care to Michael, both on the racecourse and in Cork University Hospital.

"Michael's family took the decision to donate his organs at this incredibly difficult time, but in doing so made a choice that will make a real difference to the lives of other patients and their families.

"I have had the privilege of knowing Michael through his amateur and professional career, and his dedication, modesty and kind nature always made him a pleasure to be around. Michael's success and humility will have inspired many and I share the feeling of loss with all those who knew him.

"Michael's family would like to reiterate their gratefulness for all the support they have received in the last couple of days and express their appreciation to the local community and racing family."

★ ★ ★ ★

O'SULLIVAN had emerged as one of the brightest young talents in the weighing room, enjoying a crowning moment when guiding Marine Nationale to Supreme Novices' Hurdle glory at the 2023 Cheltenham Festival. That was one of three Grade 1 winners he rode.

Having ridden Marine Nationale to a pair of bumper wins for Barry Connell, he elected to join the paid ranks with Connell's support in 2022 and the partnership enjoyed a number of memorable days before they went their separate ways last November. He had since been plying his trade in the freelance ranks, including being on Willie Mullins' roster.

The champion trainer expressed his heartfelt regret at the loss of the talented young rider. "We are devastated by the news," said Mullins. "Michael had been riding out here for the past three

years, since he was a 7lb claimer. He had become an integral part of our operation and his role was getting bigger. He was a credit to his family.

"He was a natural horseman and a great rider who loved the game and was going to be a big name. He was very modest and understated. He put his head down and grafted and took every chance he got. He's a big loss to racing."

An immensely popular, charismatic and mature young man from Lombardstown near Mallow in north County Cork, who attained an Agricultural Science degree at University College Dublin before devoting himself to riding, O'Sullivan hailed from a family immersed in racing.

His father William was an accomplished amateur rider who rode Lovely Citizen to a famous Cheltenham Festival success in the 1991 Foxhunter Chase. Lovely Citizen was trained by William's brother Eugene, who replicated the feat by producing It Came To Pass to win the same race under his daughter Maxine in 2020. More recently, Eugene has been known for producing star chaser Corbetts Cross. Michael's brother Alan also rides as an amateur.

As a mark of respect, the meeting at Punchestown on February 16 was cancelled along with the day's point-to-points.

★★★★

CHAMPION jockey Paul Townend echoed Mullins' poignant sentiments in speaking on behalf of his weighing room colleagues.

"He left a positive mark on everyone and it was a privilege to know him for such a short amount of time," said Townend. "He was a good friend. He had a very intelligent wit and you wouldn't have got one over on

▸Continues page 66

'We had a magical time together'

FOR just over two years their partnership was the most successful in their respective training and riding careers, a period trainer Barry Connell described as a "magical time together". It began with a phone call from Michael O'Sullivan to Connell in May 2022.

Connell said: "Michael had ridden for me in a point-to-point the year before. We had no stable amateur at the time and we had Marine Nationale entered in a bumper at the Punchestown May meeting. Michael rang wondering if I had anyone to ride him, and asked if he could. From his perspective, he was at home working on the farm and took a chance. Often fate can just be a phone call, you don't know where it could lead.

"I was hugely impressed by horse and rider on the day. I rang Michael shortly afterwards and asked if he'd be interested in coming in and riding out for a few days a week. He started doing that and the more we saw of him, the more we liked him. I had no stable jockey as such at the time, so a couple of months later I sat down with him and told him I thought he should turn professional."

The rest is history, with the 2022-23 season highlighted by Marine Nationale winning the Grade 1 Royal Bond Novice Hurdle and the Supreme Novices' Hurdle at Cheltenham, as well as Good Land taking a Grade 1 novice hurdle at the Dublin Racing Festival.

Connell said: "It was fairytale stuff for the two of us over the next 12 months after he said 'yes' to turning pro. We just happened to have two Grade 1 horses in the yard at the time – some trainers never get a Grade 1 horse – and he really took the opportunities.

"He went from winning a bumper in May to turning professional, and even though he was still claiming 5lb I had no compunction in putting him up on those Grade 1 horses because of his mentality and professionalism. He was very easy to deal with and fitted in very well in the yard.

"His composure to win the Royal Bond on Marine Nationale, in a race where everything that could have gone wrong did go wrong, was the main thing everyone took out of that race. We went straight to Cheltenham after that.

"They were a unit, he and the horse. They understood each other. He got as much advice as he could get from the senior jockeys about riding at Cheltenham, and I think the race was won at the first hurdle.

"Michael had one plan in mind, and that was to track the favourite Facile Vega, but the horse put in a tremendous leap at the first to take him upsides Facile Vega. However, he reined him back as he wanted to track that horse and have one go at him. He stuck to his plan, had one go coming down to the last, and won.

"When he was interviewed afterwards he was very level-headed, talking about his family and everything his parents and grandparents had done for him. He showed a lot of humility given the occasion."

Connell added: "One of my abiding memories was standing in the parade ring before the Ballymore on the second day of that meeting. Michael was riding Good Land in the race for me, and one of the officials came out to me with the gold armband and asked me to put it on Michael, as he had been the leading rider on day one. It was an enormous achievement and showed how far he'd come in less than a year.

"We had a magical time together and I'll always cherish the memories."

Justin O'Hanlon

◀Special day: Barry Connell congratulates Michael O'Sullivan after Marine Nationale's Supreme win

him too quickly. He was professional and intelligent in his approach to everything. He had a big personality and will be a loss to everyone."

O'Sullivan's death resonated to the highest office, with the Taoiseach Micheal Martin also offering his condolences. "Deeply saddened to learn of the tragic death of jockey Michael O'Sullivan," said Martin. "A talented rider who inspired many. My sincere sympathies go to Michael's family, his friends and colleagues in the racing world."

The O'Sullivans are one of the most decorated and respected families on the point-to-point scene and Michael was champion novice rider in the sphere in 2019. His exploits since taking the plunge in the paid ranks had been a source of great pride for them, with a glittering CV also featuring the 2023 conditional jockeys' title at the end of his first season as a professional.

O'Sullivan was the first jockey to die following a fall at an Irish track since Jack Tyner in 2011 as a result of injuries he sustained in a point-to-point, while in 2016 John Thomas McNamara died three years after the Cheltenham Festival fall that left him paralysed.

All three were deeply rooted in the point-to-point community, so this latest catastrophe was another terrible blow to those at the grassroots of the industry, following as it did the appalling 2022 death of 13-year-old Jack de Bromhead after a pony racing fall. It is 22 years since the death of 25-year-old Kieran Kelly, another Cheltenham Festival-winning rider, following a fall at Kilbeggan.

In all, O'Sullivan rode 95 winners in Britain and Ireland. His first success on the racecourse came on Wilcosdiana, who was trained by his uncle Eugene, in the hunter chase held in Tyner's memory at Cork in April 2018.

These are edited versions of articles that appeared in the Racing Post on February 17

Overwhelmingly likeable human, horseman and gentleman who had the racing world at his feet

Ireland editor Richard Forristal paid tribute to the hugely talented jockey

AFTER more than a week spent longing for a different outcome, the horseracing community and its many supporters mourn the loss of a rising star in the wake of Michael O'Sullivan's harrowing death. An extraordinarily talented jockey in the prime of his life robbed of the promise of everything that lay ahead, his family left bereft.

That, put simply, is the visceral tragedy of his passing. However, what many of the sport's well-wishers might not be privy to are some of the more intimate traits of a young man with the world at his feet.

Michael was an inherently decent guy, a well-mannered, witty and deeply intelligent person who distinguished himself with a university degree and spoke French fluently on his riding excursions there. He enjoyed all manner of sports and was someone who exhibited all of the humility imbued in him by his family, down-to-earth people who are the embodiment of the grassroots point-to-point fraternity. His father William and mother Bernie are dairy farmers first, and Michael was of the earth too.

When he made the decisive phone call to Barry Connell looking for the ride on an unraced five-year-old son of French Navy in a Punchestown bumper three years ago, he did so in between fixing clusters to udders in his father's milking shed. To the parlour born.

His subsequent glorious association with Marine Nationale elevated him to stratospheric heights, yet Michael's feet never left the ground. There was a charismatic, slightly languid swagger to him but not a hint of arrogance. He was just an overwhelmingly likeable human, a horseman and a gentleman who recognised the privilege of the position he had put himself in and embraced the responsibility that came with it.

A year ago, I sat down with him in his car at the Racing Academy and Centre of Education. He apologised at length for the inconvenience of having to conduct the interview in the car, but we both had busy schedules and he wanted to accommodate me, and at one point we touched on how, in contrast to some of his more guarded peers, he did everything he could to indulge the media's requests.

"My father tells me I talk too much sometimes, but, you know, with the way racing is at the minute I feel we need to engage with the public and fans, and get people into the sport," he said. "It's important, very important, when you look at all the problems we're facing."

He was 23 years of age, yet understood the role he could play in the bigger picture, already giving something back. That was a mark of the man, a mark of how well reared he was, and he deserved better than this in return from the sport he loved. We all know horseracing's fates are indiscriminate, but this is an appalling blow that will reverberate far beyond the confines of our parish.

It is unthinkably cruel that any family should have to mourn the loss of a 24-year-old grandson, son, brother, nephew or cousin, yet this brutal reality is exacerbated by the sheer dignity of the departed.

The very same was true of John Thomas McNamara, Jack Tyner and young Jack de Bromhead, all lost in the last decade and a half, and there is no underplaying the extent to which this latest trauma will devastate the grassroots community in the Munster pocket from which they all hail.

Only two and a half years have passed since Michael turned professional. He had a quiet, determined ambition about him. The easy option would have been to stay in the comfort zone of point-to-points and capitalise on his growing reputation with the support of his family, but he took a leap of faith. What an impact he made in such a short space of time.

The stylish composure he demonstrated in the eye of the storm with that swashbuckling double on day one of the 2023 Cheltenham Festival when, having just turned 23, he delivered a masterclass beyond his years aboard Marine Nationale, epitomised his ready-made potential. He was just a kid but he looked the finished article and conducted himself accordingly.

Michael's association with Connell duly ran its course, but it says much of the regard in which he was held that he was sought after by both Gordon Elliott and Willie Mullins, the latter providing what would prove his last big winner in Embassy Gardens at Tramore on New Year's Day.

Sadly, at the final fence of a two-mile handicap chase at a nondescript Thurles fixture, the merciless vagaries of this sport conspired to rob him of what should have been a new beginning.

The grim reality of the risks jockeys live with on a daily basis does not make such a dire outcome any easier to reconcile and will be absolutely no consolation to his family.

To them, we send nothing but love, and to Michael in his eternal resting place we send forth our gratitude for him being the man he was. May he rest in peace.

◄ Paul Townend wins the renamed Michael O'Sullivan Supreme Novices' Hurdle and embraces Charlotte Giles, the late jockey's girlfriend, in the winner's enclosure

A *smooth* finish...

Richard Hannon Jr., Pink Lily's trainer, commented:

"Pink Lily when she came in she looked great, she has managed to put on all that weight over the winter and looks better than ever. She is a month further ahead than most of mine in her coat and I am looking forward to running her. Very happy with her indeed!"

Highclere Estate premium oats are part of the botanicals making our gin one of the smoothest on the market.

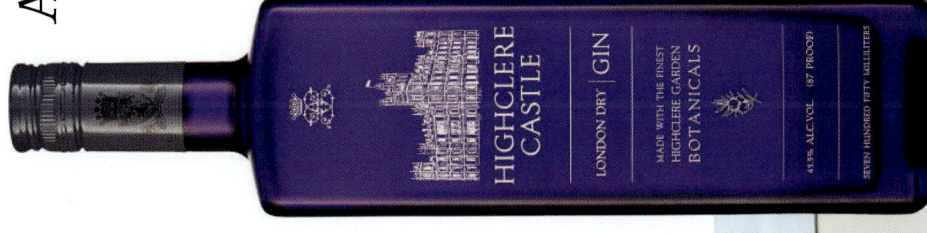

Pink Lily. 3YO (Owner: Lord Carnarvon), winning at Bath, over 1m 2f, jockey A Voikhansky, 22th May 2024.

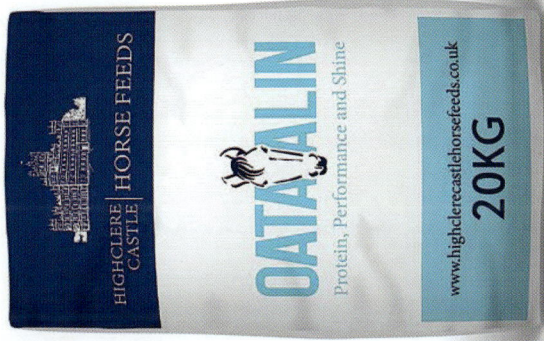

OATAALIN
by Highclere Castle Horse Feeds Ltd.

*OATAALIN mix is designed to give your horse the best performance, energy and shine, **as well as contributing to the avoidance of stomach ulcers in horses in training.***

WHY USE OATAALIN?

OATAALIN mix is designed to give horses the best of whole natural foods in three key grains: the digestibility and energy of Oats, the Calcium & Vitamins and buffer to acidity in Alfalfa.

Linseed aids skin & coat condition and is **anti-inflammatory** with slow release energy.

KEY INGREDIENTS:

- Superior Rolled Oats from Highclere Estate
- Pelletised Alfalfa
- Micronised Linseed

"At Highclere we have been feeding OATAALIN to our thoroughbreds. Highly palatable, its excellent qualities are reflected in the shine of their coats, their energy levels and their relaxed attitudes."

Pelletised Alfalfa

Office: 01635 250600 Mobile: 07950 010692
Email: office@highclereestate.co.uk
Web: www.highclerecastlehorsefeeds.co.uk

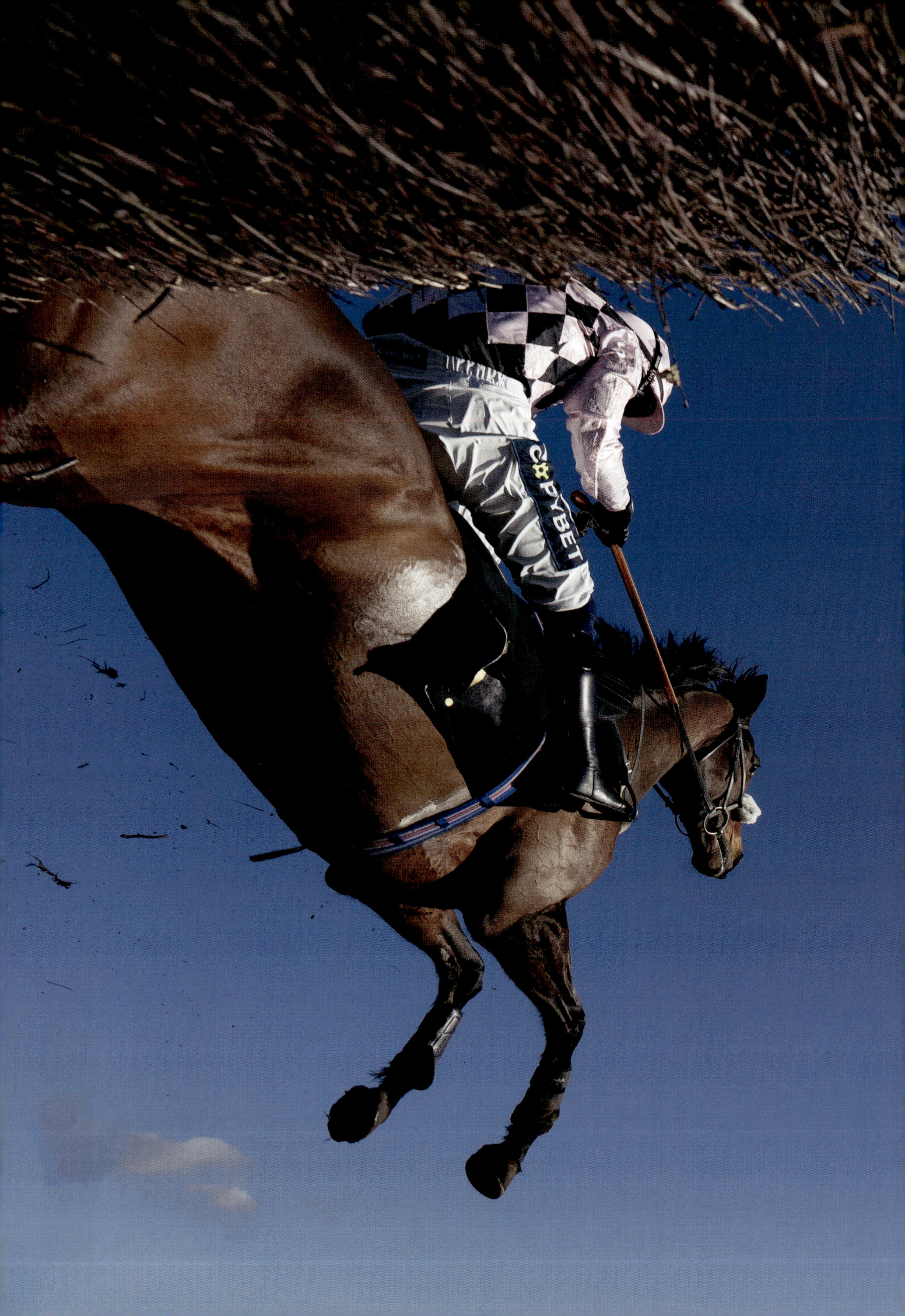

⊙ THE
BIGGER
PICTURE

Filanderer and Johnny Burke jump the final
fence on their way to a novice handicap chase
success at Wincanton in January, the middle
leg of a hat-trick spread across six months for
the Hughie Morrison-trained nine-year-old
EDWARD WHITAKER (RACINGPOST.COM/PHOTOS)

IN THE
PICTURE

Poniros sets Triumph record at 100-1 – and prompts rule change

EVEN Willie Mullins didn't expect it. The king of the Cheltenham Festival had little hope when he sent out Poniros for his jumps debut in the Triumph Hurdle and was as surprised as anyone when the 100-1 shot passed the post in front after edging out Nicky Henderson's much-vaunted Lulamba by a neck.

Poniros was the longest-priced winner in the history of the race, which dates back to 1939, and the first hurdling debutant to take the prize since the race was moved to Cheltenham in 1965 following the closure of Hurst Park, its original home.

It won't be repeated, however, after the BHA changed the so-called 'Poniros rule' in the autumn. Horses in Grade 1 juvenile and novice hurdles will now need a rating of at least 110 to be permitted a run, either via a published handicap mark or if the BHA handicapper deems them to have run to that level in at least one hurdle race.

Poniros is owned by Brighton and Hove Albion chairman Tony Bloom, a renowned punter, after being bought out of Ralph Beckett's stable for 200,000gns at the 2024 autumn sales. "If Tony Bloom backed him, it wasn't on my advice," Mullins said after the Triumph. "I couldn't believe it when I saw him flying through the middle of them. I didn't expect that. I don't think I've ever really given him a serious gallop at home. I didn't think he'd be sharp enough but his Flat-race experience came into it in the last three furlongs."

The Triumph started a new rivalry at the top of the juvenile hurdling division and the first two met for a rematch at the Punchestown festival in the Champion Four Year Old Hurdle. This time Lulamba was a decisive winner by four lengths from Poniros, stretching clear on the run-in after a fierce battle to the final flight.

There was a feeling that Lulamba – less experienced than Poniros in overall terms – could have won at Cheltenham with more time to respond to his rival's surprise late thrust but he set the record straight in convincing fashion.

"We got a bit of revenge there," Henderson said at Punchestown. "This is only the fourth race of his life and he's a big baby. I wouldn't say he was unlucky not to win at Cheltenham but he couldn't do anything about it at the time."

That victory gave Lulamba top billing in the division in the end-of-season Anglo-Irish Jumps Classifications. Racing Post Ratings had him on a mark of 154, against 147 for Poniros.

Picture: Edward Whitaker (racingpost.com/photos)

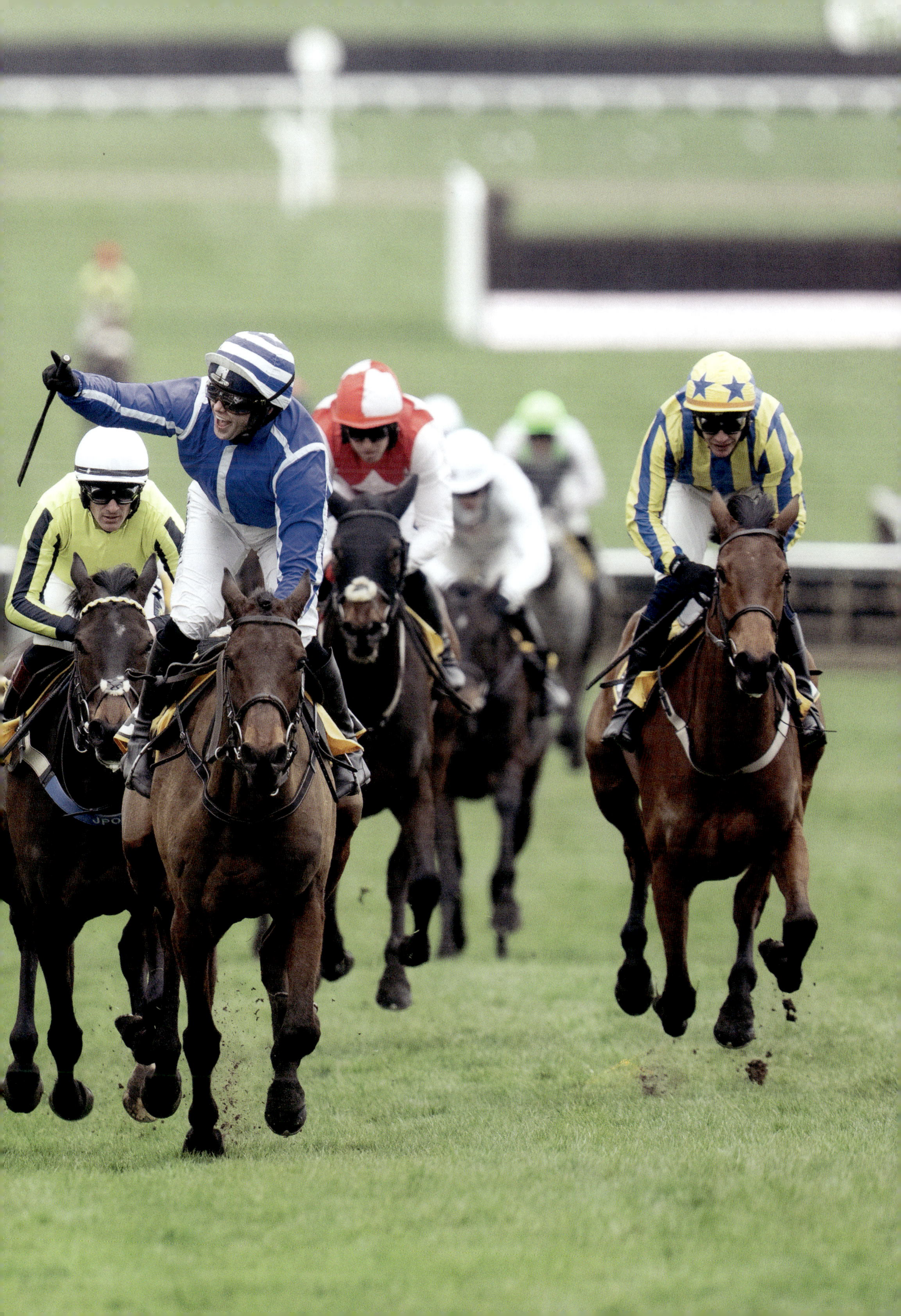

Final flourish

Rachael Blackmore's Cheltenham swansong brought her the full set of festival monuments with Stayers' Hurdle victory on Bob Olinger

By Nick Pulford
Racing Post Annual editor

RACHAEL BLACKMORE'S final fling at the Cheltenham Festival came with an old flame. No-one knew it at the time but it was fitting that her 18th and last win at jump racing's biggest meeting was on Bob Olinger in the Stayers' Hurdle. They had shared the festival love twice before but their biggest triumph together was on a different level. A special ride led to a special moment.

For both Blackmore and trainer Henry de Bromhead, the Stayers' Hurdle completed the full set of the festival's marquee events. On the jockey's side, it was a rare feat that not even the great AP McCoy had achieved – it was the Stayers' Hurdle that never featured on his incredibly long list of wins. How Blackmore did it had the hallmark of class too.

The night before the race, Robbie Power – who does race planning for De Bromhead and owners Robcour – had told her that if she was upsides at the last, she had got there too soon. The Gold Cup-winning former jockey's words were worth heeding. Even though Bob Olinger was travelling strongly from the home turn, Blackmore waited as long as she dared before unleashing him up the run-in. Their combined power was irresistible.

Teahupoo, the 2024 winner and favourite again in the Robcour colours, was overtaken just after the last and swept away by a length and three-quarters.

"Rachael was class," De Bromhead said. "She gets such a tune out of him. She asked him for two jumps and that's it. She lets him pop away and he loves doing that. He just doesn't need to be forced."

There was no forcing, just a simple bond. Blackmore and Bob Olinger were in unison, each responding to the other's wishes. The perfect couple.

★ ★ ★ ★

PATIENCE with Bob Olinger was a quality shared by the whole De Bromhead team at Knockeen down in County Waterford. They had long waited for a return to the sort of form that made him an early festival star with his wins in what is now the Turners Novices' Hurdle in 2021 and 12 months later in the now defunct Turners Novices' Chase, albeit with a huge slice of good fortune on the second occasion when Galopin Des Champs fell at the last.

As he was being prepared for his first run at the festival since then, the now ten-year-old had become a nearly horse at the top level, most notably when beaten a nose in a messy finish to the 2024 Aintree Hurdle. His last win had been in the Grade 2 Relkeel Hurdle at Cheltenham on New Year's Day 2024, he had twice been beaten by Stayers' Hurdle rival Home By The Lee in the current season and his stamina for the three-mile test was open to serious question.

Quietly, though, Bob
‣ *Continues page 74*

Olinger was being brought back to top form after what De Bromhead described as "a couple of funny old years with him". He spent important restorative time away from the yard with Power and a key role back at Knockeen through the winter was played by assistant trainer Davy Roche.

Paying tribute after all the hard work paid off with a third festival win, De Bromhead said: "It's a big team effort. I can't say enough about Davy Roche, who adores him. He would literally have him in the house with him if he could. Robbie Power got him going, and then there's all our team at home – the chiropractors,

▼Job done: Henry de Bromhead celebrates Bob Olinger's glorious return to top form in the Stayers' Hurdle, completing the full set of the Cheltenham Festival's marquee races for the trainer

physios, vets. You name it, everyone's involved in him."

Armed with the knowledge that the teamwork was beginning to bear fruit, De Bromhead approached the festival with a growing sense that Bob Olinger was being undervalued. "I remember I was at a preview and I was like 'Oh my God, he's 66-1' and I just couldn't believe it. If he'd been 20-1 then fair enough, but Home By The Lee, who had beaten him, was just much shorter."

On raceday, De Bromhead was asked by Matt Chapman on ITV Racing about a gamble that had been building on Bob Olinger. From 20-1 overnight,

he would be down to 8-1 at the off. "Is he being backed?" asked the trainer. "Really? I must admit I was surprised he was such a big price, so I'm pleased people are recognising him."

Recognition like never before was just around the corner for Bob Olinger.

★★★★

DE BROMHEAD and Blackmore had faced their own travails through the winter. The jockey spent three months on the sidelines with a serious neck injury and when she returned the Knockeen horses were badly out of form. She had two winners in Ireland in December, one in January and one in February. In the first two months of the year, De Bromhead sent out just six winners.

"We weren't in form, but I think I had 12 of these, some of our best horses, trotting in the indoor school for the whole of January," De Bromhead recalled. "So if you take them out of it, we don't have the depth to keep going when you've got your best horses out of the game. Now, obviously we still weren't in good form but we were coming to ourselves."

Cheltenham is where De Bromhead and Blackmore have hit top form so often in recent years, but it happened slowly this time. Their spring finally started to blossom in the first race on the Stayers' card when Air Of Entitlement took the Mares' Novices' Hurdle at 16-1. It was a last-gasp victory brilliantly executed by Blackmore. "You were amazing," the winning trainer told her.

Less than three hours later the plaudits were flowing again after another Blackmore masterclass in the Stayers'. Having avoided trouble at the sixth when Crambo fell outside her and the badly hampered Home By The Lee unseated, she had Bob Olinger in a

challenging position coming off the final bend but bided her time at the back of a tight leading group.

Teahupoo was the first to show up front in the Robcour colours as owner Brian Acheson watched the race unfold in his favour. The 7-4 favourite was his likely hero again and he wasn't expecting a barnstorming finish from Bob Olinger. "I didn't think he could do it," he admitted. "I thought he would come to the bottom of the hill and stop because he had never won over three miles."

This time, driven on by Blackmore, the horse described by his owner as his "third child" refused to stop as he surged past Teahupoo for a Robcour one-two. Not only had Bob Olinger proved his stamina over the Stayers' trip – "What a bloody place to do it for the first time," Acheson exclaimed – but he had reaffirmed his love of the festival.

"He's unbeaten here – one day it was a fortuitous win, but you need a bit of luck too, and he gets it here," Blackmore said. "I could have easily run into the faller. We got lucky there but you need that. He's a phenomenal horse. We were very hopeful coming here, but for him to do it is fantastic."

Power was full of praise for Blackmore's ride. "She gave him a peach," he said. "She gets on unbelievably well with Bob. They have a great association and she knows how to ride him masterfully. What can you say about her? She's now won all the Cheltenham features, as well as the Grand National, and nobody rides this place like her."

So many special days had come Blackmore's way. Her last visit to the hallowed winner's enclosure was right up there.
Additional reporting by Richard Forristal, Lee Mottershead and Jonathan Harding

Find your career in horseracing

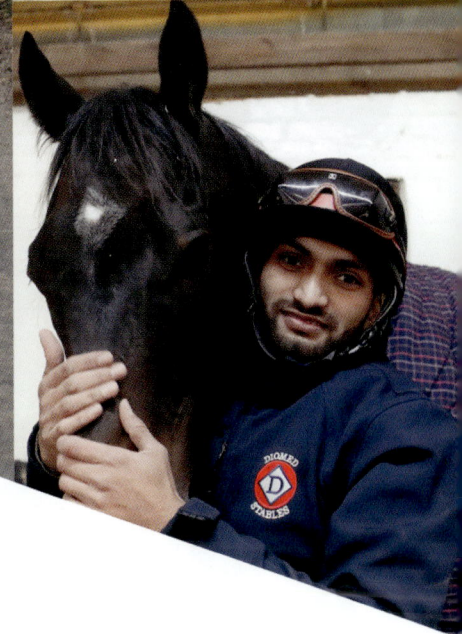

Whether it's training, apprenticeships or job roles, we are here to help you understand the industry and guide you towards making the right choice.

careersinracing.com

APPRENTICESHIP & TRAINING INFORMATION • CASE STUDIES & JOB PROFILES • FREE JOB BOARD

TRAILBLAZER

Rachael Blackmore, the pioneering jump jockey who became a global icon, announced her retirement in May at the age of 35

By Richard Forristal

"MY days of being a jockey have come to an end." With those words Rachael Blackmore, the virtuoso jump jockey who enjoyed seminal triumphs in the Grand National, Gold Cup, Champion Hurdle and Champion Chase, stunned the racing world on May 12 when she announced her immediate retirement from riding.

At the end of a season in which she completed the full house of the Cheltenham Festival's marquee events when Bob Olinger landed the Stayers' Hurdle, Blackmore decided to bring the curtain down on her career at the age of 35.

She made the announcement in a post on X. "I feel the time is right," she wrote. "I'm sad but I'm also incredibly grateful

Clockwise from left: A Plus Tard, Minella Times, Honeysuckle and Captain Guinness

▶Continues page 78

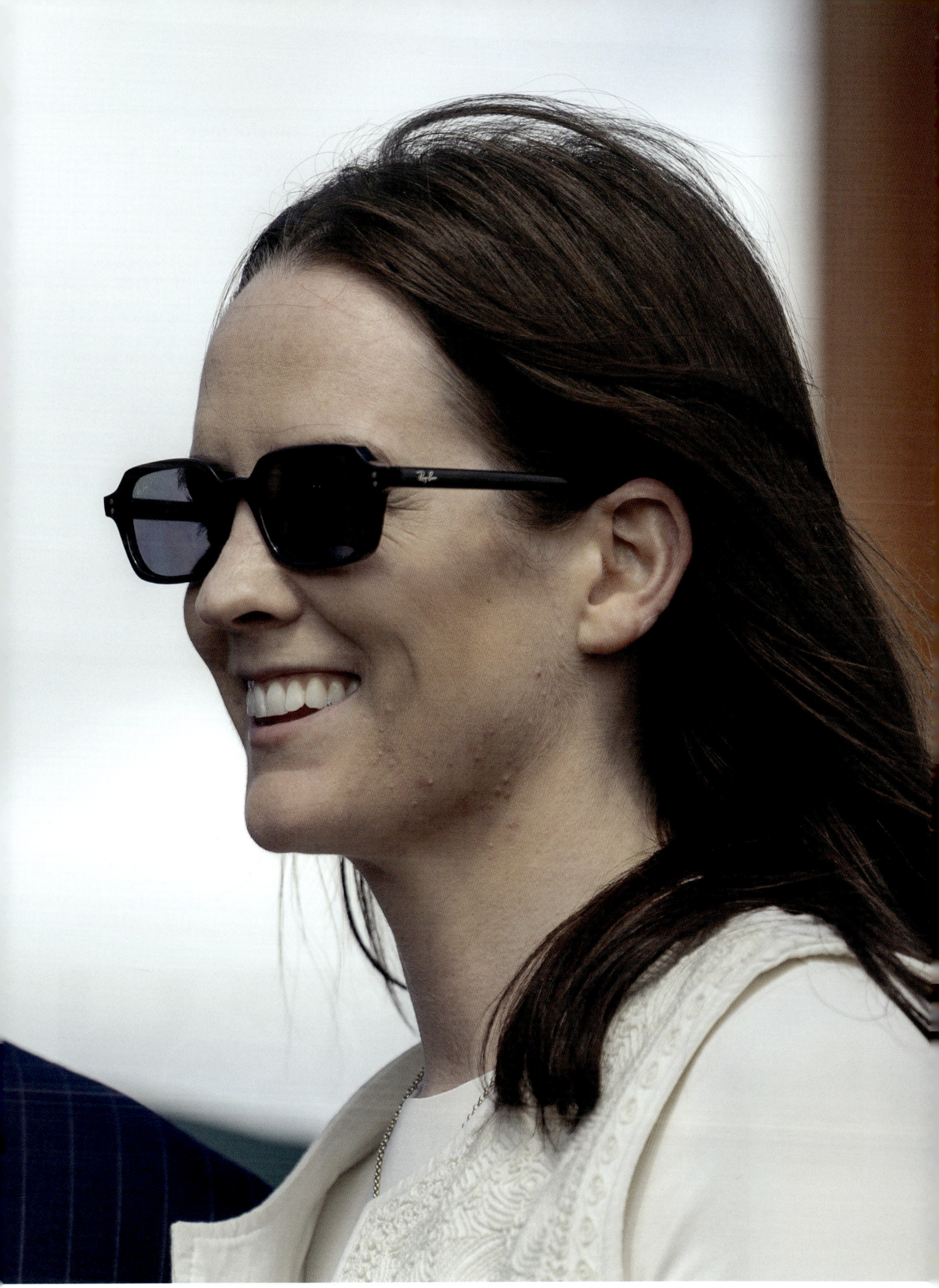

for what my life has been for the past 16 years. I just feel so lucky to have been legged up on the horses I have, and to have experienced success I never even dreamt could be possible."

Blackmore, who spent three months on the sidelines in the autumn of 2024 with a serious neck injury, departed the stage with a string of trailblazing firsts to her name. She won each of the Cheltenham Festival's feature races, famously executing one of the great Gold Cup rides of modern times to secure the sport's pinnacle event in 2022 on A Plus Tard. Like so many of her big winners, he was trained by her most devoted ally Henry de Bromhead.

"The people to thank are endless," Blackmore said. "It's not possible to mention everyone, as I don't want this to be another book, but I'm going to get a few names in here anyway and to everyone else, you know who you are, as they say.

"First, my parents who provided me with the best childhood, and a pony I couldn't hold! This set the seed for a life of racing. Aidan Kennedy gave me my first ride in a point-to-point. I spent time riding out for Arthur Moore and Pat Doyle which I loved. Sam Curling and Liam Lennon were also big supporters, as were Denise O'Shea, John Nicholson, Ellmarie Holden, Harry Smyth and Gigginstown House Stud.

▶Continues page 80

Pioneer, groundbreaker, attitude transformer

Rachael Blackmore changed everything. She is a pioneer, a groundbreaker and an attitude transformer. To properly contextualise her feats is almost impossible, yet it might best be done by saying Blackmore realised in fact what had once been deemed too fanciful for fiction.

There was a time when the 1944 film National Velvet was regularly shown on television. From one decade to the next, the movie's viewers saw Elizabeth Taylor playing a young girl who pretended to be a boy and rode a horse named The Pie in the Grand National. Hollywood being Hollywood, they stormed past the post in front, only for the victory to be quashed when Taylor fell off her mount just after the line, infringing rule 144 and leading to a medical assessment that revealed her true sex.

"A girl, ladies and gentlemen!" screamed a radio broadcaster at Aintree. "A bit of a girl clutching the neck of a bandy-legged outsider streaked across the line to win the greatest race in turfdom. A girl wins the Grand National!"

Yet a girl had not won. In the real world, women were then not permitted to ride in any races, let alone the sport's most fearsome, famous and coveted prize. It took until 1977 for a woman to don silks in the Grand National, yet in those days Charlotte Brew was regarded as little more than a novelty act, as was obvious by the words of BBC presenter Julian Wilson during a mid-1980s racing programme.

"The Grand National became a punchball in the battle for sex equality," said Wilson. "A girl called Charlotte Brew said she wanted to ride in the race. There was nothing to stop her, except, that is, the fences.

"Eventually, pretty Geraldine Rees proved that it could be done, completing the course, that is. It was a fine achievement on a moderate horse – but racing is one equestrian sport where females remain unlikely to break through, at least in the saddle."

Digested now, those words look terribly dated, but only thanks to those individuals who, in relatively recent times, have transformed the way in which female jockeys are regarded, not just outside the sport but inside. Nobody has done more to shift opinions than Blackmore, whose impact on horseracing has been at least as great as any of the outstanding riders to have gone before her.

Punters and pundits marvelled at her ability, both on quiet midweek afternoons in Ireland and on the very grandest stages. The first Grade 1 was claimed aboard Minella Indo at the 2019 Cheltenham Festival, the meeting at which Honeysuckle made her a Champion Hurdle winner on two occasions, first behind closed doors and then in front of a huge crowd that roared with delight when witnessing Blackmore's Gold Cup triumph on A Plus Tard.

That was in March 2022. Even more headlines had been made the previous April when Blackmore conquered the Grand National on Minella Times. It was a major global news story and resulted in the winning rider being named the BBC's World Sport Star of the Year, an award previously presented to the likes of Usain Bolt, Roger Federer and Tiger Woods. It was wonderful for Blackmore but also for racing.

The greatest female jump jockey of all time is not someone who craves the limelight, to the extent she has regularly turned down interview requests with the media. In that sense, the sport may not have been fully able to capitalise on her celebrity but the most valuable sign of her impact has so often been seen on racecourses, where children have sought out Blackmore and asked for an autograph or picture. They went home smiling.

Blackmore fulfilled her destiny but, more importantly, encouraged countless young girls in the same direction. Thanks to the woman who really did change everything, there is no such thing as an impossible dream.

Lee Mottershead

▶Final reminder: Rachael Blackmore wins one last time at Cheltenham on Bob Olinger in the Stayers' Hurdle

"I rode my first winner for Shark Hanlon, who then helped me become champion conditional. I will be forever grateful to Shark for getting behind me, supporting me and believing in me when it would have been just as easy to look elsewhere. He was the catalyst for what was to come.

"A conversation between [Gigginstown House Stud's] Eddie O'Leary and Henry de Bromhead in a taxi on the way to Aintree took my career to a whole new level. Eddie got me in the door at Knockeen, and what came next was unimaginable: Honeysuckle, A Plus Tard, Minella Indo, Captain Guinness, Bob Olinger, Minella Times, among many others all with one thing in common – Henry de Bromhead. He's a phenomenal trainer who brought out the best in me. Without Henry, my story is very different."

★★★★

IN 2021, Blackmore secured an unprecedented landmark when beating all her male counterparts to be crowned leading rider at the Cheltenham Festival. The following month, she rode the crest of a wave all the way to Aintree, claiming a heroic Grand National success on JP McManus's De Bromhead-trained Minella Times that resonated all over the world. Queen Mother Champion Chase victory on Captain Guinness in 2024 meant she joined an elite group comprising just Ruby Walsh, Tony McCoy and Barry Geraghty to have won jumping's four most prestigious races, and this year's Stayers' meant she achieved a quintet that eluded the mighty McCoy, who never won the race.

That victory in March, her second on the day, meant Blackmore departed with 18 Cheltenham Festival winners. She had been sitting in second place in terms of current riders, behind only Paul Townend. Just eight jockeys in the history of the sport

▸Continues page 82

'Cold, calculated precision – her piece de resistance'

Richard Forristal with three defining big-race rides

A Plus Tard 2022 Gold Cup The ride that epitomised the totality of Blackmore's brilliance. A year earlier the Gold Cup was the one that got away. Having ridden A Plus Tard patiently, she engaged too early and he came alive under her, vying to lead before they swung for home. Minella Indo relished the protracted duel.

In 2022, Blackmore still had five horses in front of her as they took the final bend in the Gold Cup. She wasn't going to get beaten for the same reason, and had a wall of horses in front of her with two fences to jump. All dressed up with nowhere to go on the Gold Cup favourite – exactly where she wanted to be.

Minella Indo had skipped away again, but Blackmore had a target on his back. She knew her mount had a searing turn of foot and needed to pick her moment. They squeezed between Al Boum Photo and Protektorat two out, and it was only on touching down that Blackmore lit the touchpaper. They finally took Minella Indo at the last, swallowing him whole to avenge their 2021 defeat to the tune of 15 lengths.

The emphatic margin belied the cold, calculated precision of the ride, because it was a subtle change that made all the difference. Her piece de resistance.

Honeysuckle 2021 Champion Hurdle When Honeysuckle faced the starter for the behind-closed-doors 2021 Champion Hurdle, no female jockey had won any of the Cheltenham Festival's marquee races and Blackmore wasn't the A-list superstar we came to know.

Honeysuckle's first Champion Hurdle win was the catalyst from which all else followed. The unbeaten mare was sent off the 11-10 market leader and, on the day, was the one required to complete a treble of short-priced favourites. The expectation was off the scale, but Blackmore stamped the occasion with the sort of calm conviction to which we would soon become accustomed.

When the need was greatest, under what should have been an overwhelming weight of pressure, Blackmore bloomed.

Despite Honeysuckle usually racing very handy, Blackmore recognised the pace was too strong and adapted accordingly, dropping in and gradually easing her mount closer.

When they pinged the third-last, suddenly Honeysuckle was in command. They led from two out and Blackmore closed the door on the challenging Aspire Tower, just to be sure.

Honeysuckle surged up the hill to glory, catapulting Blackmore into the history books.

Allaho 2021 Ryanair Chase Three days into the 2021 Cheltenham Festival Blackmore was riding the crest of a wave. She had three wins to her name after masterclasses on Bob Olinger and Sir Gerhard followed Honeysuckle's Champion Hurdle victory, and she was back in the Cheveley Park colours for Allaho in the Ryanair Chase. Paul Townend had opted for Min, but such was the irresistible force of Blackmore's onslaught that Allaho usurped his stablemate as favourite on the morning of the race.

When the tapes went up, she took no prisoners, and it was Townend who tried hardest to live with her on Min. They never stood a chance.

One of the first attributes astute judges twigged about Blackmore was how fluently and willingly horses jumped and ran for her, and this was the epitome of that trademark. The pace was ferocious, but two fine leaps saw Allaho seize the lead from the second fence and thereafter they did not relent. It was McCoy-esque.

She filled up Allaho with a couple of non-exuberant jumps five and four out, and when Townend felt he had a sniff again coming to the third-last, she went long. Allaho responded in kind and from there it was done. A complete obliteration.

▼All on her own: Rachael Blackmore comes home 12 lengths clear on Allaho in the 2021 Ryanair Chase

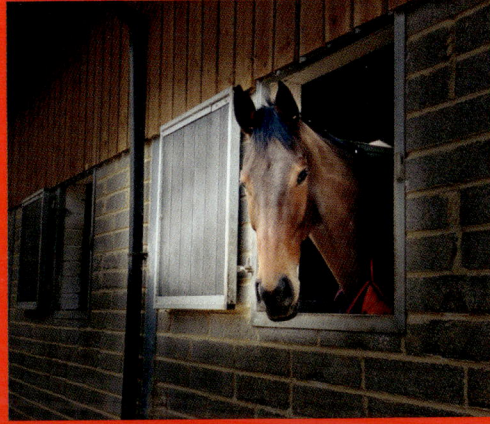

have ridden more festival winners than her.

When Blackmore had her first professional ride at the age of 25 aboard Redwood Boy at Down Royal on St Patrick's Day in 2015, she became the first female jump jockey to join the paid ranks in Ireland since Maria Cullen a quarter of a century earlier. At that stage, she had left behind an inauspicious career as an amateur, but she went on to secure her status as the most successful female jump jockey ever in sensational fashion.

In 2017, thanks in no small part to staunch support from Hanlon, with 32 wins she became the first of her sex to secure the conditional riders' championship in Ireland, and she twice went close to winning the senior title, finishing second to Townend in 2019 and 2021 with respective tallies of 90 and 92. Blackmore signed off with 564 winners, a record for a female jump jockey, as well as a further 12 on the Flat.

More than that, though, her exploits in a physically punishing sport that has long wrestled with perceptions of male bias, succeeded in transforming preconceptions about what it is possible for a female rider to achieve in jump racing.

In terms of promotion of the sport to a wider audience, Blackmore catapulted racing into another stratosphere by claiming some of the most historic sporting achievements of modern times.

Support from Michael O'Leary's Gigginstown House Stud ownership vehicle initially opened a door to her association with De Bromhead, and in March 2021, at a Cheltenham Festival held behind closed doors during the Covid-19 pandemic, Blackmore wrote herself into Cotswolds folklore when guiding Honeysuckle to Champion Hurdle glory. It was the first time a female jockey had won a British championship race, although she had by then claimed two Irish Champion Hurdles on Kenny Alexander's brilliant mare.

Blackmore went on to carry all before her in the Cotswolds after that epic Champion Hurdle success in 2021, with further wins for De Bromhead aboard Bob Olinger, Telmesomethinggirl and Quilixios supplemented by two inspired front-running rides aboard Allaho in the Ryanair Chase and Sir Gerhard in the Champion Bumper for Willie Mullins.

Those six wins meant she was crowned leading rider with a tally that only Ruby Walsh – after whom the award is now named – has bettered. She bowed out with an aggregate 33 Grade 1s.

★★★★

IN 2022, Blackmore claimed racing's greatest prize with a truly sublime ride. Tackling the Gold Cup on A Plus Tard – her first festival winner in the old novice handicap chase in 2019 and on whom she had finished second to stablemate Minella Indo in the 2021 Gold Cup – she deployed exaggerated waiting tactics on the Cheveley Park Stud-owned star.

Blackmore still had five horses in front of her turning into the straight and delayed her challenge until approaching the second-last fence. When she asked him to quicken, A Plus Tard surged clear for an emphatic victory, turning the tables on Minella Indo in devastating fashion. The 15-length margin of superiority was the widest since Master Oats' 1995 win.

The momentous success meant Blackmore emulated McCoy by becoming the first rider since the 20-time champion to complete the Champion Hurdle-Gold Cup double in the same year. Three days earlier, she and Honeysuckle had completed back-to-back wins in the Champion Hurdle.

Her 18th and final win at the meeting came aboard Bob Olinger, and now her legacy was complete. It might never be emulated, and so much has her status defined her identity that she concluded the announcement of her retirement with an existential thought.

Historic firsts

Born County Tipperary, July 11, 1989

Parents Charles Blackmore (Tipperary farmer) & Eimir Blackmore (schoolteacher)

Educated University of Limerick (degree in equine science)

Apprenticeship amateur rider with Shark Hanlon

First winner under rules Stowaway Pearl, lady riders' handicap hurdle, Thurles, February 10, 2011

First winner as professional Most Honourable, Clonmel, September 3, 2015

First Pattern winner Blow By Blow (2018 Michael Purcell Memorial Novice Hurdle)

First Cheltenham Festival winner A Plus Tard (2019 Close Brothers Novices' Handicap Chase)

First Grade 1 winner Minella Indo (2019 Albert Bartlett Novices' Hurdle)

Grand National winner Minella Times (2021)

Cheltenham Gold Cup winner A Plus Tard (2022)

Champion Hurdle winner Honeysuckle (2021, 2022)

Irish Champion Hurdle winner (Leopardstown) Honeysuckle (2020, 2021, 2022)

Punchestown Champion Hurdle winner Honeysuckle (2021, 2022)

Queen Mother Champion Chase winner Captain Guinness (2024)

Ryanair Chase winners Allaho (2021), Envoi Allen (2023)

Stayers' Hurdle winner Bob Olinger (2025)

Last winner Ma Belle Etoile, Cork, May 10, 2025

Highest-rated mount A Plus Tard (RPR 181 in 2022 Cheltenham Gold Cup)

Top jockey at Cheltenham Festival 2021 (6 wins)

Cheltenham Festival wins 18

Champion conditional jockey 2016-17

Runner-up in jump jockeys' championship 2018-19, 2020-21

Most wins in a season 100 in 2020-21 (Ireland 92, GB 8)

Total wins over jumps 564 (Ireland 527, GB 37) plus 12 Flat

Sportswoman of the Year 2021 (Irish Times/Sport Ireland)

World Sport Star of the Year 2021 (BBC Sports Personality awards)

Compiled by John Randall

▲ The Racing Post front page the morning after Rachael Blackmore announced her retirement from the saddle

"It is daunting, not being able to say that I am a jockey anymore . . . who even am I now?" she said. "But I feel so incredibly lucky to have had the career I've had. To have been in the right place at the right time with the right people, and to have gotten on the right horses – because it doesn't matter how good you are without them. They have given me the best days of my life and to them I am most grateful."

These are edited versions of articles that appeared in the Racing Post on May 13 and 14

MOORCROFT

Equine Rehabilitation Centre
Charity No: 1076278

Here at the centre in West Sussex, we have over 20 years' experience at retraining ex-racehorses, and we have difference schemes available depending on your needs or your horse's needs. We would love to help, and we do a very thorough caring job with great results. Please come and visit us or call Mary on 0792 666408 for more information and/or to discuss how we can help

www.moorcroftracehorse.org.uk

Huntingrove Stud, Slinfold, West Sussex RH13 0RB Tel:07929 666408

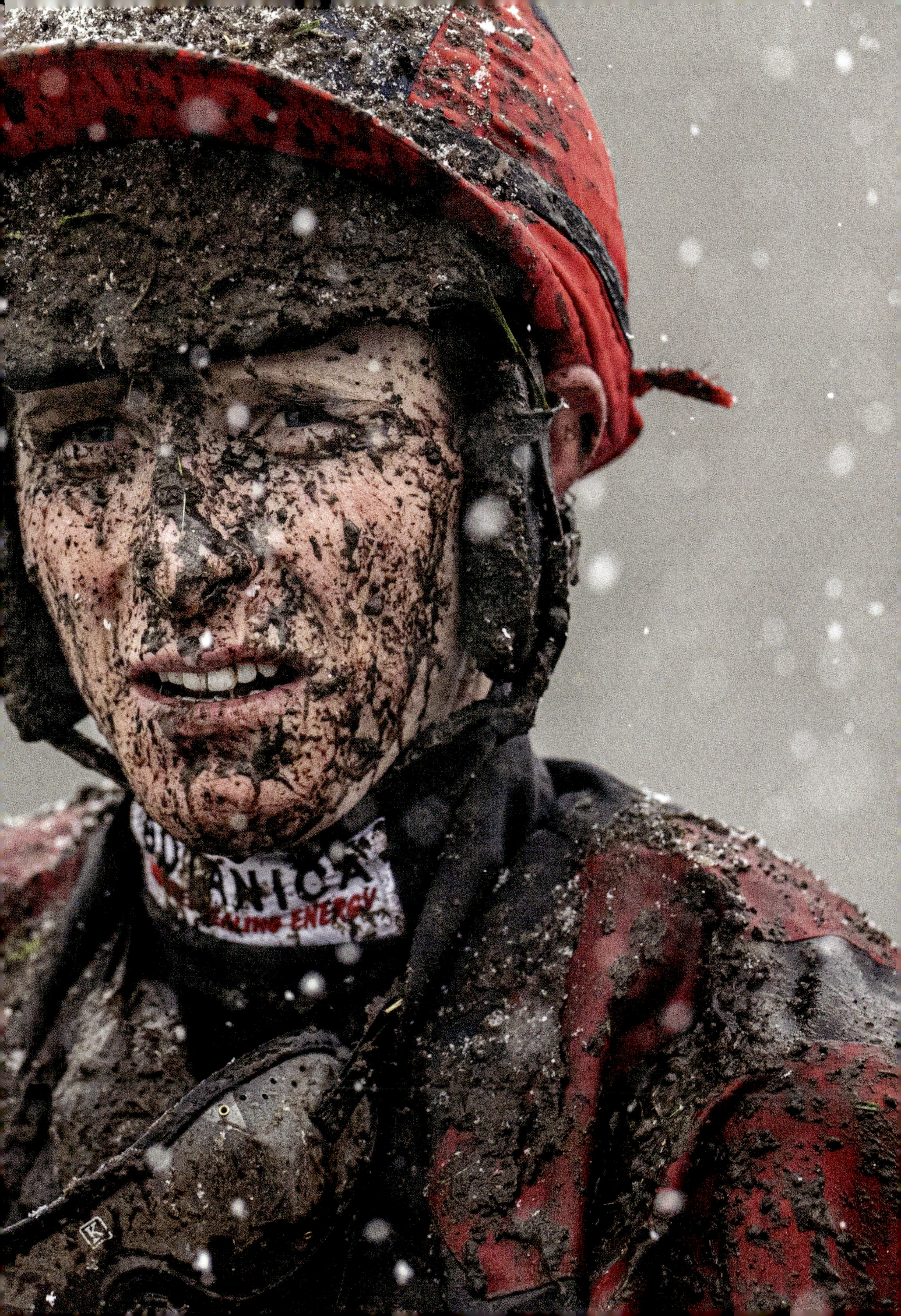

Hayley Turner, a groundbreaker for female jockeys on the Flat, retired in April with the news that she was expecting a baby. The following month she gave this interview to the Racing Post

'I was ready and I felt like I'd done pretty much all I wanted to do as a jockey'

By Catherine Macrae

HAYLEY TURNER'S calendar has a distinct new look. Where once her days revolved around early mornings and race meetings, the schedule on the kitchen wall is now pencilled in with social calls – an appointment, an upcoming family visit and a weekend barbecue with friends.

Free time is a commodity not afforded to jockeys, yet despite Turner being focused on her profession for more than two decades she has found the change of lifestyle rather easy

▶ *Continues page 88*

to adapt to. Endless treks across Britain have been replaced by quiet afternoons like today, when a bout of vacuuming is about as taxing as things are due to get at her charming home in Newmarket.

"I expected it to be worse than it is, but I've been really comfortable with not being as busy," says Turner, 42. "As a jockey, you miss out on so much without even realising it, because you need to be fully in the job, there's no way around that. You need to make a lot of sacrifices and your family and friends have to be very understanding.

"The amount of christenings, barbecues, birthdays that I've sacked off – it's good I've been able to mould my family to understand, especially since they've never been involved in racing. Now I have time to do things I'd never have been able to do before, like having the girls round on a Saturday. I couldn't even remember the last weekend I had off, so I'm really just adjusting to a normal life."

In the 25 years since Turner first won under rules, she has gone on to become a household name in racing, breaking many barriers for female jockeys on the way to becoming a Group 1-winning rider and claiming more than 1,000 winners in Britain.

She ended her incredible career with a final winner at Southwell, announcing her retirement the following week with immediate effect, alongside the news she is expecting a baby in October. While the prospect of quitting the saddle had been some time in the making, the final decision was made only in the aftermath of that unassuming Wednesday evening success.

"I think it's always been in the back of my head I was running out of time to have a child," she says. "I was ready, and I felt like I'd done pretty much all I wanted to do as a jockey. I had a scan that morning and then a winner at Southwell in the evening, and when I was driving home I

thought, 'I don't think I'm going to ride now.'

"Southwell may not be Ascot, but it's quite a sentimental place for me and it felt right. I went to school there and my nana used to come all the time to watch me ride there. She's not with us anymore but we've got a bench for her at the track. As I drove home, I realised all of a sudden I wasn't going to be doing this ever again. I got quite emotional and rang my mum, as I always do, and the decision was made."

★★★★

THE intervening weeks have been largely regret-free for Turner, but she still misses some aspects of her old life. "I think it'll get easier the more I'm detached from it, but it was never going to be entirely easy and I'll miss the banter from the weighing room a lot," she says. "At the same time, I know I'm lucky that I've always had a job I've enjoyed and had so many good memories. When I announced my retirement I don't think I've ever had as many messages from people, even when I had Group 1 winners, and that's been really lovely too."

A photograph of her final winning ride on Spirit Of Jura, gifted by the owners, occupies a temporary spot on the kitchen counter, but it has some stiff competition for a more permanent place among the many accolades decorating Turner's home. Some of the mementos are predictable: photographs of significant winners for David Simcock and Andrew Balding, an illustrated racecard from Dream Ahead's 2011 July Cup win and the Nunthorpe trophy of the Michael Bell-trained Margot Did that same year. Other keepsakes, however, are more unusual, such as a sporting achievement prize from the 2012 Glamour Women of the Year Awards.

"That was a strange one," recalls Turner. "I was sat at a table with Little Mix, people like Kylie
▸Continues page 90

Landmark moments

Full name Hayley Turner

Born January 3, 1983

Apprenticed to Michael Bell, Newmarket

First winner Generate (trainer Mark Polglase), Pontefract, June 4, 2000

July Cup winner Dream Ahead (2011)

Nunthorpe Stakes winner Margot Did (2011)

Beverly D Stakes winner I'm A Dreamer (2012)

Group 2 winner Barshiba (2010 Lancashire Oaks)

Group 3 winners Lady Deauville (2008 Lando-Trophy), Caledonia Lady (2012 Sprint Stakes), Shaden (2015 Firth of Clyde Stakes)

Listed winner for Queen Elizabeth II Momentary (2012 Swettenham Stud Fillies' Trial at 33-1)

Royal Ascot winners Thanks Be (2019 Sandringham Handicap), Onassis (2020 Sandringham Handicap), Latin Lover (2022 Palace of Holyroodhouse Handicap), Docklands (2023 Britannia Handicap)

Other big-handicap winners Furnace (2008 Totesport Cup, Ascot), Brunston (2010 Newbury Spring Cup), Boom And Bust (2011 Totesport (Golden) Mile), Ripp Orf (2018 Victoria Cup)

1,000th winner Tradesman, Chelmsford, November 21, 2023

1,000th winner in Britain Expressionless, Yarmouth, July 25, 2024

Last winner & last ride Spirit Of Jura, Southwell, April 2, 2025

Highest-rated mounts (RPRs) 124 Dream Ahead (2011 July Cup), 118 Docklands, 117 Margot Did, 115 Bonus, Wigmore Hall, 114 Sovereign Debt, I'm A Dreamer

Richest win £278,710, 2012 Beverly D Stakes, Arlington Park (I'm A Dreamer)

Champion apprentice 2005 (joint with Saleem Golam)

Champion woman jockey 11 times (2005 to 2015)

Group/Grade 1 wins 3

Pattern wins 7

Royal Ascot wins 4

Most wins in a year in Britain 100 in 2008

Total wins in Britain 1,022

Official honour OBE (2016) for services to horse racing

Compiled by John Randall

Minogue were there, and when you go up you have to do a speech. I had no idea what to say, so I just went up and said, 'None of you know who I am, do you?' And they just started laughing because no-one had a clue, and there's me sat with all these famous people."

Pride of place on the dining room table goes to the iconic Shergar Cup, a prize gifted to Turner four years ago after becoming the most successful rider in the history of the international jockeys' competition. The sculpture sits alongside her three Alistair Haggis Silver Saddle trophies, awarded to the leading rider at the meeting each year, the last of which was won in August 2024.

Turner's catalogue of accolades from the Shergar Cup and beyond showcase a career well lived but, like many in her profession, it has not always been an easy path to walk. In 2015 she broached the idea of retirement for the first time and quit the saddle for two years before returning to race-riding in 2017, first in France and then in Britain a year later.

"I should have had a break, rather than retire," she admits. "I wasn't doing very well and I felt like I'd tried everything. I was training so hard, riding out for everyone, and I just couldn't make a change. I'd had a bad fall at Doncaster two years earlier, when I broke three vertebrae and my pelvis, and I didn't have enough support when I got back from it. I needed to take some time off and regroup but I said I would retire instead, and after quite a short amount of time I was keen to get back.

"When they brought out the allowance in France for female jockeys, I thought that was my chance to get back into riding and I've never regretted coming back. I felt like there was more I could do, and I've had four Royal Ascot winners and so many good rides, so it worked out all right. There was relief more than anything when I retired the first time, whereas I'm more content this time round. That's a much better feeling."

★★★★

TURNER'S willingness to leave her riding career behind for good is boosted by the feeling there are other female riders able to take up the baton she has long carried. As well as being the first woman to ride 100 winners in a year and win a Group 1 race outright, Turner long held the title of Britain's most successful female jockey, but her record of 1,022 wins was recently surpassed by Hollie Doyle, who spearheads what Turner sees as the encouraging rise of women within the sport.

"People often asked me who my female role model was and there was never anyone, because there weren't any jockeys to follow," says Turner. "It meant I was never disappointed because I didn't expect too much, and I was never sucked in by the female jockey narrative because my friends have always been the lads. They worked as hard as I did and travelled as far, so how am I an exception when we're all doing exactly the same thing?

"The difference now is there are some really good girls riding and that's great to see, and Hollie has certainly helped with that. It was really nice to see her break the record, and I do think it's only the start of things. The next ten years are going to get so much better.

"I hope I've made it a little easier for women to get those big breaks and I think it'll just get easier and easier for them as long as they're good riders. Now at least the girls have got a target, and they know that if they're working hard then it's not impossible to succeed."

A magnitude of possibilities await as Turner embarks on the next phase of her life. After a groundbreaking career as a jockey, she is glad to be able to rely on others this time round as she prepares for the arrival of her

▲ Turner prize: Hayley Turner celebrates one of her many successes at the Shergar Cup; below, a winning moment with Queen Elizabeth II at Newbury; thumbs up after her Group 1 breakthrough in the July Cup on Dream Ahead in 2011

baby and whatever the future may bring.

"I have two older sisters who have nothing to do with racing but have had kids, so it's nice that I'm doing something they've done for once instead of going off and doing my own thing," she says. "They've not thrown loads of information at me, but if I'm stuck they're pretty keen to help.

"It's a big change and it's a journey I'm going on. I'm not really sure what I'm doing, but my older sister said if I ever get stuck, just google it, it's that easy. I'm just making it up as I go along, but all I know for sure is I'll look back in years to come and be really thankful I stopped riding when I did. I'm proud of what I've achieved and I've got a new chapter of my life waiting to start."

This is an edited version of an article that appeared in the Racing Post on May 25

Sam Hawkens (red cap, centre) wins the
Summer Handicap over 1m6f at Glorious
Goodwood in August for trainer William
Haggas and jockey Tom Marquand

EDWARD WHITAKER (RACINGPOST.COM/PHOTOS)

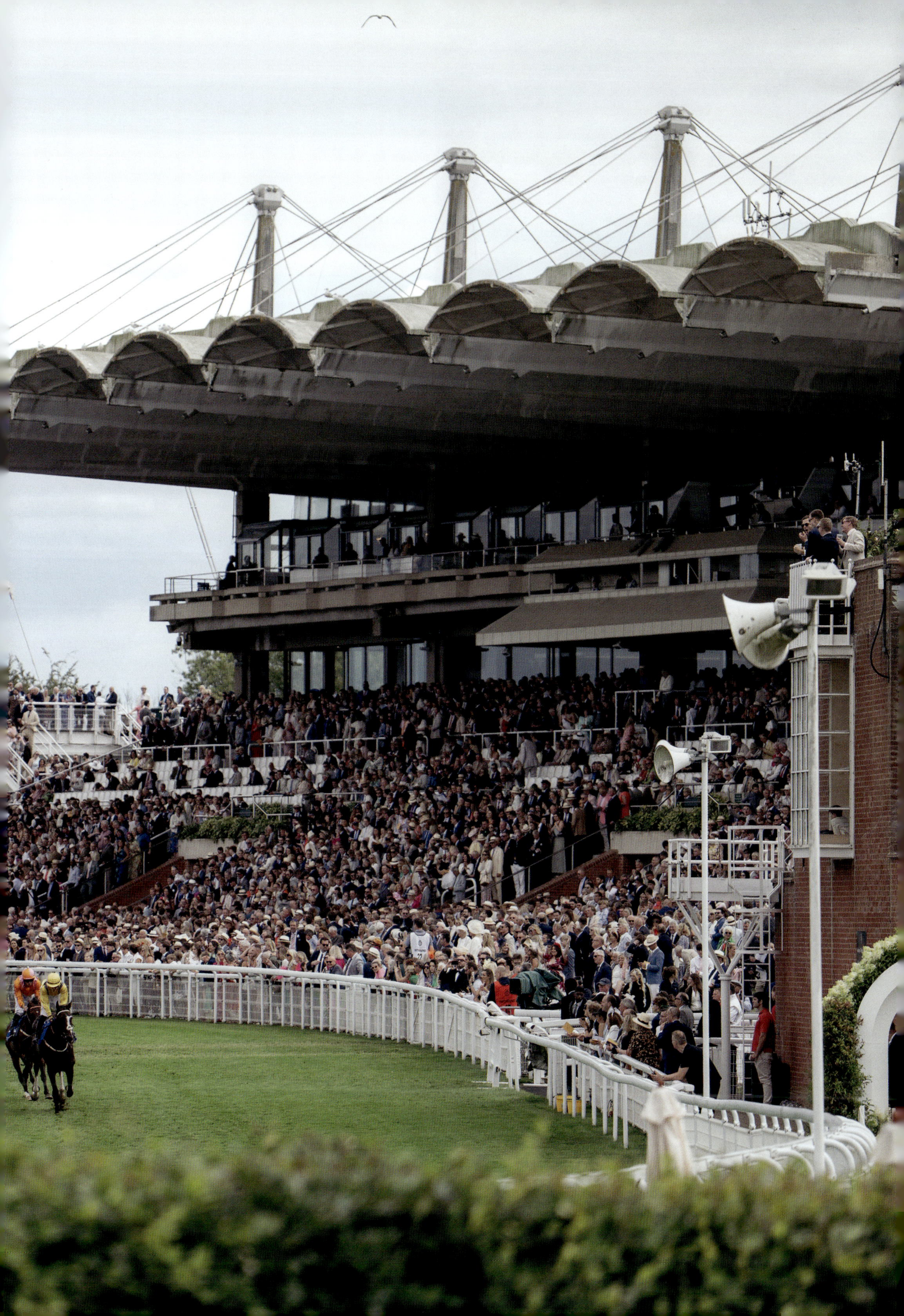

Cercene's Coronation gives Murphy a first Group 1 win at 70

A FIRST Group 1 victory is big. When it comes in one of Royal Ascot's historic contests and at the age of 70, after a lifetime of trying, it is huge. That was the story for County Tipperary trainer Joe Murphy thanks to Cercene's tenacious success in the Coronation Stakes.

"I suppose this is 50 years of work," Murphy said as he was showered with congratulations in the winner's enclosure after scoring with only his second runner at the meeting. "Along with my wife and family we've grown it from a small yard, switching from National Hunt to Flat, and we've always believed in the horses we've bought. This is Mecca day for us and our lifetime ambition to have a Group 1 winner."

Cercene might be on the small side, but the €50,000 yearling purchase showed enormous heart to battle back against 6-4 favourite Zarigana and claim a famous win by half a length at 33-1.

"If she was an inch bigger I wouldn't have her," said Murphy, alluding to the fact that most horses by a Derby winner like Australia would be out of his price range. "But size doesn't matter and Gary Carroll gave her a great ride. He said she was headed but came back again. She's tough and resilient. She's a dream to train."

Murphy's yard is built on the foundations of his family and arguably the proudest person in the winner's enclosure was the trainer's son.

"He's given a lifetime to it, so he deserves this reward," said Joe jnr. "He's had a couple placed in Group 1s and Classics, so to win one is fantastic. He's a grafter and this is the culmination of a lifetime's work. I'm proud of my dad and I'm proud of the filly."

It was also a red-letter day for 35-year-old Carroll, who matched the winning trainer by striking at the highest level for the first time.

"I'm delighted this is the year to get a Group 1, but I'm more delighted for Joe," the jockey said. "I've been riding for him since I was a 7lb claimer and he said only last week I was part of the family. It's unbelievable.

"When I hit the front she waited a little bit and I got headed, but she's got a huge heart. She battled back and stuck her head out for me. A Group 1 is something I've been striving to achieve all my life. I started riding in 2007 and have hit the crossbar plenty of times, but to finally win one is a marvellous feeling."

Reporting: Lewis Porteous and Nick Pulford
Pictures: Patrick McCann (racingpost.com/photos)

Daryz fulfilled his destiny with an epic and emotional Arc triumph in the Aga Khan's famous silks a few months after the death of the legendary owner-breeder

BORN TO RUN

▲ Photo finish: Daryz runs down Minnie Hauk in a thrilling Arc; main, Mickael Barzalona takes him to the winning post for a second time

By Scott Burton
France correspondent

THERE is a frenzied rush to get to the winner's enclosure at the centre of a chaotic Longchamp paddock. Everyone is straining to catch a glimpse of Mickael Barzalona and Daryz returning in triumph after running down Minnie Hauk in the final strides of a mesmerising Prix de l'Arc de Triomphe.

At my side I am suddenly aware of a tall young man attempting to forge his way through the melee, the most important person of all hanging on to his arm. Princess Zahra Aga Khan and her son Iliyan finally make it into that hallowed spot, joining Barzalona, trainer Francis Graffard and the rest of the team, past and present.

Fanning out in a line almost as broad as the limits of the enclosure are the Aga Khan Studs' chief lieutenants in France and Ireland, Nemone Routh and Pat Downes, as well as the current stud manager at Haras de Bonneval, Pierre Gasnier, and his predecessor, Georges Rimaud. Work-rider and groom Guillaume Nugou and Aiglemont's unflappable travelling head lad, Antoine Creton, remain at the winner's head. It takes a village.

Graffard is joined by his wife Lisa-Jane and their two daughters. The joy is palpable. Did the couple ever dare dream of this in the autumn of 2011 when they struck out on their own with just three horses in the yard?

Arc victory seems the most impossible end to a year that started with the death of the man almost none of us could remember not being the head of the racing and breeding empire that bears his title. As Daryz stares out at the crowd, the late Aga Khan's fingerprints are all over this moment in time. Cheers and shouts of congratulations will accompany Princess Zahra and her racing team all the way through the carriage ride and the trophy presentation on the course to the post-Arc press conference.

There will be many clues as to how we got here in the words of Graffard and the princess in that meeting with the media. But first we need to look back at where Daryz came from and what he achieved even to make the line-up in Europe's grand final.

★★★★

FOALED on May 2, 2022, the tall and powerful light bay son of Sea The Stars hails from an Aga Khan female line shot through with Group 1 pedigree. His mother Daryakana landed the 2009 Hong Kong Vase, while granddam Daryaba won the Prix de Diane and Prix Vermeille a decade earlier.

Daryakana has foaled a remarkable series of top-class horses, including Prix Ganay winner Dariyan, although an Arc winner is undoubtedly her masterpiece to date.

Daryz was bred to be a later developer – Daryaba didn't make her debut until late April of her three-year-old career yet was a Classic winner just seven weeks later – and the Prix Juigne in early April was an opportunity to make up for lost time with an imposing colt who never made it to the track at two.

For Barzalona and Graffard, there had been urgent business in Dubai 24 hours before Daryz's debut at Longchamp, with the later-than-usual date of the Dubai World Cup meeting requiring a quick flit back to Paris following Calandagan's second place in the Sheema Classic.

It was worth the dash home as Daryz finished off in a rapid 22.36sec for the final two furlongs to begin a winning run through his first four starts. Daryz earned an opening quote of 50-1 for the Arc after his second success a month later and had already done enough

▸ Continues page 98

by mid-May to be among the 81 entries for Europe's greatest all-aged race.

It was arguably his four-and-a-half-length victory in the Listed Prix Ridgway in early June that really put him on the road to the Arc. Graffard often referred back to the fast pace that day having allowed his developing colt to drop the bit for the first time.

A defeat of Bay City Roller in the Group 2 Prix Eugene Adam demonstrated the same lesson, although in reverse. A tame pace set by Christophe Soumillon on Scorthy Champ saw Daryz fight for his head down the back straight, making his finishing effort even more noteworthy; 33.57sec for the final 300m showed Daryz had the potential to be among Europe's best over a mile and a quarter.

It was at this point that Graffard showed why he has become such a complete trainer. Speaking after Calandagan had landed the Grand Prix de Saint-Cloud later on the same card, he defied expectations that Daryz would head to the Grand Prix de Paris over a mile and a half and against his own age group, while his stablemate would naturally bid to go one better at York than when second to City Of Troy in 2024.

"If you want to talk about the Juddmonte International, it's a race I'm thinking about for Daryz," Graffard said. "I'll ask Princess Zahra where she wants to go but I'll make an entry for Daryz in that race. He's a horse I like a lot and I need to make him tougher and give him experience, and I think he'll get that if he goes abroad. With Calandagan I'll focus on the King George and see where we go after that."

Only Aidan O'Brien among Europe's very top practitioners is quite so willing to risk defeat in the pursuit of future gain. While the International turned into a non-event for Daryz after the field ignored the pacemaker Birr Castle, the colt was exposed to an entirely different experience in

▸Continues page 100

Rich legacy of racing excellence

PRINCE KARIM, AGA KHAN IV, died at the age of 88 on February 4. He was the spiritual leader of the 15 million Nizari Ismaili Muslims and was among the world's pre-eminent owner-breeders for most of his life.

His pursuit of excellence resulted in a long list of champions, notably Shergar, his spectacular 1981 Derby winner.

His grandfather, Aga Khan III, bought his first yearlings in Europe in 1921, had five Derby winners including Bahram, Mahmoud and Tulyar, and was champion owner 13 times in Britain. His father, Prince Aly Khan, was also a notable owner-breeder.

When Aga Khan III died in July 1957, his will bypassed his playboy son and appointed his grandson as successor to his worldly and spiritual duties. The new Aga Khan was 20 then and still only 23 when, in May 1960, he was pitched into the racing world by a car crash in Paris that killed his father, who had inherited the old Aga Khan's horses.

It was by no means certain that the young man, with all his responsibilities, would continue the family's deep involvement in a sport he had no interest in, but he was soon hooked.

His long list of notable successes included four Prix de l'Arc de Triomphe wins with Akiyda (1982), Sinndar (2000), Dalakhani (2003) and Zarkava (2008), who was an unbeaten world champion and the best filly or mare he raced.

He also made an indelible mark on Derby history with five winners – Shergar, Shahrastani (1986), Kahyasi (1988), Sinndar (2000) and Harzand (2016). Shergar, who won the Derby by a record ten lengths, was a truly great champion and the benchmark of excellence by which all subsequent winners of the race have been measured.

Among his other stars were Charlottesville, Petite Etoile, Blushing Groom, Darshaan and Shardari. He also bred the great champion Daylami, whose big-race wins included the King George VI and Queen Elizabeth Stakes, Irish Champion Stakes and Breeders' Cup Turf in 1999. Charlottesville and Dalakhani were among his eight Prix du Jockey Club winners, while Shergar was the first of six Irish Derby winners and the first of three King George winners.

He was champion owner in France 16 times, in Britain twice and Ireland once. He was also champion breeder in France 12 times and five times in Britain. Calandagan's victory in the 2024 King Edward VII Stakes at Royal Ascot was his last in Britain.

A statement from the Aga Khan Studs on his death said: "For 65 years, His Highness has been at the head of his family's breeding and racing operation, which is today one of the most prestigious in Europe. Guided by his passion for horses and the sport of horseracing, he carefully developed and shaped his studs and bloodlines in a quest for excellence. His memory will endure at the Aga Khan Studs through the horses he has bred and the families he has nurtured."

Calandagan and Daryz both come from those families. In the year of their breeder's death, their victories in the King George, Champion Stakes and Arc were a reminder of his rich legacy.

John Randall

▲Premier league: clockwise from top left, the late Aga Khan's Sinndar, Harzand, Dalakhani and Kahyasi; right, trainer Francis Graffard with the Arc trophy after Daryz's victory

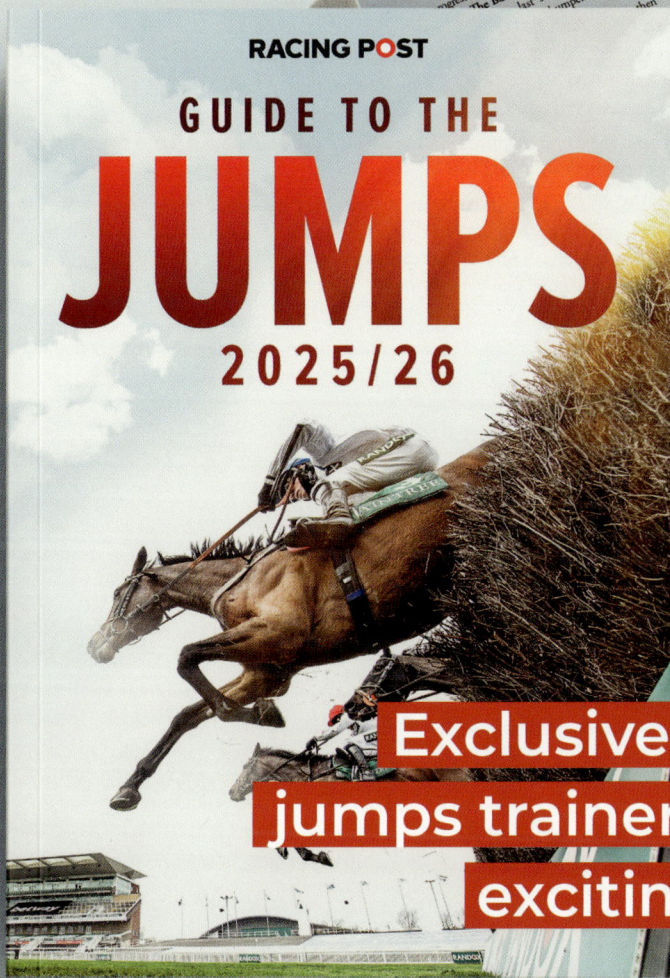

going to the races. It made a man of him. As Routh reflected the day after the Arc: "He really grew up for it and, although we learned nothing, he did learn something."

That's easy to say after the event, but Graffard, Routh and Princess Zahra faced a dilemma after York. They couldn't head straight to the Arc with a horse who had just finished last of six on his first try at Group 1 level, while sending him for one of the Arc trials would mean some tight turnarounds. Once again, fortune favoured the brave. Daryz was pointed at the Prix du Prince d'Orange over a mile and a quarter – 25 days on from York and just 21 days before the Arc.

The clash with Japan's Derby winner Croix Du Nord came on much softer ground than the three traditional trials run at Longchamp a week earlier and provided plenty of positives for both camps.

Yuichi Kitamura kicked Croix Du Nord into what looked like a winning lead but Daryz had cut it to a short head by the line despite a troubled passage. Most importantly, he had behaved well in the preliminaries and travelled more economically than had been the case in the Eugene Adam and the International. The fact that he had shown he could operate in very soft ground was an additional piece of evidence to take on board, given how fast he had shown himself on a really quick surface through the summer.

Still there was much water to flow under the bridge in the final three weeks before the Arc.

The Monday before his date with destiny, Daryz eased through his final breeze around Les Aigles in Chantilly on very deep ground, leaving smiles all round. On the Thursday he was drawn in stall two, meaning the dream was very much alive.

★★★★

IN THE moments before Barzalona climbs aboard for the Arc, Daryz looks calm in his red

▶Continues page 102

Fight to the finish
How the jockeys saw the epic Arc battle

Mickael Barzalona, Daryz The race went perfectly. The horse was in a rhythm where he was doing everything easily. We were in our own bubble. Minnie Hauk made quite a lot of effort in front of me, and when Daryz pulled out from her slipstream, he showed tremendous fighting spirit. I didn't know exactly when we'd get on top but I never doubted that we would. She quickened more sharply than we did but Daryz responded immediately – I could feel his strength and his reserves.

Christophe Soumillon, Minnie Hauk She's a big galloper and she took the front so easily. When she came on the bit I thought, "Now it's time to go and we're going to win easy," but I was squeezing her to keep going. If you take Daryz out, she would be one of the most impressive fillies to win the Arc, but that's racing. Sometimes you just have to accept you get beaten by another one. Unfortunately it's in this race, but what can you do?

And Barzalona on his first Arc victory It's a privilege to wear these famous colours and I try to give my best every time. I'm thrilled to win my first Arc for such a historic ownership.

▼Winning team: Daryz and Mickael Barzalona after their Arc success

IRISH INJURED JOCKEYS

Providing appropriate support, financial or otherwise, in a prompt and sympathetic manner to those jockeys past or present who are injured, unable to ride or generally in need.

KEY INITIATIVES

✓ **IIJ Rehabilitation Suite**

On site Physio, strength & conditioning programs and dietetics .

✓ **Bursary Scheme**

To provide jockeys with enhanced career prospects when they leave racing.

✓ **Gear safety subsidy**

Ensuring all jockey's gear is up to safety standards.

Scan to donate

📞 045-533011

🌐 irishinjuredjockeys.com

✉ info@irishinjuredjockeys.com

DARYZ

hood and is giving no trouble to Nugou and Creton, a signal that he is in his own bubble and not being troubled by all the hoopla going on around him.

Those who look for signs in the natural world could not have wished for more. A sharp shower douses Longchamp as the parade breaks, revealing a rainbow in an arc from the windmill to the starting stalls away to our left. There is also something heavenly in what unfolds next.

With only Minnie Hauk to his inside in the stalls, Barzalona is able to slide straight on to the rail and follow the favourite the whole way round. He is confident that arguably the best stayer in the field – a three-year-old filly with the lightest weight – will take him deep into the race.

Barzalona is sitting on a colt with an explosive turn of foot but the question in many minds is whether he will stay on his first start over a mile and a half in what has become pretty testing ground.

Standing on the press balcony my mind darts back to a conversation with Routh two days earlier, when she pointed out that both Sea The Stars and Daryakana won over the mile and a half of Longchamp's Grande Piste on the same weekend in October 2009. "He was bred for this race," she had told me.

As the field levels for home, Daryz is about to do exactly what he was born to do. Minnie Hauk has got first run but the break is not a decisive one. Barzalona goes in pursuit and, as their 15 rivals quickly recede into the background and battle is joined, Daryz appears to be taking ever longer strides. He is devouring the sodden turf and Minnie Hauk's lead.

At the end of a suspenseful 20 seconds, Daryz is ahead for maybe the last two strides. No more than that but, no matter, his destiny is fulfilled.

★★★★

TWENTY-FIVE minutes later little of the initial euphoria has drained away by the time Barzalona, Graffard, Routh and Princess Zahra arrive at the press conference. They are cheered and clapped to the stage, all pretence of impartiality joyously cast aside by those gathered to record the words of the winners.

Graffard speaks with warmth and wonder. "When I was a boy in Burgundy, watching the races with my grandfather, I dreamed of these horses, these silks and this race," he says. "This sport is built on emotion and today is the ultimate example.

"We've had big victories before, but today I realise just how special the Arc truly is. The emotions are magnified — by the crowd, the atmosphere, and especially by these colours with such history."

On the six-month journey with Daryz from debut to destiny, he says: "We've always held him in high regard. He has that dazzling turn of foot but he wasn't mature enough for a race like the Jockey Club earlier in the season. We always thought that if we ever had a colt good enough for the

▲ Star of the show: Daryz with Mickael Barzalona and groom Guillaume Nugou after the Arc; below, the next day's Racing Post front page

Arc, it would be him. To get here, we took the long road. And today it all paid off."

Princess Zahra is quick to give credit to Graffard's skill and planning. "I want to thank Francis for bringing him here through such an unusual but effective campaign," she says.

How fitting that the campaign had ended with the famous emerald green and red silks back on the top step of the podium after a race cherished so dearly by the late Aga Khan.

"It's really the summit of your ambitions as a breeder to win a Prix de Diane or an Arc," says Princess Zahra. "It's a step change. It's the pinnacle and a huge moment for the operation and everyone involved in it. My dad was always so over the moon to win an Arc and I never knew what it felt like. But now I know what he felt like."

The rainbow may have been a fleeting vision in the sky above Longchamp, but the memories of Daryz soaring to greatness are imperishable.

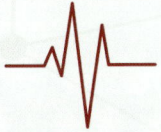

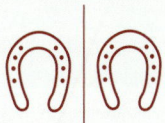
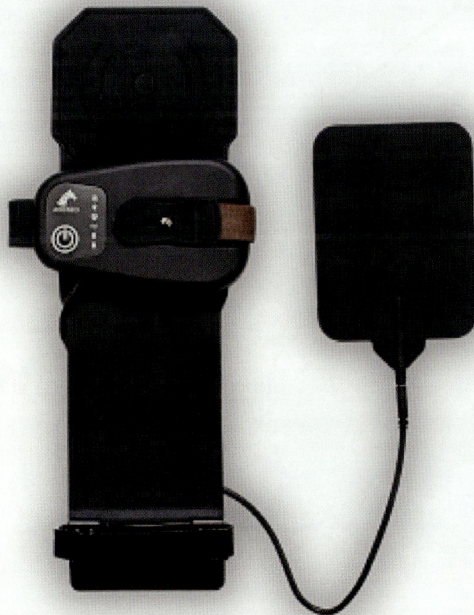

THE
BIGGER
PICTURE

The Ian Williams-trained 9-1 shot Silent Age (Marco Ghiani) leads
the field around the bottom bend en route to an all-the-way
victory in a 1m2f handicap at Sandown in June

EDWARD WHITAKER (RACINGPOST.COM/PHOTOS)

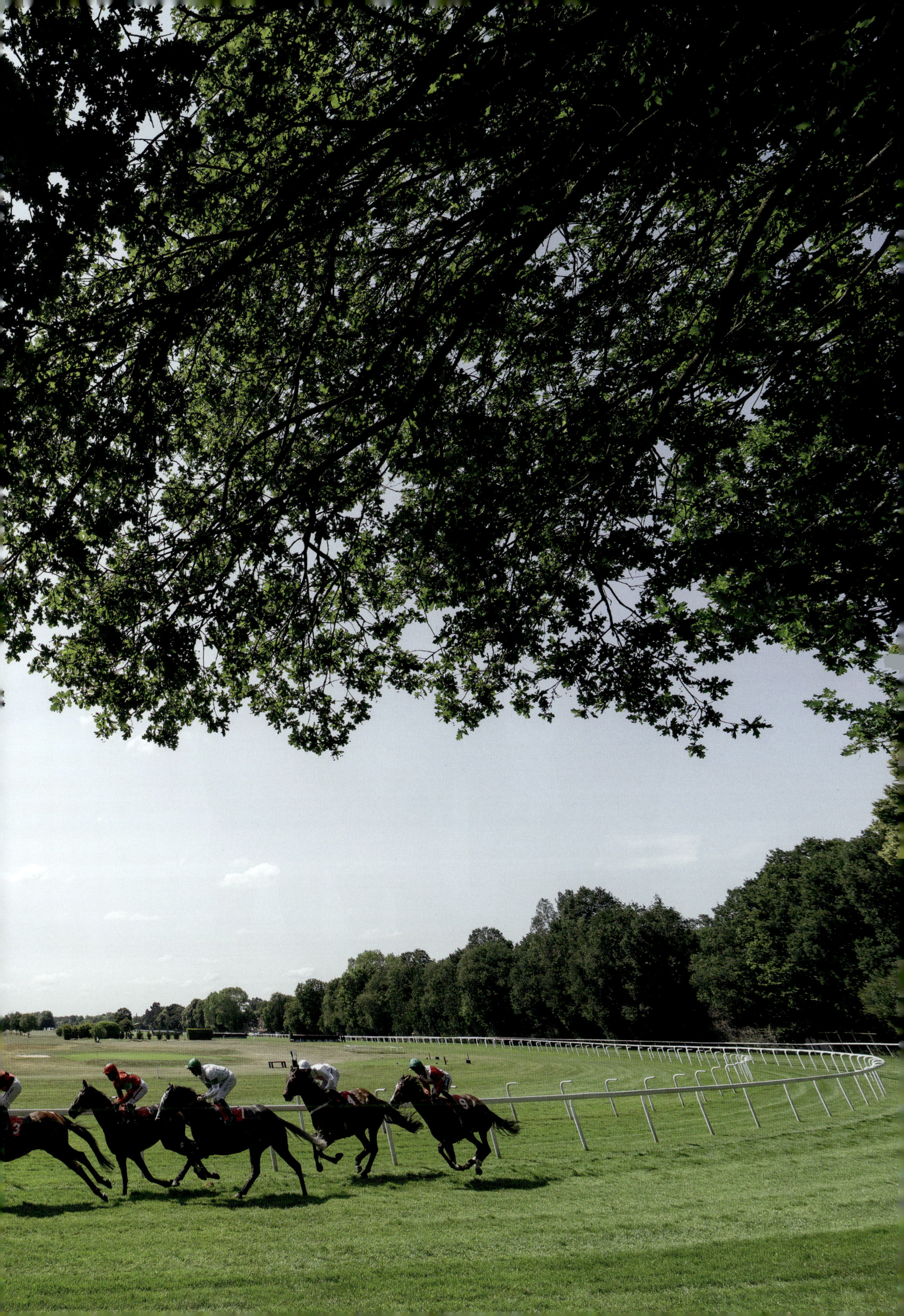

KING
OF ASCOT

Calandagan was another star for the Aga Khan Studs and trainer Francis Graffard with his King George and Champion Stakes triumphs

By Scott Burton

IN AN exceptional year for the emerald green and red of the Aga Khan Studs, the constant at the centre of it all was Calandagan.

A brilliant six-length winner of the King Edward VII Stakes at Royal Ascot as a three-year-old in 2024, he now shouldered the responsibility of carrying the flag around the world. He bore the weight like a feather.

Ascot was his playground again. This time he was even better than before. Not once but twice.

Gelded after his very first racecourse appearance, the son of Gleneagles is not the biggest horse at Aiglemont, the Aga Khan Studs' Chantilly stable. But he is undoubtedly the bravest, although not everyone would have agreed in the first week of June 2025. At that time the defeats were piling up and the critics were piling on.

In two more starts in 2024 Calandagan had produced a pair of excellent runner-up efforts at Group 1 level, both back at a mile and a quarter; first he pushed the joint-world champion City Of Troy all the way in the Juddmonte International, then he succumbed to a late ambush by Anmaat in the Champion Stakes.

If Calandagan has a fault – or at least a tactical vulnerability – it is that he can get himself quite a long way back early in his races, and as Graffard and jockey Stephane Pasquier discovered in the 2024 Champion Stakes, trying to give him the hurry-up earlier on is largely counter-productive.

He came from a long way back on his 2025 seasonal debut in Dubai to finish a clear second to a resurgent Danon Decile, but by the time he arrived at Epsom on June 6 for what looked on paper his easiest Group 1 assignment yet, a few commentators were beginning to murmur that the

row of twos next to his name was more than just a case of repeatedly running into top-class opposition.

When he got outmuscled by the Aidan O'Brien-trained Jan Brueghel in the Coronation Cup, the knives were out. Indeed barely had Mickael Barzalona got the saddle off before ITV's Matt Chapman was putting it to both Graffard and Princess Zahra Aga Khan that Calandagan wasn't putting everything in; that he was somehow not that fussed about winning races.

Both owner and trainer played their parts in an entertaining interview while defending their horse, although they might have preferred not to have had to reprise the same three-hander a few weeks later when Zarigana got worried out of the Coronation Stakes by Cercene at Royal Ascot. Chapman suggested then that Graffard might need to reach for the sheepskin cheekpieces for those two star players.

Calandagan finally got a deserved and delayed Group 1 success in some style, running away from Arc runner-up Aventure and 2023 Hong Kong Vase winner Junko in the Grand Prix de Saint-Cloud in late June. It was clearly a relief for Graffard to put an end to a frustrating sequence, although he was clear afterwards that he had never felt let down by the horse in any of those four defeats.

"I never lost confidence in him and you have to remember that he has been making a sort of comeback both times this season," the trainer said. "In Dubai he was beaten by a horse who had already run twice and he needed the race. At Epsom he had a few little things against him, including the ground and the last little uphill stretch, and he was only just beaten.

"The only regret I have is from the Champion Stakes last year when they switched to the inner track and he was

drawn inside, so we tried to rush him into the race to take advantage. I think that cost us the win. We might have won if I hadn't given the wrong instructions."

The bookmaker quotes had already started to come in for a return to York and the Juddmonte International, but Graffard had other thoughts as he stood in the Saint-Cloud winner's enclosure. He suggested Calandagan would be staying at a mile and a half for the King George in just four weeks' time.

★★★★

THE King George has been something of a forgotten mark in the calendar for most French trainers but Graffard had shown he was unafraid to take on the best anywhere when springing a 25-1 shock in the race 12 months earlier with Goliath.

While the title-holder had been laid low when an eased-down last of five in the race at Saint-Cloud, Graffard had Calandagan back to peak fitness and was confident he would be able to run him again quickly in pursuit of back-to-back successes.

O'Brien relied once again on Jan Brueghel as his main challenger, only this time the layers thought the clash with Calandagan would have a very different outcome to the one at Epsom. Graffard's gelding was sent off the 11-10 favourite and Jan Brueghel was 5-2. It was far from a two-horse race, with the Andrew Balding-trained Kalpana and Godolphin's evergreen Rebel's Romance also legitimate contenders.

Calandagan got his favoured fast ground and, having now ridden him three times since taking on the role of first jockey to the Aga Khan Studs, Barzalona had a much better handle on his partner.

Ryan Moore and Jan Brueghel cut out the running, with supposed hare Continuous taking sentry
▶Continues page 108

station on his better-fancied stablemate's shoulder. Whether the steady pace made much difference in the end is debatable, such was the margin of Calandagan's superiority. He once again showed that long kick, which he was able to sustain all the way to the line.

Oisin Murphy and Kalpana circled the field and set sail for home but, once Calandagan dipped his white-snipped nose a little lower to the ground, he seemed to grow in stature as his stride lengthened. Barzalona had bided his time as the O'Brien plan fell apart and the rider's confidence in Calandagan was absolute. The winning margin was a length over Kalpana.

Princess Zahra was not in attendance but Graffard was ready for Chapman, bringing up his cheekpieces suggestion before the ITV man had mustered a question.

Graffard went on to say: "Every time we've been beaten in the past we've had excuses. I couldn't say it was because he doesn't want to try and his jockey never reported that to me either. I think there's no more doubt about his will to win."

★★★★

THE next question was whether Calandagan could set the record straight in the Champion Stakes. It was a red-hot line-up, much stronger than the year before. Much of the talk centred on the third clash between Ombudsman and Delacroix, but Graffard made sure his challenger was part of the conversation.

"I hope he can be very competitive against them and prove he's one of the best

horses in Europe, which I think he is," the trainer said in the build-up. "I think it's fantastic for racing to see all of them competing."

Crucially, there was no rushing Calandagan into the race this time. Barzalona was content to settle him second-last of the 11 runners off a strong tempo, with the Ombudsman and Delacroix teams both fielding a pacemaker.

The big three were close together near the back rounding the home turn. As Delacroix started to struggle, Barzalona was the first of their riders to strike for home, forcing William Buick on Ombudsman to give chase.

Calandagan was too quick and too strong. He powered to victory by two and a quarter lengths over Ombudsman in surely the race of the season on the Flat.

"We love horseracing and that was a beautiful race to watch," Graffard said. "He loves this track. He was very good today." So good that he joined the great Brigadier Gerard as the only horses to achieve the King George-Champion double in the same season.

Barzalona's view from the saddle was that it had been "a tough race", adding: "I'm proud of Calandagan showing his best against Delacroix and Ombudsman. He proved he's the best again. I could feel Ombudsman coming but when he finds his rhythm, he's a powerful horse."

Top-level performers

IT IS rare to see two horses achieve a mark in the 130s on Racing Post Ratings in the same season. Even rarer for them to go head to head in the race of the year.

That is what happened in the Champion Stakes. Ombudsman went into the race having already reached the elite grade with an RPR of 130 for his Prince of Wales's Stakes victory at Royal Ascot.

Calandagan was a little behind on 127 but on a high after his joint-career-best display in the King George. His decisive Champion win took him up to another level. Beating Ombudsman by two and a quarter lengths earned him an RPR of 131.

Their two signature performances were the first rated in the 130s on turf in Europe since Baaeed's phenomenal RPR of 136 when he won the Juddmonte International at York in 2022. William Haggas's superstar is the standout in the years since the unmatched career of Frankel (143 in 2012).

The only others to reach the 130s in the past decade were Cracksman (trained by John Gosden) in the 2017 and 2018 runnings of the Champion Stakes and Ghaiyyath (Charlie Appleby) in the 2020 Juddmonte International.

130+ Racing Post Ratings
Flat turf in Europe last ten years

RPR	Horse	Race
136	Baaeed	2022 Juddmonte International
131	Calandagan	2025 Champion Stakes
131	Cracksman	2017 Champion Stakes
131	Cracksman	2018 Champion Stakes
131	Ghaiyyath	2020 Juddmonte International
130	Ombudsman	2025 Prince of Wales's Stakes

* Covers 2016 to 2025 * 2025 RPRs subject to end-of-year revision

For Barzalona and the whole team, October had brought an incredible fortnight from the Arc to Champions Day. "It has been absolutely unbelievable," said Princess Zahra at Ascot. "I could never have thought things would happen this way. It's amazing."

There was no doubt about how important Calandagan was for the Aga Khan Studs

team in a year that started with such sadness. He may not add to their future riches in the breeding shed but, like Daryz, he carried the famous colours with the utmost distinction.

▲Ascot ace: Calandagan wins a high-quality Champion Stakes from Ombudsman (blue), Almaqam (yellow) and Delacroix

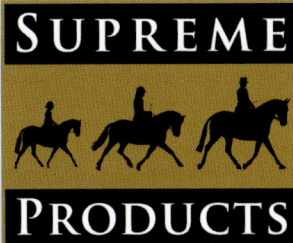

The scene on St Leger day at Doncaster in September as Treble Tee (blue with yellow cap) eases down after winning the opening race, a mile handicap, for trainers Simon and Ed Crisford and jockey Oisin Murphy

EDWARD WHITAKER (RACINGPOST.COM/PHOTOS)

MIGHTY MINNIE

Minnie Hauk landed a Classic Oaks double in her glorious summer and ran her heart out in a pulsating Arc

By Nick Pulford

SHE nearly got there. Minnie Hauk's procession through a summer of Oaks triumphs of varying magnitude ended with a dramatic, desperate battle up the sodden Longchamp straight in the autumn. The queen of Chester, Epsom, the Curragh and York was within touching distance of the ultimate glory in the Prix de l'Arc de Triomphe. Agonisingly, in her first race against the colts, one of them was just too good. Hard as she tried, she could not hold off Daryz. She fell short by a head.

Heads could be held high after such a valiant effort. Minnie Hauk had shown her class time after time. Now, on very soft ground that favoured her opponent, she had proved herself a warrior of the highest order. "We're very proud of Minnie Hauk," said co-owner Michael Tabor. "She just got caught. She's run a blinder. I thought she'd won."

Aidan O'Brien didn't admit to allowing any such thought to creep into his mind – "I'm never sure, I never expect anything" – but was equally proud of his filly. She had given her all in an unsparing finish. "She ran a great race. We're delighted with her," he said.

Minnie Hauk had spread delight wherever she had gone all year. This time it was tinged with disappointment, for sure, but she could not have done any more. She was beaten but brave to the very end.

▶Continues page 114

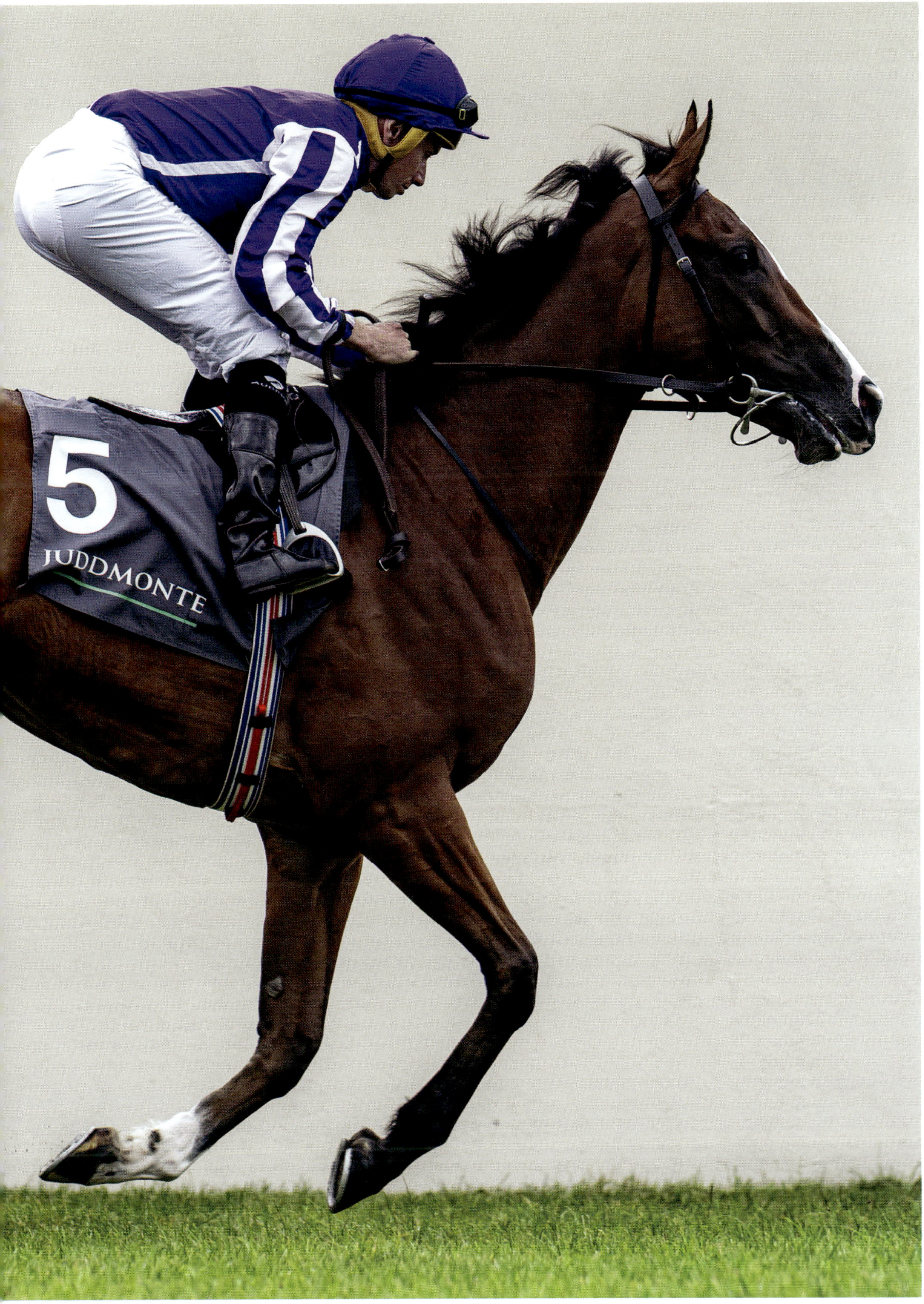
5
JUDDMONTE

◄Driving force: left to right, Minnie Hauk shows her class and bravery to win the Oaks at Epsom, the Irish Oaks at the Curragh and the Yorkshire Oaks before losing narrowly to Daryz in the Prix de l'Arc de Triomphe

★★★★

EVEN before she was named Minnie Hauk, the daughter of Frankel and Multilingual was expected to be something special. She was the top lot in the elite section of the Goffs Orby Sale as a yearling, fetching €1.85 million. The price tag was not surprising for one of the finest pedigrees in the stud book. Her sire was a peerless champion, her dam was a half-sister to champion miler Kingman and her granddam was French 1,000 Guineas winner Zenda, a half-sister to champion sprinter Oasis Dream.

Yet the blue-blooded filly took some time to establish herself at the top of the tree. She was beaten on her debut at Cork – as it transpired, by a high-class filly in Wemightakedlongway – before rounding off a short juvenile season with a narrow victory in a Leopardstown maiden. She began to make significant progress with her reappearance victory in the Cheshire Oaks, often favoured by O'Brien on the educational path to Epsom. Asked at Chester whether she was the stable's leading hope for the Oaks, Coolmore's Paul Smith said: "We don't know if she is yet and we'll see how all the trials go, but she has to be in the mix."

When the mix was finished, it turned out Minnie Hauk was Ballydoyle's number one – and the pick of Ryan Moore at Epsom – ahead of Musidora winner Whirl. The hot favourite, however, was Godolphin's Desert Flower, the 1,000 Guineas winner. This would be the test of whether

Minnie Hauk was up to scaling the peaks after her steady climb.

Moore's selected ride was more than ready. In a driving finish that foreshadowed the Arc battle to come, Minnie Hauk engaged in a sustained duel with Whirl from more than two furlongs out. The difference this time was that Minnie Hauk narrowly won the day, holding off her determined stablemate by a neck. None of the others could get into the argument. Desert Flower was third and Wemightakedlongway fourth.

"I'm delighted with Minnie Hauk," said O'Brien after winning his 11th Oaks. "She's very classy and Ryan gave her a beautiful ride. She's very exciting."

Just how exciting became clear when O'Brien spoke openly about the ability he had been seeing at home and where it might take her. "There's every possibility she could run in an Arc," he said. "She can go at a much stronger tempo than today, so it's definitely a possibility. The improvement she's shown from Chester to here is a little bit abnormal. She's a middle-distance filly who was working like a Guineas filly."

★★★★

BALLYDOYLE'S middle-distance fillies went on to dominate the summer in their division. Minnie Hauk stayed on the mile-and-a-half road to the Curragh and York. Winning the Irish Oaks was harder than expected for the 2-11 favourite, even if it confirmed that two things she loved were a strong pace and a

challenge. She didn't get the first of those elements but the sedate fractions helped Wemightakedlongway to push her until the end.

From the furlong pole Minnie Hauk always looked likely to prevail but the final margin was only a length and a quarter. "Ryan was very happy and she's one of those fillies you're probably never going to see the best of until the tempo is very strong," O'Brien said. "When you see her work, she has a very high cruise and until the pace is really on, she doesn't really open up into that cruise. She's never won by very far. It was the same at Chester and Epsom."

By the time Minnie Hauk turned out for her next assignment in the Yorkshire Oaks, Whirl had completed a Group 1 double since her narrow Oaks defeat. Having stepped out of the fray with her stablemate, she went down to a mile and a quarter to land the Pretty Polly at the Curragh and the Nassau at Goodwood, where Coronation Stakes winner Cercene was five lengths back in second.

The Nassau performance made Whirl the better of the Ballydoyle pair on Racing Post Ratings with a mark of 123. Minnie Hauk responded by going higher still at York. Sent off the 8-15 favourite in a field of four, her only serious rival was the four-year-old Estrange from the David O'Meara stable. It was the first time she had faced an older opponent and she rose to the challenge with the most clear-cut win of her career.

After stablemate Garden Of Eden had set the pace to the

two-furlong pole, Minnie Hauk was sent to the front by Moore and remorselessly drew three and a half lengths clear of the pursuing Estrange. "Ryan always said the stronger the tempo, the better we're going to see of her, so this wasn't going to be a Mickey Mouse race," O'Brien said. "She's not made like a typical mile-and-a-half filly, she's built like a miler, as she's so round and strong. She always finishes her race no matter what and she's always going through the line."

An RPR of 124 put Minnie Hauk top of the fillies not just among the three-year-olds but of any age, including King George VI and Queen Elizabeth Stakes runner-up Kalpana. That four-year-old was being pointed at the Arc by Andrew Balding and Paris was the obvious destination for O'Brien's year-younger star. Supplementing her for the Arc for €120,000 was a no-brainer.

A week before the Arc, O'Brien reflected on her season in a Racing Post interview. "She hasn't had a rigorous campaign and she hasn't had a grueller yet," he said. "She didn't even have a hard race in the Oaks. We do think that you haven't seen the best of her yet. But we'll see."

What we saw at Longchamp was one of the races of the season. It was heart-pounding. Minnie Hauk could not quite hold off Daryz in an epic duel. That was heart-wrenching. But in defeat, as well as in her run of victories, she won so many hearts.

Additional reporting by Scott Burton, Matt Rennie, Jonathan Harding, Conor Fennelly and David Jennings

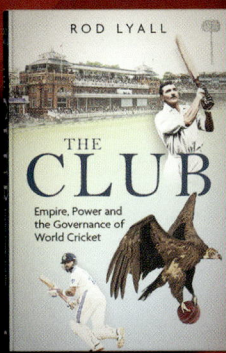

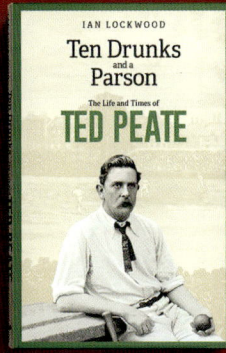

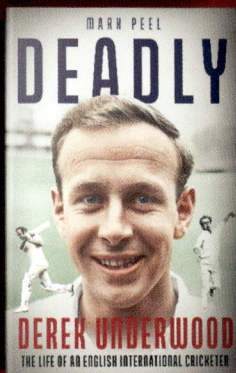

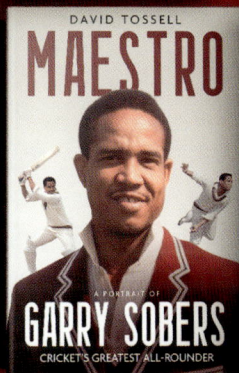

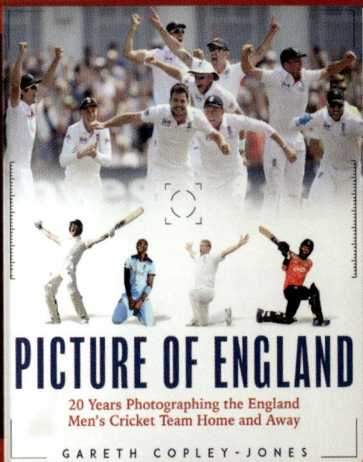

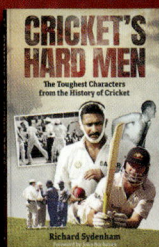

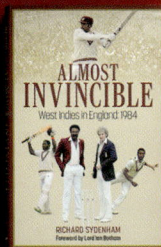

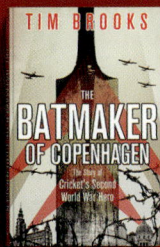

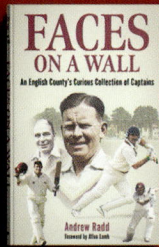

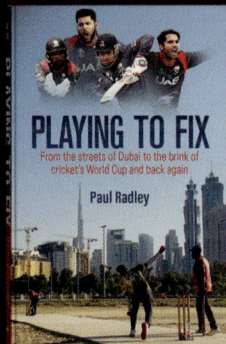

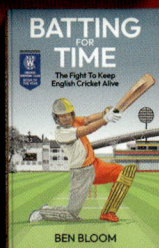

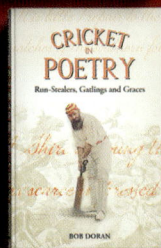

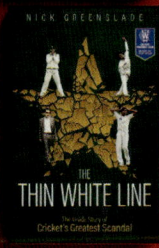

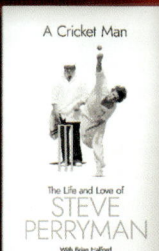

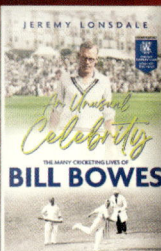

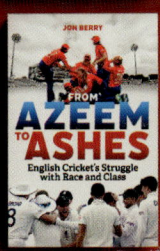

Lambourn became another dual Derby winner for Aidan O'Brien and an

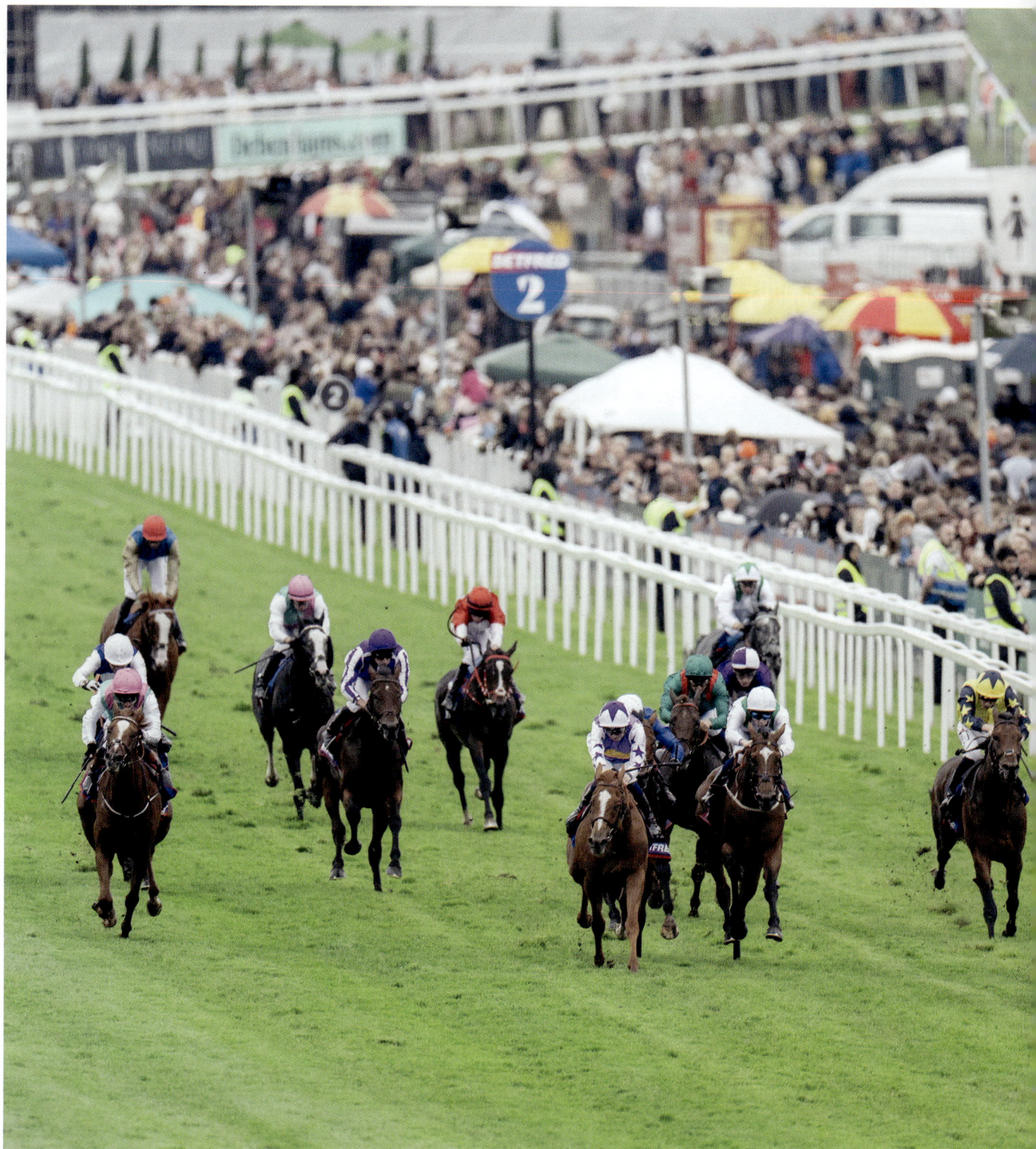

Epsom first for jockey Wayne Lordan with a brilliant front-running ride

ALL THE WAY

By Nick Pulford

★★★★

HE CARRIED the name of an English training centre and represented Ireland's most famous establishment with distinction. Lambourn became the 17th Derby winner in Ballydoyle's hallowed ranks and a record-extending 11th for Aidan O'Brien. His place on the honours board was augmented when he added the Irish Derby a few weeks later; he was O'Brien's 17th winner and the 24th from Ballydoyle.

More rarely, Lambourn was just the eighth dual Derby winner trained at Ballydoyle – either by Vincent O'Brien, its founding father, or by the namesake who followed him. Yet this latest Classic hero of Epsom and the Curragh was not the best three-year-old colt of 2025 in Ballydoyle, nor did he rank above all the fillies. Delacroix, Minnie Hauk and Whirl all sped past him as the summer heated up. He was far from one of the greats.

In the record books, however, it is the name of Lambourn that sits alongside Nijinsky, Galileo and all the other exalted Derby kings of Ballydoyle. A resolute march through the early summer earned him that divine right.

LAMBOURN crossed swords with Delacroix when they took their first steps on the road to the Derby in the Ballysax Stakes at Leopardstown on March 30. Their relative standing showed in the betting – Delacroix was 4-7 and Lambourn 9-1 – and it was confirmed in the race. The hot favourite eased home by two and a quarter lengths from his lesser regarded stablemate.

Delacroix may have won the battle, but it was to be Lambourn who won the war. While Ballydoyle's number one stayed at home for the Leopardstown Derby Trial, Lambourn was sent further afield to the Chester Vase. On the fifth start of his career, he had a fifth different rider. For the first time, Ryan Moore was on board.

This was Lambourn's big chance to earn a place on the Epsom teamsheet, over a similar trip to the Derby test, and he put in a solid enough performance.

Sent off the 11-8 favourite, he beat the largely unconsidered 25-1 shot Lazy Griff by a length and a half, albeit after being the first off the bridle and forcing Moore to work hard. "As you can see,

▶Continues page 118

he's very lazy in the way he runs and a little bit green, but he would have learned a lot from the track," said Coolmore representative Paul Smith.

The learning process at Chester was a strong reason for sending Lambourn there, according to O'Brien, and the trainer was satisfied. "He looked a thorough stayer and, while he was a little on and off the bridle, once the penny dropped he came home really strongly," he said. Lambourn was still as big as 25-1 for the Derby, way behind stablemates The Lion In Winter and Delacroix. On the same day, Minnie Hauk won the Cheshire Oaks to go into single figures for her Epsom assignment.

The pecking order at Ballydoyle was taking shape and at that stage Lambourn's victory seemed less a pointer to the Derby and more a yardstick for the Ballysax form. "We like Delacroix," O'Brien said in his post-race comments on the Chester Vase. By the end of the following week, after the Ballysax winner had followed up at Leopardstown and The Lion In Winter had disappointed on his reappearance in the Dante Stakes, Derby favouritism had passed to Delacroix.

★★★★

IN A far from vintage Derby, Delacroix had shortened to 2-1 by the off after the rain-softened ground prompted the late withdrawal of Ruling Court, the 2,000 Guineas winner. Dante winner Pride Of Arras was 4-1, Lambourn 13-2 and The Lion In Winter 7-1. The proven stayer among them was Lambourn and Wayne Lordan – riding him for the first time since a winning debut at Killarney the previous July – wanted to make sure the race would be a proper test. If it seemed an obvious plan, Lordan turned it into a masterclass.

From his middle draw in stall ten, Lordan urged Lambourn through the first furlong to establish a lead. Tracking him on the inner was none other than Chester Vase runner-up Lazy

Griff, this time a 50-1 shot. That was about to prove the key formline. Lordan pushed on into a comfortable lead and began to stretch further on the run down to Tattenham Corner.

"He was enjoying it in front and in a good rhythm," Lordan said. "I just wanted to see the three-furlong pole so I could get going on him because I knew whatever was going to go by me would have to deserve to get by me and stay."

None of Lambourn's 17 rivals could even get close. Lazy Griff ran on to finish second, beaten three and three-quarter lengths, with the rest strung out behind. Delacroix was left floundering in ninth. Lambourn simply did not stop. Lordan said: "When I got a flick into him passing the two he

▲Headline maker: Wayne Lordan after his brilliant front-running win in the Derby; below, the jockey's masterclass is saluted on the front page of the next day's Racing Post

went forward and I knew that if I gave him another one he'd go forward again. He was still galloping strong in that last furlong."

Forty years on from Steve Cauthen's mould-breaking all-the-way victory on Slip Anchor, the Derby had been won against the clock again. "Wayne got the fractions 100 per cent perfect," O'Brien said. Coolmore's MV Magnier marvelled at the sight. "I watched Slip Anchor's Derby this morning and then watched this Derby, thinking, 'Oh my God! Steve Cauthen's riding him'," he said.

O'Brien had his 11th Derby, and his ninth in the past 14 runnings, but he was happy to heap the praise on the 43-year-old jockey who had just landed

▶Continues page 120

his first. "Wayne is a massive part of the team," the trainer said. "He's there every day and it's a privilege to have a man like him. He's an unbelievable fella; so uncomplicated and so committed."

The last comment was equally true of Lambourn, who had justified Lordan's faith in him. "Wayne rides him in all his work and, after his last piece, he told me he was absolutely there," O'Brien said.

★★★★

LORDAN was thankful to be there himself. A fall in the 2023 Irish Derby forced him to spend eight months on the sidelines, having been knocked unconscious and suffered fractures to his legs and elbow, and his return to race-riding hung in the balance.

"I had a lot of tests to pass. If the doctor had decided I wasn't going to be able to take another fall, that would have probably been it," he said at Epsom. "It's a tough game and a lot of the lads go through it. Thankfully I was the lucky one who overcame it and came back." Looking at Lambourn, he added: "I suppose when you're getting back to ride horses like that, your focus is even stronger."

As is the fate of support riders, Lordan passed on the baton to Moore in the Irish Derby. The stable jockey took the laurels this time, while it was Lordan who was ninth on stablemate Puppet Master. The 8-13 favourite was almost upset by 28-1 shot Serious Contender – another from the O'Brien team, ridden by Gavin Ryan – but got home by three-quarters of a length, matching the Derby double achieved by his sire Australia and grandsire Galileo. Lazy Griff was three lengths behind Lambourn in third.

Moore was never worried. "He was having a bit of a laugh with me," he said. "I just had to keep him awake. He was just a bit lazy, but he has loads of ability and was always in control."

▼Double up: Lambourn takes the Irish Derby under Ryan Moore

O'Brien concurred. "He's just so laid-back, I can't tell you," he said. "He's like his dad. If you put him in first gear, he stays in first gear; if you put him in third gear, he'll stay in third gear."

Unlike his dad or grandad, Lambourn was unable to kick on from his Derby triumphs through the summer. Aimed towards the St Leger, he was fifth in the Great Voltigeur Stakes at York and then fourth in the Doncaster Classic behind stablemate Scandinavia. On the same day, across the sea, Delacroix cemented his elevated status with victory in a thrilling Irish Champion Stakes. How their fortunes had turned.

Lambourn had been outperformed by more illustrious stablemates. Yet there will always be the memory of how he left everything in his wake in the Derby. For Lordan, with one of the rides of the season, it was a crowning achievement.

'The most incredible horse'

AIDAN O'BRIEN lost one of his stars in May when brilliant stayer Kyprios was retired at the age of seven due to injury.

The dual Gold Cup winner won no fewer than 17 of his 21 starts and was last beaten in October 2023. Of all O'Brien's Flat horses, he has the triple distinction of ranking first for Group 1 wins (eight), total Pattern victories (12) and longest winning streak, having won the last nine races of his career. He finished on an official rating of 122, identical to O'Brien's four-time Gold Cup winner Yeats.

The decision to retire him was made due to an aggravation of an old ringbone lesion, which he picked up when winning the Saval Beg Stakes at Leopardstown for a third time on May 16. That victory made him O'Brien's most prolific Flat Pattern winner, surpassing Yeats and Magical.

Reflecting on a stellar career, O'Brien said: "Kyprios was just the most incredible horse. We had to be ultra-respectful of him. Always. When he was a little bit sore after his run at Leopardstown, we were never going to take any risks with him. Everybody felt the same way."

Asked what made Kyprios (below) such a sublime stayer, the master trainer replied: "It was his attitude combined with his ability to stay. Then it was the class he had to go along with those things. He was an incredibly sound horse and his mind was absolute concrete."

According to Racing Post Ratings, Kyprios's best display came in the 2022 Prix du Cadran on Arc weekend. He won by an astonishing 20 lengths despite drifting all the way across the track.

"The day he won the Cadran was something else," O'Brien said. "Then the two Gold Cups were incredible. They were both great days too."

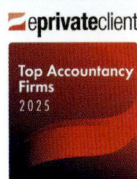

RISING STAR

THE RETIREMENT of Kyprios left Ballydoyle looking for a new staying star. They did not find one in time to hold on to the Ascot Gold Cup but soon their search ended in Scandinavia. He turned into something of a Scandi thriller.

The opening episode was low key and the second didn't promise much, but the excitement mounted from there. Each new episode had an ending that prompted thoughts of what would come next, leading from glorious drama to a Classic conclusion.

By the autumn, when Scandinavia lined up as the short-priced favourite for the St Leger, Aidan O'Brien noted how this slow-burner had "come forward in leaps and bounds with every day, every week. Every time you see him he gets better."

He was better again at Doncaster in the most nail-biting conclusion of all. A neck was all he had to spare over the battling Rahiebb, but victory in the final British Classic belonged to Scandinavia.

Once again it had been compelling viewing.

★★★★

KYPRIOS was still around when Scandinavia reappeared as a three-year-old in May with a Navan maiden win over a mile and a quarter. At Leopardstown the previous evening, Kyprios had made it two out of two for the season and seemed firmly on course for a third Gold Cup. Not for long. Inside a fortnight he had been retired.

Scandinavia's own target at Royal Ascot was the Queen's Vase but he was only fifth there, albeit not beaten far behind Carmers and with Rahiebb only just ahead in third. That turned out to be a good line of form, although it took some time to develop.

O'Brien aimed lower on Scandinavia's next run in the Group 3 Bahrain Trophy at Newmarket and, significantly, he added cheekpieces to the raceday armoury. A notable step forward was the result. Scandinavia powered clear from the Dip to win impressively by eight and a half lengths, taking his Racing Post Rating up by 9lb to 117. That put him firmly in the hunt for the top staying prizes.

Trawlerman might still have been a little out of reach on 123 after his dominant Gold Cup win but Illinois – Scandinavia's year-older

Scandinavia developed quickly into a leading stayer for Aidan O'Brien with Group 1 wins in the Goodwood Cup and St Leger

stablemate – had the whippersnapper at his heels after recording 118 in victory at Chester and 116 when runner-up to Trawlerman at Royal Ascot.

O'Brien immediately put them up against each other in the Group 1 Goodwood Cup, which had been won by Kyprios after each of his Ascot Gold Cup triumphs and no doubt would have been the target again if his season had gone to plan.

Illinois was the 7-4 favourite with Ryan Moore on board, while Scandinavia – the mount of Wayne Lordan and the sole three-year-old in the eight-runner field – was 4-1 joint-second in the market alongside Sweet William.

It was set up for a close contest and that is what ensued. Illinois tried to run the sting out of his rivals from the front and succeeded with all bar his younger stablemate, to whom he was conceding a stone in weight. Battle was joined from a furlong out and Scandinavia slowly but surely inched his way into the lead. He crossed the line three-quarters of a length to the good.

A first Group 1 victory

prompted Lordan to make reference to Kyprios in his post-race comments. "I think in the future he could step into Kyprios's shoes, but I suppose if Kyprios was here today it might have been a tougher task," the jockey said. "That's the way it goes. Kyprios has gone, so this could be the man for the next few years."

★★★★

SCANDINAVIA'S progress had been so impressive that he was made 2-1 favourite for the St Leger ahead of his dual Derby-winning stablemate Lambourn. The first three from the Queen's Vase – Carmers, Furthur and Rahiebb – were also in the line-up. Even though he was back against his own age group, it would be another stiff test for Scandinavia.

With O'Brien having to shuffle his jockeys to cover injury to Moore and suspension for Lordan, Tom Marquand was called up for the ride. He was quite the supersub. He was familiar with Scandinavia, having partnered him in a Newmarket maiden at two, and he knew the feeling of

wearing the St Leger winner's cap after his victory on Galileo Chrome for Joseph O'Brien in 2020.

Again it was a hard-fought battle. Again Scandinavia prevailed. This time he was the target up the long straight, having taken over from the front-running Lambourn with two and a half furlongs still to go. He did not flinch for a moment, not even when Rahiebb made a late charge against the far rail. Classic victory was his.

Marquand, who had come in for the winning ride in 2020 only when Shane Crosse tested positive for Covid, had made the most of his opportunity again. "It's a shame someone has to miss out for another person to have an opportunity, but the ride has to fall to someone and luckily it was me," he said.

Wearing the cherished cap again, Marquand confirmed he had clear memories of his mount from that Newmarket maiden. "You don't forget horses like Scandinavia," he

said. "I don't ride tons of horses for Aidan, so when I do ride them I remember every single one. He was a beautiful horse who was always going to have a future over staying trips – but I'd be lying if I said I thought then that he'd be a Leger winner."

This was O'Brien's ninth Leger winner and his third in a row. He has nine wins in the Ascot Gold Cup too and that is where he is aiming Scandinavia, who was put away for the year after the Leger. The trainer saw the qualities in Scandinavia to be a Cup horse but with something extra too. "He has a beautiful temperament and he stays, but he'll probably have no problem coming back to a mile and a half as he has loads of gears," he said. "And the better the ground, the better you'll see him."

Classic success secured, the outlook was bright for Scandinavia.

Reporting by Andrew Dietz, Lee Mottershead, Catherine Macrae and Nick Pulford

◀Scandi thriller: Scandinavia holds off Rahiebb (yellow) and Stay True in the St Leger; inset, Tom Marquand in the winner's cap

'A wonderful racehorse'

SCANDINAVIA'S Goodwood Cup was marred by a fatal injury to Trueshan, the 2021 winner. The Alan King-trained nine-year-old was having his 35th start, and fourth run in the Goodwood Cup, when he was pulled up by Hollie Doyle after sustaining an injury six furlongs out. Doyle described the popular campaigner as a "special, special horse" who gave her some of her best memories.

As well as the Goodwood Cup, Trueshan had two more Group 1 wins in the Prix du Cadran in 2021 and 2023. He had Group 2 victories in the Long Distance Cup (2020, 2021 and 2022) and Doncaster Cup (2023) and put up a tremendous weight-carrying performance to land the 2022 Northumberland Plate under 10st 8lb.

The day after Trueshan's death, King said there had been an outpouring of sympathy. "I've been blown away by the messages this morning and last night," he said. "I've had over 200 of them and there are a lot of kind people out there. It meant a lot to me and the team here at Barbury that he touched a lot of people.

"When he won the Goodwood Cup, which was my first Group 1 in England, it was very special. He was a wonderful racehorse."

◉ THE
BIGGER
PICTURE

Oneforthegutter after his victory in the
valuable 1m6f heritage handicap at the
Newmarket July meeting for trainer Ian
Williams and jockey Silvestre de Sousa
EDWARD WHITAKER (RACINGPOST.COM/PHOTOS)

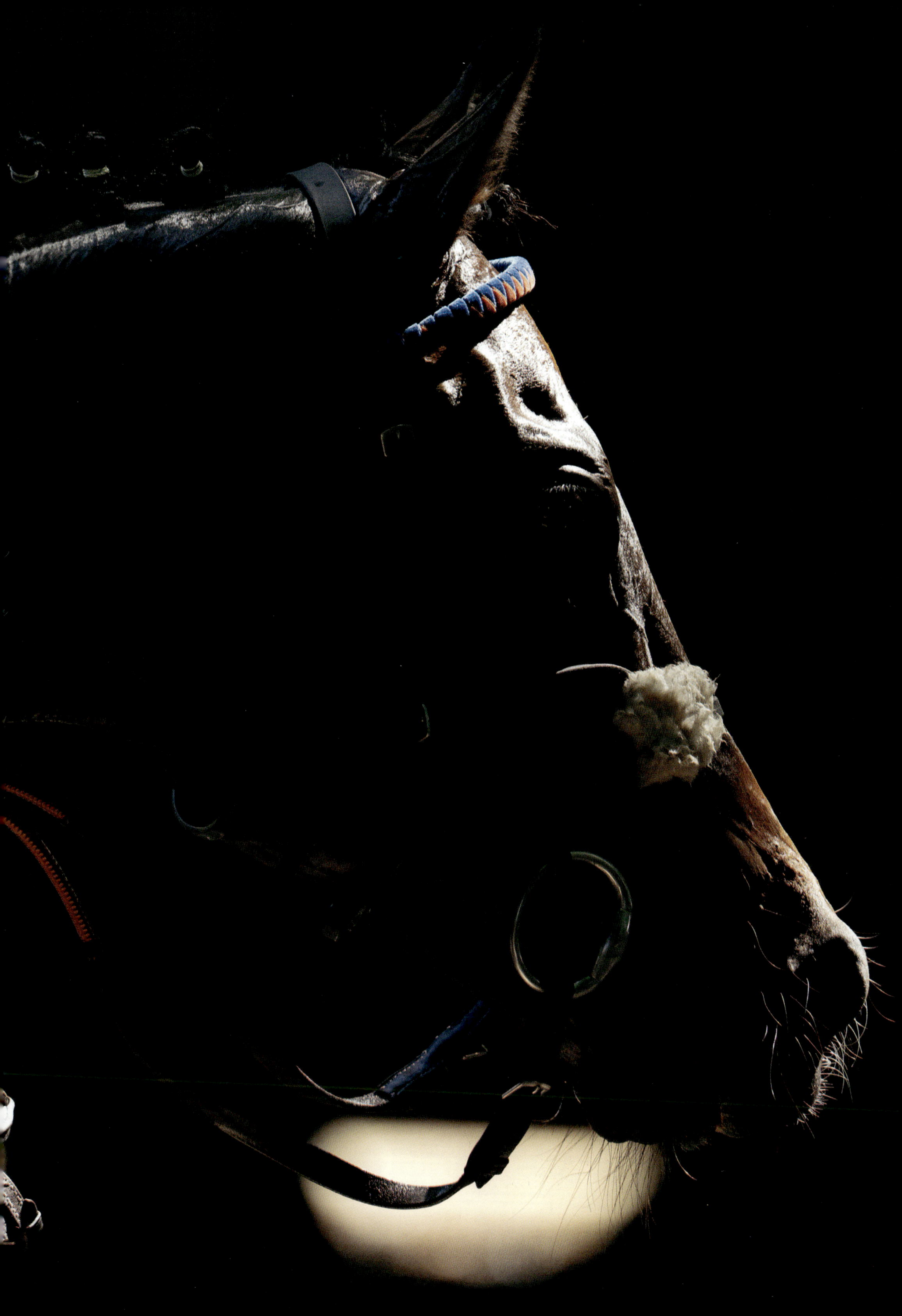

Poignant success at Royal Ascot for Johnson Houghton

TEARS flowed after Eve Johnson Houghton's Royal Ascot victory with Havana Hurricane in the Windsor Castle Stakes, which came just four months after the death of the trainer's father Fulke.

"I'm missing my dad; he'd be the first person I'd ring. He'd have been proud," the trainer said after her third Royal Ascot success. Winning jockey Charlie Bishop paid his own tribute. "That one's for Fulke," he said. "He was amazing to all of us."

Johnson Houghton took over the historic Woodway Stables near Blewbury, Oxfordshire, in 2006 on the retirement of her father but he continued to play a key role in the operation until his death in February at the age of 84. He trained more than 1,200 winners in a 46-year career and his stars included 1978 King George VI and Queen Elizabeth Stakes winner Ile De Bourbon and champion milers Romulus and Habitat.

He also trained Ribocco and Ribero to win consecutive runnings of the St Leger and Irish Derby in 1967 and 1968. Like all of his best horses, they were owned by Charles Engelhard or bred by the widow of the US gold and platinum tycoon.

Speaking after her Royal Ascot win with Havana Hurricane, his daughter opened up on how much she missed him. "It's tough for anyone who loses their father," she told Neil Clark in the Racing Post Weekender. "I used to see him every day and he was a very good sounding board as well as being great fun. We really miss him. But he'd be proud, I think."

Bought for just 9,000gns, Havana Hurricane was a second Windsor Castle winner for Johnson Houghton – after Chipotle in 2021 – and she had Group 1 success at Royal Ascot in 2018 with Queen Anne Stakes hero Accidental Agent, who was bred and owned by her mother Gaie.

Johnson Houghton said of her latest victory: "I said to the owners, win, lose or draw, he cost you 9,000gns. You've made more than that already and you're here to play. We've had a great day."

Remarkably, there was an even better two-year-old at Woodway. Zavateri won two Group 2s before going to the Irish Champions Festival to land the Group 1 National Stakes.

"I'm so lucky," Johnson Houghton said at the Curragh. "It has gone really well this year. We don't have the biggest budget but we get it done. I've got a great team and an amazing place to train."

In a year that started with grief, her father's legacy was in good hands.

Pictures: Patrick McCann (racingpost.comphotos)

Desert Flower rounds off epic Classic

EVEN for a global operation as powerful and successful as Godolphin, the first weekend of May was extraordinary.

In less than 42 hours Sheikh Mohammed's team in royal blue notched Classic doubles on both sides of the Atlantic. The first leg of the quadruple was Good Cheer's Kentucky Oaks, then more headlines were made by Ruling Court's 2,000 Guineas and Sovereignty's Kentucky Derby, and finally Desert Flower completed the sequence with 1,000 Guineas victory.

Charlie Appleby, the first trainer to do the Guineas double since Aidan O'Brien in 2019, said: "It's been an amazing weekend for Godolphin. It's not just what we've achieved here, but what we've achieved over in America."

After being left with the task of rounding off the four-timer, Appleby added: "I said thanks to the team in the US this morning as I'm usually laid-back but they'd tightened the screws a bit."

In truth, Appleby felt secure in his work. "I'm in an incredibly lucky position," he said. "Outside the team there's a huge amount of pressure, but for me it's enjoyable and to be able to speak to His Highness [Sheikh Mohammed] every day is incredible."

He also had a high level of confidence in his filly, who headed to the Guineas with a perfect four-from-four record as a juvenile. "To be brutally honest, I think she's pretty bulletproof," he said with bold directness on the eve of the race.

Desert Flower, sent off the even-money favourite, proved him right. Having made all, she was threatened briefly by 28-1 shot Flight at the furlong pole before pulling out more to score by a length. "Watching it, you'd have said we had a battle on our hands, but I knew as soon as she hit the rising ground she'd find another gear," Appleby said.

Victory in the 1,000 Guineas left the trainer with only the Oaks missing from his Classic CV in Britain and there were high hopes for Desert Flower when she lined up as the 11-10

weekend for Godolphin

favourite at Epsom a month later. Her unbeaten record was ended, however, and so was Godolphin's run of Classic success.

Desert Flower was beaten just over four lengths in third in the Oaks behind Aidan O'Brien's duellists Minnie Hauk and Whirl and, while that pair went on to have golden summers, Appleby's filly was forced on to the sidelines.

"Epsom took its toll on Desert Flower," the trainer reported in the autumn, making clear that she was too valuable a broodmare prospect to risk.

That high value was secured with her Guineas victory on Godolphin's magical weekend.

▼Flower power: Desert Flower (William Buick) wins the 1,000 Guineas at Newmarket for Godolphin and Charlie Appleby

Washed silks hang on the line to dry at Joe Murphy's Crampscastle yard in Fethard, County Tipperary in July – a world away from the glamour of the 70-year-old trainer's first Group 1 win with Cercene in the Coronation Stakes at Royal Ascot a few weeks earlier

PATRICK McCANN (RACINGPOST.COM/PHOTOS)

FLYING COULEURS

All smiles: Sean Bowen and
Rebecca Curtis (inset) celebrate
their Irish Grand National
success with Haiti Couleurs

Rebecca Curtis's small Welsh stable got back in the big time with impressive Irish Grand National winner Haiti Couleurs

By Nick Pulford

BRITISH-TRAINED staying chasers have found it tough to compete against their Irish rivals in recent years, but Haiti Couleurs made it look supremely comfortable. He was travelling so well when he passed the winning post in the Irish Grand National that jockey Sean Bowen wondered for a moment if he had miscounted and there was still another circuit to go.

Never mind that there was a Willie Mullins-trained favourite or that Gordon Elliott had seven runners in Ireland's richest jumps race. Haiti Couleurs brushed them all aside with contemptuous ease. Bar his possible slip-up on the simple maths, Bowen never had a moment's concern as he cruised home by three and a quarter lengths.

It was a crushing victory. The dominance was complete and utter. Trainer Rebecca Curtis was as much in awe of her brilliant winner as anyone else. "He looked like he was in second gear the whole way, didn't he?" she said. "It was amazing."

For Curtis and Bowen, this was an important step forward in their ambition to compete more regularly on the big stage. To mount Britain's first successful raid on the Irish Grand National since 2014, and to do it with such authority, seemed a significant moment. Amid so much gloom around British racing, Haiti Couleurs had become a strikingly bright flagbearer.

★★★★

BEFORE Fairyhouse, there was Cheltenham. Curtis's new stable star played a leading role at the festival too, landing the National Hunt Novices' Handicap Chase on the opening day. Much had been expected of the eight-year-old – he was 7-2 joint-favourite – and he delivered victory in great style by four and a half lengths.

In a sign of things to come, the view from the saddle was serene. Ben Jones was on board this time and he had it just as easy as Bowen would at Fairyhouse. "It was a walk in the park really," Jones said. "He was a dream of a ride. I felt like I had loads left and he galloped all the way to the line. It was a very good performance and I still don't think we've seen the very best from him."

Curtis had been less calm in the build-up to the race. With only around 20 horses in her team, she did not have the luxury of multiple opportunities on the big days. There was intense pressure to make the most of this one for the "three amazing owners", collectively known as The Brizzle Boys, who had invested in Haiti Couleurs.

"I felt nervous beforehand," she said. "He was one of the favourites and I wanted him to win so much for these owners because they've been my best supporters."

The trainer's feelings during the race were entirely different, such was the control exerted by Haiti Couleurs and Jones. "It was one of the weirdest races I've ever watched," Curtis said. "It was almost like it was in slow motion because he just seemed to do it so easily."

This sixth Cheltenham Festival success was vindication of Curtis's belief in her ability. In the previous year she had invested heavily to upgrade the gallops and facilities at her Pembrokeshire yard. "It was shit or bust, basically," she said in a Racing Post interview after Cheltenham. "It was a big risk but if you want to keep moving forward you've got to do something. Things had started to become a bit stale and we needed to have a fresh start, to revamp and go again."

Curtis had also backed herself when buying Haiti Couleurs for £68,000 in 2022, going against the advice of others. "His price tag looks cheap now," she said after

▸Continues page 134

Cheltenham. "Watching his point-to-point videos, I loved the way he travelled and jumped. I remember at the time I was told not to buy him for one reason or another but I loved him straight away and I try not to be influenced by what other people say."

✦✦✦✦

CURTIS also brushed away any negative thoughts when she lined up the next target for Haiti Couleurs. Looking out across the sea from her base on the coast of south-west Wales, the next stop is Ireland and that was where she would send her Cheltenham hero.

She was unfazed by Britain's recent record in the Irish Grand National and positively excited by the opportunity of mounting the first successful raid since Jonjo O'Neill with Shutthefrontdoor 11 years earlier. "I just think he'll be suited by the race," she said. "It's a brilliant distance for him, novices have a good record in the race, he's on a perfect mark, it's nice timing and it's something a bit different for the owners. I love Irish racing and the whole experience."

There would be a change of jockey at Fairyhouse. Bowen had been on board for both of Haiti Couleurs' chase wins before Cheltenham but was claimed by Olly Murphy to ride against him at the festival on Resplendent Grey. The soon-to-be-champion

had to sit and suffer as Jones and Haiti Couleurs went away into the distance, leaving Bowen's mount back in fourth.

For all his successes over the season, Bowen was winless at the festival again. He had also missed the ride on Curtis's 2020 Stayers' Hurdle winner Lisnagar Oscar, due to a broken collarbone, and frustratingly a festival first continued to elude him.

The Irish National was a chance to show what he could do on the big stage, just as it was for Curtis to issue a further reminder of her training talent. Bowen, always in control out on the track, was coolness personified. The trainer, her job done in getting Haiti Couleurs there in top shape, could do no more than watch in hope.

"I watched it in the parade ring on the big screen," she said. "I was going to go out to the front in the stands, but it was so busy that I stayed where I was. I was calm until the last two fences and then I started to let out a few roars."

This meant a lot. "It feels like one of our best wins," Curtis added. "I'm delighted for Sean. Although he's ecstatic to be champion jockey, he said one

▲ Big splash: Haiti Couleurs gallops in the sea near Newport, Pembrokeshire; inset, with trainer Rebecca Curtis and work-rider Adam Janes; below, on his way to a crushing victory in the Irish Grand National under Sean Bowen

thing he's missing is some big wins and he's just had one."

✦✦✦✦

BY THE autumn, Curtis had her eye on the biggest races of all for Haiti Couleurs. The Cheltenham Gold Cup and the Grand National at Aintree. "The two races are just a thought," she said, "but there's a slight possibility we'll end up looking at both because he's the right sort of horse who could do it. He thrives on racing; three days after his races he's as fresh as anything."

Having gone up more than a stone in the ratings for his wins at Cheltenham and Fairyhouse, Haiti Couleurs had summered so well that his trainer felt he could go higher still.

"I'd like to target him as a Graded horse; we'll find out more as the season goes on," she said. "He's not slow, so going back in trip would be fine. He got to the front so easily in the Irish National and can go a real good gallop. The Gold Cup is an endless gallop and you want a horse who stays like he does and jumps well."

Curtis and Bowen are eager for more big-race success. Haiti Couleurs might well deliver it.

SEAN BOWEN simply didn't want the 2024-25 jumps season to stop. By the end, in an unforgettable April for the 27-year-old rider, he was on such a roll that anything seemed possible.

The British season had its usual finale at Sandown and it came with Bowen crowned champion for the first time. He capped his title triumph with big-race victory in the bet365 Gold Cup aboard Resplendent Grey, trained by chief ally Olly Murphy. That Sandown success came only five days after Bowen's most valuable win in the Irish Grand National with the Rebecca Curtis-trained Haiti Couleurs.

"Amazing. The best two weeks of my life. I hope it carries on forever," Bowen said after his victory on Resplendent Grey. "There have been plenty of good days but the last two weeks have been something I never want to stop."

The final week was a whirlwind finish to a season in which Bowen set a searing pace at the top of the table. He finished on 180 winners, 38 clear of Harry Skelton, as he seized the title from third-placed Harry Cobden. It was all the sweeter after the heartbreak of the previous season. Bowen held a peak lead of 47 over Cobden then but had to miss the whole of January with a knee injury and had been overtaken by the time he was back in the fray, handing the momentum to his opponent.

In a major Racing Post interview heading into that triumphant final week of the latest season, Bowen described the Sandown finale 12 months earlier as one of his worst days in racing. "The longest I've ever been annoyed for was after Sandown," he told Lewis Porteous. "I was depressed for three days but after that I kicked on again. You have to get over losing very quickly and keep as level as you can."

This time Bowen had eased to victory long before the final day. On receiving the coveted trophy at Sandown, he said: "I can't quite believe this has happened. I'm so grateful to everyone. This day here last year was one of the worst I've had in racing, but this is definitely one of the best."

Resplendent Grey's victory made it even better. After a disappointing run in the National Hunt Novices' Handicap Chase at the Cheltenham Festival, there was a rethink with the talented seven-year-old and cheekpieces were applied to help him get into a better rhythm. Bowen was at his best in the saddle to deliver his mount late and clinch victory from a phalanx of Willie Mullins-trained challengers.

This was the last of the 103 winners Bowen rode for Murphy out of his seasonal total of 180. The trainer was delighted it was a big one for the new champion. "Today is his day," he said. "I've been a very small cog in his wheel. We've had a really good relationship together for the last two years. These are the races you want to win."

He added: "I'm unbelievably proud of Sean. There wouldn't be too many trainer/jockey combinations that have the sort of relationship we do. He respects me and I respect him and I think that has contributed to our success. I love working with him."

The feeling was mutual. In his Racing Post interview, Bowen said: "I wouldn't have been champion jockey without Olly and his yard is going from strength to strength. He knows how to train winners and it's a matter of time until the big winners come. We're so hungry for winners together and I think that's a massive part in why the yard is doing so well. He was as depressed as I was when I wasn't champion last year and no-one wants me to be champion jockey more than Olly does."

GLORY DAYS

On what it meant to reach his goal after two consecutive second places in the championship, Bowen made his drive and determination crystal clear. "I've never made any secret that I wanted to be champion jockey but I suppose some people don't want to put that pressure on themselves," he said. "It's something I've always wanted and luckily now I'm fulfilling that dream. If you don't believe it's going to happen one day, it probably won't."

A special day away from the track awaited Bowen in July when he married long-time partner Harriet Matthews, yet there was little let-up in his relentless quest for winners. Two days after the wedding, he rode a double for Gordon Elliott at Perth.

Come the autumn, Bowen

Sean Bowen wound up his first title-winning season with big victories on Haiti Couleurs and Resplendent Grey in an incredible final week

▲Living the dream: Sean Bowen takes the champion's walk and rides Resplendent Grey to victory in the bet365 Gold Cup on the final day of the 2024-25 jumps season at Sandown

had a commanding lead in his bid for back-to-back titles. In September he took the prize as leading rider in the inaugural summer jumps championship and by the end of that month had racked up 93 winners in all. His brother James was a distant second on 40.

The champion's ultimate aim was to ride 200 winners in the season. "That's why we've been having such a big go of it and it's something I really want to do," Bowen said. "It's been done before but not very often, particularly nowadays, and to have my name alongside some of the greats to have done it before would be fantastic."

He also had major ambitions for Haiti Couleurs and Resplendent Grey, the standout performers of his title-winning season. "Those are my big two," he said. "I read the other day that Becky was aiming Haiti Couleurs at a Gold Cup campaign and, jeez, wouldn't it be lovely if I ended up with a Gold Cup horse in Haiti and a Grand National horse in Resplendent Grey?"

As the man himself said, if you don't believe it's going to happen, it probably won't. With Bowen driving ever onwards, anything seems possible.

Reporting by David Carr, Lewis Porteous, Lee Mottershead, Sam Hendry and Nick Pulford

THE
BIGGER
PICTURE

The sun is setting at Windsor on August 4 as runners in the final race, off at 8.28pm, head for the line. On a good evening for favourite backers, victory in the mile handicap goes to 9-4 chance Radical Design – the fifth market leader to win on the seven-race card

EDWARD WHITAKER (RACINGPOST.COM/PHOTOS)

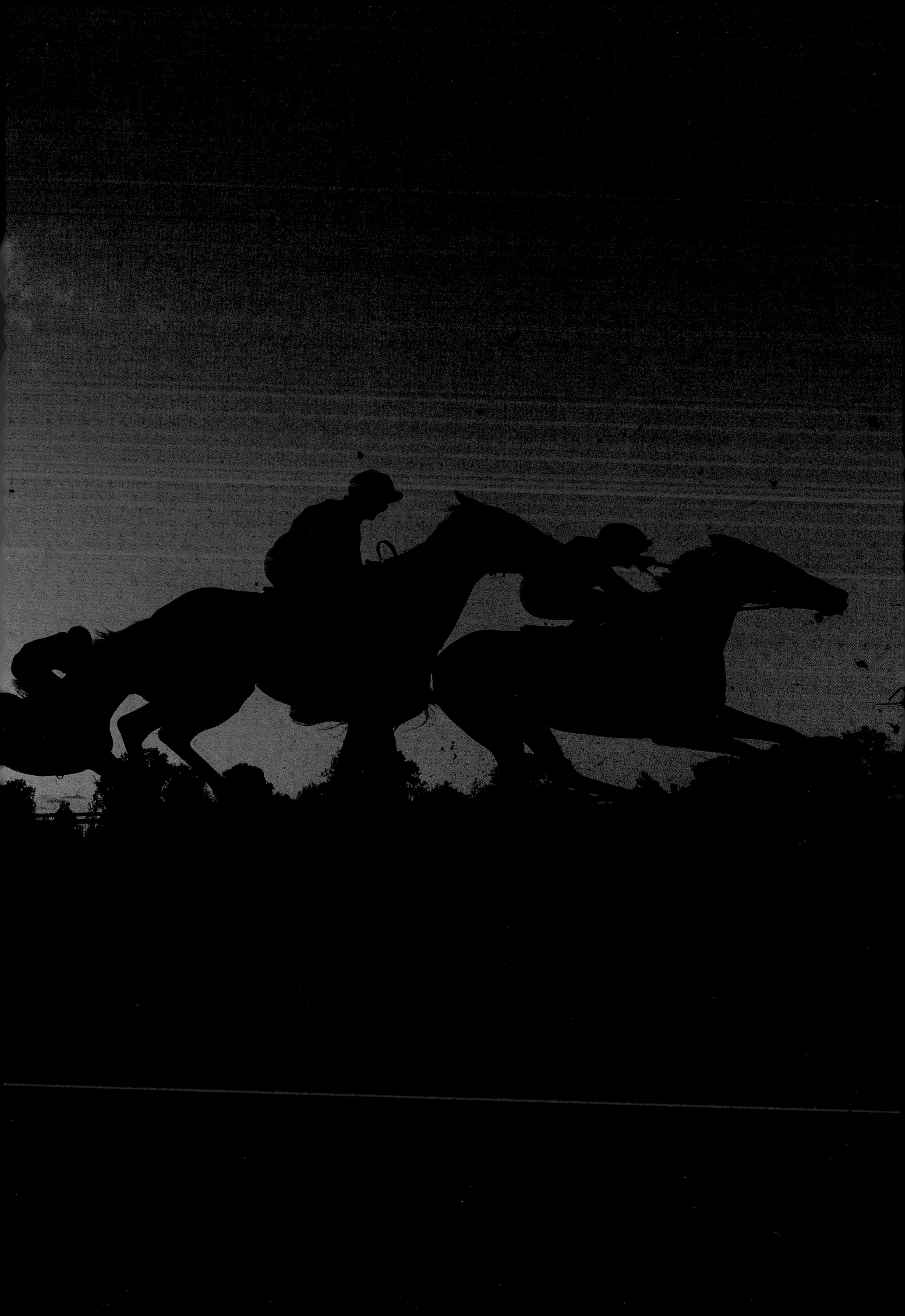

IN THE PICTURE

Doddiethegreat wins big for charity at Cheltenham

DODDIETHEGREAT was a popular winner of the Pertemps Network Final Handicap Hurdle at the Cheltenham Festival even though he was a 25-1 shot who denied favourite backers of runner-up Jeriko Du Reponet.

It was a one-two for the Nicky Henderson team headed by a yard favourite, another Cheltenham win in the colours of Honeysuckle's owner Kenny Alexander and a rare festival success for three-time champion jump jockey Brian Hughes. Jeriko Du Reponet turned the tables in a reverse one-two at the Punchestown festival a few weeks later, but the day in the Cotswolds belonged to Doddiethegreat.

For many, the biggest winner was the My Name'5 Doddie Foundation. Alexander donates all prize-money won by the horse named after Scotland rugby great Doddie Weir to the charity, which funds research into motor neurone disease (MND). The foundation was set up by Weir – who wore the no.5 jersey for club and country – following his diagnosis with MND in 2016. He died in November 2022.

Henderson had long targeted valuable races with the aim of winning as much prize-money as possible for the foundation, but the quest looked over when Doddiethegreat severed a tendon in late 2021. His return after two years off was great credit to Henderson and his team.

"We all like Doddie, there's something about him," the trainer said in the Cheltenham winner's enclosure. "He had to spend 18 months at Kenny's farm in Scotland. It didn't look like he'd get back to the racecourse, but he's done it and it's lovely."

There was delight all round that Doddiethegreat had risen to the occasion with his tremendous victory in such a worthy cause, which benefited by £62,000 from the Cheltenham win. "It's been a while," said Hughes after riding his first festival winner in seven years, and his thoughts also went to the rugby giant behind the foundation. "I was lucky enough to meet Doddie one time, he was a very inspirational man," he said.

The nine-year-old was the first homebred winner at Cheltenham for Alexander, whose broodmares are based at New Hall Stud in Ayrshire. "I'd almost forgotten I'd even bred him as I've had him so long, it's been nine years going," he said.

Peter Molony, a key cog in Alexander's breeding operation, purchased Doddiethegreat's dam Asturienne for £30,000 in 2011. "She was the first mare I ever bought for Kenny," he said. With the back story and what the Pertemps win had delivered for the foundation, it was no wonder that Molony added: "It's a wonderful result in every way."

Reporting: Catherine Macrae, Tom Peacock and Nick Pulford
Picture: John Grossick (racingpost.com/photos)

SECOND COMING

Australian mare Asfoora returned to Europe to take major honours again in a sprint season of shocks, breakthroughs and topsy-turvy form

By Andrew Dietz

THE new queen of Australian sprinting came, stayed and conquered again. Asfoora is no Black Caviar but she scaled incredible heights of her own. Her Prix de l'Abbaye triumph took her into the history books as the first Australian-trained winner in France. Not only that, she was the first sprinter since Lochsong 32 years earlier to complete the Nunthorpe-Abbaye double in the same season. She is no Lochsong either, yet her achievements have been momentous.

Trainer Henry Dwyer and owner-breeder Akram El-Fahkri have been on the journey of a lifetime. They had brought Asfoora to Britain the previous year and secured the holy grail of Royal Ascot success in the King Charles III Stakes. Victory in the Nunthorpe on their return trip made Asfoora the first Australian-trained horse to win Group 1s in Britain in consecutive seasons. Creating more history in France was "a real bucket-list thing", as Dwyer put it after the Abbaye.

"It means a whole lot," said the trainer, who is based in Ballarat, about an hour and a half from Melbourne. "It's about experience. We've tried to experience new things. I've never been to the races in France and here we are winning a Group 1 on Arc day. I'm not a massive trainer, but trying to do something different is what motivates us. When you're lying on your deathbed you're not going to think about the things you didn't do but about the things you did do."

★★★★

THE second British tour had stuttered and stalled. It was always going to be tough to repeat the glory of Royal Ascot but the 2025 visit was starting to look like a wasted journey. Asfoora was fifth in her King Charles III repeat bid and, even worse, only seventh in the King George Stakes at Goodwood. She had been a short-head runner-up in that Group 2 the previous year. This was a pale imitation of the Asfoora who had introduced herself to British racegoers in such explosive fashion first time around.

Heading into the Ebor meeting, Dwyer was all out of excuses for his star sprinter. Royal Ascot was her first run off the plane – unlike the previous year – and she had needed it. Then the rain had arrived at the worst possible time at Goodwood. They had been satisfactory runs, but Dwyer wanted spectacular. The time had come for her to deliver. It was win or bust – simple as that.

Asfoora was 11-1 for the Nunthorpe, by far the biggest price she had been in her British starts. Those who had lost faith in her were about to miss out. The old Asfoora was back and, such was her dominance on York's slick sprint track, Dwyer said he knew she was going to win with two furlongs still to run. Oisin Murphy had her in the front line at that point and

soon eased her into a clear lead. The winning margin was a convincing length and a quarter.

"It's an incredible buzz to be validated with what you think," Dwyer said in the winner's enclosure.

"A few people were doubting her and it's hard to keep faith when they're not winning, but we made sure to never lose it. We really thought she was on song this time. We knew there were no excuses for this – it was win or be retired."

Dwyer needed a sporting owner when he floated the ambitious idea before the maiden voyage and he still had

one on the repeat trip. "I've really been on a holiday with her the last two years," he said. "If I'm 100 per cent honest, if I owned her I wouldn't have come back. Akram was very insistent that we did and that she deserved another chance."

★★★★

IN BETWEEN York and Longchamp, Asfoora broke new ground again when she became the first Australian-trained runner to compete in Ireland. She could not claim a historic win, however. The flame dimmed again and she was seventh, albeit not beaten

far, in the Flying Five at the Curragh.

The City of Light would reignite her on Arc weekend. This was where Asfoora burned brightest in her 2025 campaign. And yet she almost didn't have Paris.

The biggest obstacle to her historic victory in the Abbaye came just before the race when it was discovered that she had arrived at Longchamp with another horse's passport. Panic ensued. With the clock ticking down to the race, Dwyer realised the document was at Amy Murphy's yard in Chantilly.

Murphy, a great support to

▸Continues page 144

Dwyer since the start of Asfoora's adventure, contacted Francis Graffard's assistant and she in turn handed the vital ID to an Uber driver, who made it across the city just in time.

The race, by contrast, presented little difficulty. The Abbaye can be a minefield for any top-class sprinter, but it was a relative breeze for Asfoora from her advantageous low draw. Murphy angled out off the rail with a furlong and a half to go and his mount accelerated smoothly for a half-length victory over the Czech-trained outsider Jawwal.

Asfoora's previous Group 1 wins had been on good to firm ground but she showed her class and versatility to cope with very soft going at Longchamp. "The sprint track took the rain really well and she was able to cruise through the race with a good draw," Murphy said. "I got a little bit of space when I needed it and never really had to get too serious with her. I truly believed she was in the form of her life. She's a star and the people connected with her are the same."

★★★★

THE Uber drama dominated much of the post-race talk. "It's just surreal really," Dwyer said in the winner's enclosure. "We were within a minute and a half of not running – I had the Uber driver on a retainer to get it here in time. I've driven back and forward from Chantilly to Longchamp four times in the last three days and it's never taken me shorter than an hour. He did it in 52 minutes. Hopefully he appreciates his €200 tip because he did a good job."

The trainer's anxiety must have been through the roof before the race as he explained the situation to El-Fahkri, who coincidentally owns a taxi firm in Melbourne among his other business interests.

"I tracked Akram down at the races to tell him she more than likely wouldn't be running, which was a tough conversation to have," Dwyer said. "We were beside ourselves – it was going to be an absolute balls-up – and I thought it was an 80-20 chance against us, but luckily the passport got there at the last minute and we were good."

Excitement followed by dismay followed by relief followed by hysteria. After a rollercoaster day of Disneyland proportions, Dwyer was ready to let his hair down in the French capital.

"Akram went back to his hotel for a mug of tea, but we went to a few places and ended up in a piano bar, which was very enjoyable," he said. "The evening was pretty big. There was a good contingent of Aussies with us and we celebrated accordingly."

More celebrations may lie ahead. A third instalment of the European adventure is in the works, following the decision to keep Asfoora in training as an eight-year-old. "Akram's very intent on racing her on next year," Dwyer said after Longchamp. "On the back of the

▲Aussie rules: above and previous pages, Asfoora and Oisin Murphy land the Nunthorpe; below, a second Group 1 win of the year in the Prix de l'Abbaye

Abbaye, you'd be hard pressed to say she hasn't got another year in her."

Asfoora will never match Black Caviar, the iconic Australian mare who conquered Royal Ascot in 2012 and retired undefeated in 25 starts. Nor will many hold her in the same regard as Nature Strip, Takeover Target and Choisir, who are other well-known names from the band of Australian sprint winners at the royal meeting. That has never fazed Dwyer. "We know what the days of Black Caviar were like and we're under no illusions, we're not her or Nature Strip," he said. "But she's picked her market and runs her race when circumstances are right. It's special."

Dwyer was right about that. Asfoora and all her team, including devoted groom Chenelle Ellis, had achieved something unique. The new fans she has made in Britain and France will look forward to welcoming her back again.

FIRST GROUP 1 FOR GOLDIE WITH AMERICAN AFFAIR

THREE decades of triumph and toil as a trainer for Jim Goldie reached a new high when homebred sprinter American Affair landed a memorable first Group 1 for his East Renfrewshire stable in the King Charles III Stakes.

Goldie has trained three generations of the sprinter's family but the improvement shown by this five-year-old in less than two years has been off the charts.

Unraced at two, American Affair gained his first win in the spring of his three-year-old season in 2023 and his second came in a handicap over six furlongs at Carlisle off a mark of 67 in September that year. The official handicapper feels he has improved by more than three stone since then.

Dropping back to the minimum distance has been key, with connections believing he continues to get quicker with age. American Affair won the Portland Handicap at Doncaster at the back end of the 2024 campaign and racked up big sprint handicap victories at Musselburgh and York this season before an unlucky Temple Stakes fifth at Haydock teed him up for the royal meeting.

On his first attempt at the highest level, Goldie's

▼ Competitive edge: American Affair has a neck to spare over Frost At Dawn (15) in the King Charles III Stakes at Royal Ascot

flagbearer was well suited by the big field and stiff finish, showing a terrific attitude to repel Frost At Dawn by a neck for an 11-1 success under Paul Mulrennan.

The rider has been a vital cog in the sprinter's rise through the ranks, having been aboard for seven of his eight victories, and it was Mulrennan's first Royal Ascot winner since Dandino landed the King George V Handicap in 2010. The grey-haired rider, 43, joked the colour was jet black for his last success.

Goldie, who had the race in mind from as early as April, said in a Racing Post interview in July: "I knew he was a player, but everything had to go right. It didn't at Haydock, and afterwards you could have backed him at 100-1 for Royal Ascot. We went from vying for favouritism in a Group 2 to that, which is mad, but some folk were clever enough to get those odds."

A bone issue curtailed American Affair's season, with a planned run in the Nunthorpe and a trip to the Breeders' Cup put on the back burner, but Goldie is confident his stable star will be fully firing on all cylinders again next season. There could still be more to come.

▼Rise and fall: Lazzat (red cap) blasts home in the Queen Elizabeth II Jubilee Stakes, the second of Royal Ascot's all-aged Group 1 sprints; inset, James Doyle is dumped on the turf after the race before Lazzat heads off around the course

LAZZAT ZIPS HOME IN THE JUBILEE – AND KEEPS ON RUNNING

IN A season full of shocks in the sprint division, the Queen Elizabeth II Jubilee Stakes proved the outlier.

Having not met his reserve when unsold for £2.25 million at the 2024 Goffs London Sale, it can be safely assumed that the transfer fee paid by Wathnan Racing to acquire fast-improving French sprinter Lazzat in the lead-up to the royal meeting was substantial.

Jerome Reynier's stable star was best on Racing Post Ratings and joint top-rated on official figures, yet the presence of Japanese ace Satono Reve and the previous year's Commonwealth Cup scorer Inisherin ensured he was sent off the 9-2 third favourite.

The race itself was fairly straightforward. Lazzat was quickly away from stall 11 and made all in the centre of the track, beating Satono Reve by half a length. The drama came afterwards.

Spooked by a bright winning rug unfurled by Reynier, Lazzat proceeded to dump rider James Doyle on the turf and embarked on an extended tour of the Berkshire track, evading officials and groundstaff for several minutes.

The ITV cameras lapped it up, with the terrestrial channel's social media team posting popular 'Lazzat on the loose' clips on TikTok and Instagram.

The rider, rather bizarrely,

returned to the winner's enclosure on foot as attempts to catch Lazzat, who was gelded at two in the hope of making him more tractable, continued in the back straight.

Doyle, who went into the meeting feeling Lazzat was his banker, said: "I apologised to the King and Queen when I went to collect my prize. I told them I should have stayed in Pony Club longer than I did, so we had a good laugh about it."

For Reynier, who has also enjoyed Group 1 wins in France, Dubai and Germany with the likes of Facteur Cheval and Skalleti, this was a breakthrough success at the royal meeting and cemented a new partnership with the powerhouse owners.

Lazzat received his lap of applause in the winner's enclosure just ten minutes before the off-time of the following Jersey Stakes and was the fifth and final winner of a highly successful Royal Ascot for Wathnan Racing.

The Qatari operation were denied the leading owner award only by virtue of a countback of placed horses in favour of Coolmore. In just their second full season in Britain, that was an impressive feat.

HUGHES SPRINGS 66-1 SURPRISE WITH NO HALF MEASURES

BOOKMAKER delight with a 66-1 winner was nothing compared with the elation of Richard Hughes after he had landed his first Group 1 success as a trainer with No Half Measures in the July Cup. "We've done it, we've done it," he said in the Newmarket winner's enclosure. "Finally, finally."

Hughes's filly, whose previous career best was a Group 3 win on heavy ground at Newbury, relished her first start over six furlongs in almost a year, combined with a fast surface, to become the longest-priced winner of the July Cup since it was first run in 1876.

At the time only three British Group 1 winners had returned bigger odds since the Pattern was created in 1971, although three more were added before the end of the season – Powerful Glory (200-1, Champions Sprint), Qirat (150-1, Sussex Stakes) and Cicero's Gift (100-1, Queen Elizabeth II Stakes).

July course regulars may have followed the progress of No Half Measures after an impressive handicap success at the track the previous summer, after which Ryan Moore, described as a "realist" by Hughes, told the trainer he had a smart prospect on his hands.

The Richard Gallagher-owned four-year-old was an unconsidered July Cup

▼Full on: No Half Measures (orange cap) is brought with a perfectly timed challenge by Neil Callan to beat Big Mojo by a neck in the July Cup

outsider by many – although Racing Post tipster Robbie Wilders highlighted her chance in his column – and much of the pre-race interest revolved around the drop back to sprinting for Notable Speech, the previous year's 2,000 Guineas and Sussex winner.

That plan didn't come off – Notable Speech was fifth – but Hughes's did. He told Neil Callan to ride No Half Measures with patience, ensuring she finished off well, and the rider executed the tactics to perfection. Produced inside the final furlong, the filly held subsequent Haydock Sprint Cup scorer Big Mojo by a neck.

Hughes, who won the race as a rider on Oasis Dream in 2003 and is in his 11th season as a trainer, said: "At halfway, I thought she was going okay and then I just held my head as I couldn't believe what was happening. I had nearly given up thinking it [a Group 1 win] would happen but I knew if a good one came along, we would be able to do it."

The trainer bought No Half Measures for £34,000 as a yearling, showing his eye for a bargain and then demonstrating his ability to maximise the potential of a talented filly. Surely it is long odds the three-time champion jockey will have to wait another decade for his next Group 1.

▼Big moment: Mick Appleby's Rutland yard claims a first Group 1 in Britain when Big Mojo lands the Haydock Sprint Cup; right, Appleby with winning jockey William Buick

'THIS MEANS MORE' – APPLEBY STRIKES WITH BIG MOJO

A FIRST top-level win can be a whirlwind experience for a trainer – particularly when it comes away from home. Mick Appleby was able to take it all in the second time around when he celebrated a domestic Group 1 breakthrough with Big Mojo in the Sprint Cup at Haydock.

Appleby has built a fine reputation for improving horses from other stables over the years and has been among the top trainers on the all-weather for more than a decade.

The Rutland trainer's career took a sharp upturn when Big Evs burst on to the scene as a juvenile in 2023, winning the Windsor Castle, Molecomb and Flying Childers before securing a first for Appleby at the top level in the Grade 1 Breeders' Cup Juvenile Turf Sprint.

Less than two years on, Appleby and owners Paul and Rachael Teasdale were back in the limelight at the highest level with Big Mojo. Having proved he was better than ever at three when narrowly beaten into second in the July Cup, their new star bounced back from a lesser effort on easier ground at Glorious Goodwood with a career-best performance at Haydock.

In a race dominated by those drawn high (the first five were drawn in stalls 15, 19, 16, 13 and ten), Big Mojo continued the sprinting merry-go-round. Positioned prominently under William Buick, who was riding him for the first time, the 16-1 shot hit the front over a furlong out and repelled all challengers to score by a length and a quarter.

"It's a big moment and it does mean more this time," Appleby said. "It's absolutely great for the whole team to get a Group 1 over here. We were disappointed with his run at Goodwood and there were a lot of question marks by his name, but we put it down to the ground. He's gone and proved he's still at the top. It took William half the track to pull him up."

There was a sea of Wathnan Racing silks in behind, with the operation responsible for the second, third and fifth – including Kind Of Blue, who was runner-up for the second year in a row.

Even amid the glamour of training a Group 1 winner, Appleby, in typically down-to-earth fashion, was not one to forget his roots. "It's great to have these nice horses," he said, "but we'll be back on the all-weather this winter."

ARIZONA BLAZE TOO HOT TO HANDLE IN FLYING FIVE

ANOTHER Group 1 sprint, another country, another breakthrough winner. The Flying Five, Ireland's only top-level sprint for older horses, brought a home win for the Adrian Murray-trained Arizona Blaze. The three-year-old had long promised to land a Group 1 prize and finally it arrived.

David Egan kept the faith. He had partnered Arizona Blaze in all but one of his 16 starts – the exception being a half-length second in the Grade 1 Breeders' Cup Juvenile Turf Sprint the previous November – and wasn't going to desert him now.

Egan could have chosen stablemate Bucanero Fuerto, who was a little shorter in the betting, but he stuck with the colt who had carried him close to top-level success at Royal Ascot when a neck second in the Commonwealth Cup.

Both in the purple of Kia Joorabchian's Amo Racing, Arizona Blaze and Bucanero Fuerte were disputing the lead as they passed the two-furlong pole. Asfoora, the 7-2 favourite after her Nunthorpe Stakes win, was tucked in behind and looked a big threat.

This time, however, nothing was going to get past Arizona Blaze. Egan's mount stayed on strongly on the yielding ground in the final furlong, holding off the late-finishing

▼Flying finish: Arizona Blaze has a clear break on his pursuers in the Flying Five; inset, Amo Racing boss Kia Joorabchian, right, celebrates with assistant trainer Robson Aguiar

Nighteyes by a length. Bucanero Fuerte was third and Asfoora faded into seventh.

It would have been easy for Egan to have switched saddles to Bucanero Fuerto, who came into the race off a career-best win over the Curragh's six furlongs. Arizona Blaze, by contrast, had disappointed on his latest run when only 11th

as the 9-2 favourite in the Nunthorpe. Egan, however, continued to believe their luck would turn.

"That defeat in the Commonwealth Cup was hard to swallow," he said. "He's a top-class horse and really deserved that [a Group 1 win].

"Leading up to the race, a lot of people were saying

Bucanero was the pick of the two. It was a flip of a coin but I always had a lot of faith in this horse."

Murray agreed it had been a difficult call to make. "They're two brilliant horses," he said. "It was a tough decision for David and I thought there was a good chance he was on the wrong one, but he was right. I

was confident Arizona Blaze would bounce back as he very rarely runs a bad race. At York he was a little slow out of the stalls and got on the back foot."

Egan and Arizona Blaze were very much on the front foot in the Flying Five. That elusive Group 1 victory was theirs at last.

200-1 STUNNER

THE biggest shock of all was saved for last. In a sprint season of ever-changing fortunes, the history books were rewritten in the most dramatic fashion when the final Group 1 was won by Powerful Glory at an incredible 200-1.

A neck the other way and the 2-1 favourite Lazzat would have prevailed in the British Champions Sprint. As it was, that was the slim margin by which the Richard Fahey-trained three-year-old became the longest-priced winner of any European Group 1 race since the Flat Pattern was created in 1971.

Disbelief was the overriding feeling – not least for winning jockey Jamie Spencer. "I thought I was going to be placed and then all of a sudden, I thought 'I've got a chance'," he said. "He jinked a little bit left and I put my whip away, and we held on. I'm just shocked. It's disbelief really."

Spencer has long been acknowledged as a master of the Ascot straight track, especially with a waiting ride, and this was another perfect demonstration of his craft. He settled Powerful Glory in the back three of the 19 runners in the early stages before gradually manoeuvring into position to launch his challenge from the two-furlong pole.

Lazzat was the target up ahead and Spencer's mount ran

Longest-priced British Group 1 winners

200-1 Powerful Glory 2025 British Champions Sprint

150-1 Qirat 2025 Sussex Stakes

100-1 Hittite Glory 1975 Flying Childers Stakes

100-1 Sole Power 2010 Nunthorpe Stakes

100-1 Cicero's Gift 2025 Queen Elizabeth II Stakes

80-1 Khaadem 2023 Queen Elizabeth II Jubilee Stakes

66-1 Maroof 1994 Queen Elizabeth II Stakes

66-1 Billesdon Brook 2018 1,000 Guineas

66-1 No Half Measures 2025 July Cup

Since European Pattern created 1971 (Theodore 200-1, 1822 St Leger)

POWERFUL GLORY, at 200-1, became the longest-priced winner of any European Group 1 race since the Flat Pattern was created in 1971, beating the record of 150-1 by Qirat in the Sussex Stakes in July. Long before the Pattern, Theodore won the St Leger at odds of 200-1 in 1822, *writes John Randall*.

The world record for the longest-priced Group/Grade 1 winner is held by Lunar Fox, who won the 2021 Australian Guineas at Flemington in Melbourne at 300-1.

Powerful Glory is also the longest-priced winner of any European Group race, beating the record of 150-1 by Nando Parrado (2020 Coventry Stakes), Valiant Force (2023 Norfolk Stakes) and Qirat. He also equalled the record for the longest-priced winner of any Flat race in Britain, being the eighth to be returned at 200-1.

him down in the final 100 yards to propel himself into the record books. "It was a Spencer special," said Fahey, who deserved much credit too for guiding Powerful Glory to Group 1 success on just his fifth start.

"Did I think he would come here and win? I thought he would need to be at his very best because he's still an immature horse," the trainer said, adding: "It was the plan all year, genuinely. We had a blip halfway through and we had to stop with him, and we were running out of races."

Fahey's only remaining chance was the Champions Sprint, where Powerful Glory was up against three of the year's Group 1 sprint winners – Lazzat, No Half Measures and Big Mojo. The late-comer to the show beat them all. Also behind him were three more Group 1 winners from the previous season – Inisherin, Montassib and Kind Of Blue.

In that sense, the result could be read as further evidence of the topsy-turvy nature of the top sprints. Powerful Glory's shock success was also proof of Spencer's special alchemy in the saddle.

As Lazzat's rider James Doyle put it: "When Jamie Spencer is riding on the straight course at Ascot, he can create a bit of magic and I think you've just seen it."

Seeing was believing.

Two Tribes stars at Goodwood for top handicap team

TWO TRIBES went to war in the midsummer handicaps, landing two big pots in the space of a week for trainer Richard Spencer and justifying an almighty betting plunge in the Stewards' Cup at Glorious Goodwood.

Having landed the International Handicap at 25-1 over seven furlongs at Ascot on July 26, Two Tribes dropped back a furlong for the Stewards' Cup seven days later under a 6lb penalty. He was 20-1 overnight but a gamble developed rapidly on raceday. His price had halved by 1.25pm and in the last 12 minutes before the off at 3.05 it went to 9-1, 7-1, 13-2, 6-1 and finally to an SP of 11-2.

In the 70 seconds it took to complete the race, Two Tribes made the 27-runner heritage handicap look simple. He thundered down the stands' side to come home two and a quarter lengths in front under David Egan, taking his prize-money in a week to more than £200,000.

Owner Phil Cunningham, who also had the Spencer-trained Run Boy Run and Twilight Calls in fourth and fifth, was delighted with the result. "Absolutely amazing," he said. "It was a lovely victory last Saturday and we weren't going to run him after that, but there was a change of plan on Wednesday. It was a big pot and he was going to sneak in at the bottom under a penalty, so we said we'd have a crack at it. It's worked out perfectly.

"The clever lads who bet the horses clearly picked the right one because he was the market mover," added the owner, who admitted he had got involved in the plunge but kept coy about the amount.

Remarkably, the Spencer-Cunningham team had another big handicap double at Ayr in September, landing not only the famous Gold Cup but the Silver Cup too. That was another £125,000 in win prize-money banked in little more than an hour.

This time Run Boy Run stepped up from his Goodwood fourth to take Gold at 12-1, while 8-1 chance Candy earned Silver.

"We've been targeting all the major festivals this year," Spencer said. "Phil wanted to give it a really good kick, coming racing and enjoying the weeks of festivals. It's been a great season for us. We haven't had a lot of winners, but prize-money is up and we've been targeting winners on the big days."

Cunningham was stunned by the double success on his first-ever visit to Ayr. "I don't know what to say; it's quite emotional," he said. "We're just getting stronger and stronger. I think we'll come back!"

Reporting: Maddy Playle, Catherine Macrae and David Carr
Picture: Edward Whitaker (racingpost.com/photos)

By Rodney Masters

LAMBOURN LEGEND AND HEAD OF A MAJOR RACING DYNASTY

Barry Hills died at the age of 88 on June 28. The story of his remarkable training career was captured in these Racing Post extracts

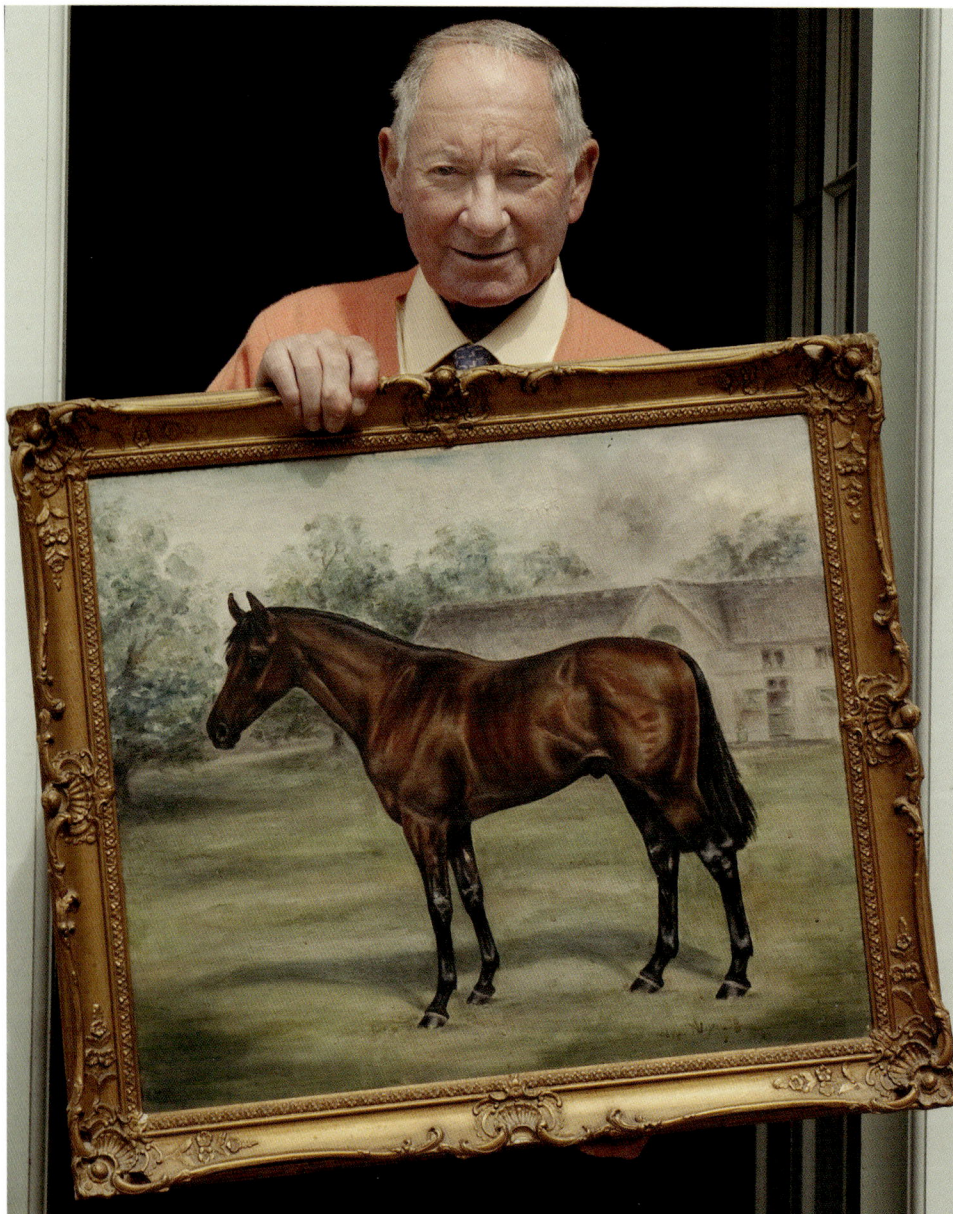

▲In the frame: Barry Hills with a painting of Frankincense, the gambled-on Lincoln winner who made him the money to start his training career

HE WAS christened Barrington W Hills because his mother considered the name would look perfect on a brass plaque outside a solicitor's office. A career in law was spurned by the teenager, but Mrs Hills was to take immense pride in the twin achievements of her boy. After a brief period as a featherweight apprentice with trainer George Colling, which yielded eight winners, Hills became a consistently successful trainer. He also founded a dynasty. The Hills family are to British Flat racing what the Rockefellers were to US industry.

The story of how Hills set himself up as a trainer is like no other. In 1968 he was in his tenth year as head groom to Newmarket trainer John Oxley. Hills took a shine to a tough miler named Frankincense, whom he considered well handicapped.

Having quickly grown a considerable punting kitty from the previous season, with bets that included Sky Diver at 50-1 in the Stewards' Cup, he went for a life-changing touch on Frankincense in the Lincoln. Ridden by Greville Starkey and carrying 9st 5lb, Frankincense was sent off at 100-8 and came home half a length in front, beating 30 other runners.

He already had a plan scripted on how best to spend his Frankincense pot. He invested £15,000 to buy South Bank Stables in Lambourn, the now demolished yard – replaced by executive houses – from where Lester Piggott's father, Keith, had trained the 1963 Grand National winner Ayala.

From South Bank he teed off a career that was to collect almost every major Flat prize in Europe, including the Prix de l'Arc de Triomphe with Rheingold in 1973. The one

▶Continues page 162

BARRY HILLS
1937-2025

missing piece of the jigsaw was the Derby, in which he provided the runner-up on no fewer than four occasions with Rheingold, Hawaiian Sound, Glacial Storm and Blue Stag. All four came so agonisingly close that their combined losing distances were less than the length of the trainer's horsebox.

In 1978, Hills was convinced that the front-running Hawaiian Sound, a first Derby ride for US legend Bill Shoemaker, had held the challenge of Shirley Heights. Owner Robert Sangster, who had watched the race from just beyond the winning post, went over to Hills and said: "Bad luck, Barry. We just got beat." Hills thought otherwise: "Don't be silly, we've won."

Some 20 years later when telling the story, Sangster said that when the result was announced the colour drained from the trainer's face and there was a look of utter dejection.

Hills had been training for 17 years at South Bank when Sangster, one of his closest friends, asked if he would take over from Michael Dickinson at the Manton estate on the fringe of Marlborough in Wiltshire. With the team having expanded on the back of his success, it was a timely challenge he grabbed with relish.

Hills adored Manton. Among the improvements he supervised was the restoration of the Manton House stable block and construction of an indoor equine pool.

The relocation was an outstanding success, with 400 winners including Sir Harry Lewis, who won the 1987 Irish Derby, and Handsome Sailor, who took the following year's Prix de l'Abbaye.

In 1990 Sangster's company, Swettenham Stud Ltd, had a notion, which turned out little more than a whim, to sell the 2,300-acre estate for £15 million. Hills attempted to put together a package to remain in situ, inviting several other trainers, including Nicky Henderson and

Richard Hannon, to join him and share the acclaimed facilities.

His project came to nothing and Hills was £3m short of the required funding. He returned to South Bank, but his agile mind was already thinking about the next step; while South Bank had served him admirably down the years, he had outgrown the stables.

At the time, he was the only trainer in Lambourn with more than 100 horses. In addition, he was concerned about the distance from the stables to his private gallops, along an increasingly busy road. His answer was to invest several million pounds to build Faringdon Place, a superb training base just below his private gallop. Two American barns soon grew to three, plus another rank of stabling. He also pumped considerable funding into a variety of all-weather gallops. He said he had made a big investment and the place had to work; and it did.

Planning permission from West Berkshire Council for the Faringdon Place project had been far from certain, but Hills, noted for his lack of tolerance for long-winded nonsense from officialdom, made it clear he

▶Continues page 164

'We knew he'd win a long time before the race'

Barry Hills on the famous Frankincense gamble that paved the way to his training career

On March 27, 1968, Barry Hills trained his eyes down the straight mile at Doncaster to monitor Frankincense's progress in the Lincoln Handicap. Less than two minutes later he was a man of means, *writes Julian Muscat.*

Under Greville Starkey, Frankincense carried more weight to victory than any previous winner of the Lincoln, which was then one of the most hotly contested handicaps in the calendar. And as Hills lowered his binoculars he knew he had the resources to bring a long-cherished dream to life. He would never look back.

"We'd planned it from November the previous year," said Hills, who was then travelling head lad to the Newmarket trainer John Oxley. "We'd backed the horse from 66-1 all the way down to 5-1 favourite, although he drifted [to 100-8] on the day. We knew Frankincense was going to win a long time before the race. He was the right type of horse for it and his work in the build-up gave us plenty of confidence."

Hills and his cohorts had executed a proper touch. He himself netted more than £60,000 from winning bets, which equates to almost £1 million in today's values. At the time he earned less than £1,000 per year.

Some days later, after all the winnings had been collected from every point of Britain's compass, Hills turned his thoughts to the future. "I'd always wanted to train and this was my opportunity," he recalled. "The following year I gave Keith Piggott [Lester's father] £16,000 for South Bank Stables [in Lambourn]. I was on my way."

This is an edited version of an article that appeared in the Racing Post on August 5, 2020

'He ignited my passion to want to be the best I could be'

Multiple Classic-winning jockey Steve Cauthen credited Barry Hills for reigniting his riding career as he led the tributes to the Lambourn legend, *writes Lewis Porteous.*

Cauthen's career in the US had hit a low when prominent owner-breeder Robert Sangster offered him the chance to move to Britain to ride for him and Hills in 1979 and it did not take the 'Kentucky Kid' long to strike up a formidable partnership with Hills.

They enjoyed immediate success together with Earl of Sefton Stakes winner Hawaiian Sound and Gordon Richards Stakes scorer Sexton Blake before Tap On Wood won the 1979 2,000 Guineas.

As well as a winning relationship on the track, Cauthen built a watertight friendship off it with Hills, who was renowned for his combustible nature but quickly warmed to his new stable jockey.

Cauthen recalled: "When I landed at the airport I said to Barry, 'Do you want me to put my case in the trunk?' He replied, 'It's not a f***ing trunk here, it's a boot!' I thought, 'What the hell have I got myself into?' but it didn't take long for us to understand each other.

"We had great trust in each other and he really was an unbelievable trainer. He was great at placing horses and knew exactly where they belonged."

He added: "Barry taught me how to be a man and really ignited my passion to want to be the best I could be. It's easy to lose track of that, but Barry wanted to be a winner. He worked his way up and wasn't going back. He did everything he wanted to do and he did it with great people."

Before departing for the vacant position as number-one rider to Henry Cecil, Cauthen partnered Gildoran to Gold Cup success for Hills in 1984. That was arguably the win that meant most to him.

"One of the happiest moments I've ever had was walking into the winner's enclosure at Ascot on Gildoran," Cauthen said. "That was right after I'd announced I was going to Henry's and to win that for Barry and Robert was a great moment.

"There was never a tougher time for me than when I left to go to Henry's because I loved Barry and Penny. They were like family and still are. It was like leaving a mentor and a dad, but his voice will always be in my head."

would retire if the scheme was rejected. That threat certainly concentrated the minds of any dithering councillor because a departing BW Hills would have seen unemployment figures soar in the Lambourn valley.

Faringdon Place was more relaxed for the horses, and also for their trainer. He was nicknamed Mr Grumpy for good reason, and at times, particularly before breakfast, he could be as tough as last week's Hovis. He seemed more amenable after settling into a new home within a furlong of the stables.

He once said: "People say I don't get so worked up these days, and perhaps that's true, but I can still get very stroppy at times. I can accept major things going wrong, and that mistakes do happen, but it is the needless mistakes that make me angry."

Pride in appearance was a key factor with Hills, not only with his horses. He was invariably immaculately dressed and few people ever saw him without a tie.

John, the eldest of his five sons, and who trained in Lambourn until his untimely death from cancer in 2014, had said there was something of the streetfighter in his father's character.

"I've been lucky," said John. "Being the son of Barry Hills is obviously an enormous help. He had to go through a lot more than I did to get his training operation up and running. He did it all from scratch. He's a streetfighter. He doesn't suffer fools."

Hills instilled rich qualities in his sons. Between them John, as a trainer, and twins Michael and Richard in the saddle, won thousands of races at home and overseas, but the true and lasting significance of their achievements cut deeper than success on a racecourse. They earned respect throughout the sport for the professional, no-nonsense way they went about getting the job done.

The same can be said of his

▸Continues page 166

Five of the Lambourn legend's brightest stars

Rheingold Barry Hills's first star was his brightest and gave him the biggest win of his career in the 1973 Prix de l'Arc de Triomphe, just four years after he had taken out a licence.

Rheingold, owned by the war hero, nightclub owner and violin virtuoso Henry Zeisel, would have run out a clear winner of the Derby under Ernie Johnson had it not been for Lester Piggott summoning up one of the rides of his life to lift Roberto past him in the last four strides and win by a short head. Rheingold was in the right place at the wrong time; Hills never did win a Derby, with Hawaiian Sound, Glacial Storm and Blue Stag all only second best.

Rheingold – who won the Grand Prix de Saint-Cloud twice, a Prix Ganay and a Hardwicke Stakes and was runner-up in the 1973 King George to the great filly Dahlia – had Piggott on his side not against him in the Arc at a rainy Longchamp, and the result made up for the one that got away at Epsom.

Piggott kept Rheingold close to the pace in a huge field and drove him into the lead as the field turned for home, getting first run on Allez France. She showed grit and determination to close the gap but Rheingold had gone beyond recall and landed the spoils by two and a half lengths.

Nomadic Way Equally at home in staying events on the Flat or in the best company over hurdles, Robert Sangster's son of Prix du Jockey Club and Irish Derby winner Assert provided Hills with a notable success at the Cheltenham Festival in the 1992 Stayers' Hurdle.

Unraced as a two-year-old, Nomadic Way rounded off his three-year-old campaign with a gutsy victory in the Cesarewitch off a featherweight under Willie Carson, but age and maturity and eight flights of hurdles later brought out the best in him.

In February 1990 he beat Elementary by six lengths in the Irish Champion Hurdle and found only Kribensis too good in the big one at Cheltenham a month later. The following year it was Morley Street who proved his master in the Champion Hurdle and again took his measure in the Aintree Hurdle.

A step up in trip proved key to his finest hour. In his first race beyond three miles he kept on strongly in the Stayers' Hurdle to beat a classy field by three and a half lengths, reward for his previous near-misses over two miles.

Further Flight Simon Wingfield Digby's ghost-grey stayer carved an enduring niche in racing history by winning five consecutive runnings of the Group 3 Jockey Club Cup, becoming the only horse ever to win the same Group race five times.

There were better horses and faster horses around but Further Flight built a fervent following and his appearances at Newmarket in the autumn were hugely anticipated and deeply enjoyed.

His talent first flowered on a major stage with victory in the 1990 Ebor. A year later he made the transition to Group races, winning the first of nine Group 3s when landing the first of his two Goodwood Cups.

Two months later he began the five-year odyssey that would set him apart when he won the 1991 Jockey Club Cup. He completed the five-timer at the age of nine, drawing clear up the hill to beat Assessor by two and a half lengths before receiving a hero's reception in the winner's enclosure.

Cormorant Wood In the early part of her racing career, Cormorant Wood looked like being a nice filly to add to the list of nice fillies Hills had handled, but nothing to compare with Dibidale, winner of the Irish and Yorkshire Oaks in 1974, who might have won the Epsom version had her saddle not slipped.

Cormorant Wood, owned by the trainer's old pal Bobby McAlpine, was sixth in her Oaks bid in 1983 but that autumn was rerouted on the path to excellence over two furlongs shorter.

The first big moment came at Newmarket in the Champion Stakes, featuring a range of Group 1 talent, from the top miler Wassl to Arlington Million hero Tolomeo and Coronation Cup winner Be My Native. Although the field had to contend with a blustery wind, it was as nothing compared to the whoosh as Cormorant Wood surged from the back to score with authority.

Dropped to a mile as a four-year-old, she dead-heated with Wassl in the Lockinge. In her last appearance she returned to ten furlongs to slam Tolomeo, Chief Singer and Sadler's Wells in the Benson & Hedges Gold Cup (later Juddmonte International) at York.

Haafhd Hills was just seven years from retirement when he trained one of his best, Haafhd. Owned by Sheikh Hamdan Al Maktoum, the son of Alhaarth worked in scintillating fashion before his reappearance as a three-year-old in the 2004 Craven Stakes and his five-length win came as no surprise to Hills, who was adamant he was the best miler he had trained and a valid 11-2 shot for the 2,000 Guineas.

His faith was duly borne out on the Rowley Mile, as the trainer's instructions to "take the race to them" were followed to the letter by his son in the saddle. Richard Hills went into the Guineas full of confidence and was rewarded with a bold performance that yielded a definitive victory over Snow Ridge, Azamour and Grey Swallow.

Defeats followed in the St James's Palace and Sussex Stakes, but there was a return to form when Haafhd lined up as a 12-1 shot for the Champion Stakes at Newmarket in October. He was always travelling best behind the leaders and pulled two and a half lengths clear.

Haafhd was then retired to stud, leaving Hills with the memory of a crack colt who lived up to his expectations.

Compiled by Peter Thomas and Steve Dennis

fourth son, Charlie, who took over the running of the stable from his father in August 2011. Charlie trained his first Classic winner less than two years later in May 2013, with Just The Judge in the Irish 1,000 Guineas, and achieved a Breeders' Cup success with Chriselliam the same year. He has also sent out four-time Group 1-winning sprinters Muhaarar and Battaash, back-to-back Queen Elizabeth II Jubilee Stakes winner Khaadem and Irish 2,000 Guineas hero Phoenix Of Spain.

George, the youngest son, is a bloodstock insurer and the dynasty has embraced another generation as grandson Patrick, son of Richard, accumulated more than 80 winners as a jockey between 2006 and 2013.

The three eldest sons were from the trainer's first marriage to Maureen, the two youngest from his marriage to Penny, who, although publicity-shy and insistent on remaining in the background, was such a level-headed, steadying influence that she was possibly the key person in the set-up. The staff always adored her.

No wife could have shown greater support when Hills was diagnosed with throat cancer. Few outside the immediate family were aware he was undergoing treatment. He had struggled with troublesome vocal cords for 20 years, and had surgery at various times for the removal of benign nodules.

It was shortly before Christmas 2005, while he was at a festive lunch in London with his sons, that he received the news in a telephone call from his doctor that a biopsy had revealed cancer.

Like every other challenge in his life, he tackled this one with a determined spirit. After supervising the first two lots at Faringdon Place he would travel to London, with Penny always at his side, on 36 consecutive working days, Monday to Friday, to receive the treatment in Harley Street.

After each session, he set himself the mission to research which London restaurant served the best lunch, with his award going to the Dorchester Grill. The challenge focused his thoughts away from the next session of treatment.

The cancer returned in 2008, necessitating the removal of his voice box. He soon got to grips with a digital replacement.

"You can't keep a good one down, can you?" son John had sportingly said when his father's Moonax had narrowly denied his Broadway Flyer Classic glory in the 1994 St Leger, and so it proved as Hills snr came out of retirement in 2013.

First of all it was to assist John

Glittering success across the decades

Full name Barrington William Hills

Born Worcester, April 2, 1937

Father Bill Hills (head lad to Tom Rimell & George Colling; pony trainer)

Family Married (1) 1959 Maureen Newson; sons John, Michael & Richard; (2) 1977 Penny Woodhouse; sons Charlie & George

Apprenticed to Fred Rimell, Kinnersley, Worcestershire 1952-53; George Colling, Newmarket 1953-56

First mount Golden Chance (trainer Fred Rimell) 10th at Birmingham, June 3, 1952

First winner as jockey Sudden Light (trainer George Colling) Newmarket, July 14, 1954

Total wins as jockey 8 (1954-57) including 3 on Peter Pan, 1955

Travelling head lad to John Oxley, Newmarket 1959-68

Stables as trainer South Bank, Lambourn 1969-86, 1991-94; Manton 1987-90: Faringdon Place & Wetherdown House, Lambourn 1994-2011; Kingwood House, Lambourn 2014-15

First winner as trainer La Dolce Vita (ridden by Ernie Johnson) Thirsk, April 18, 1969

First big-race winners Hickleton (1970 Great Metropolitan Handicap), Golden Monad (1970 Dee Stakes)

First Group 1 winner Our Mirage (1971 Prix de la Salamandre)

First winner over jumps Love From Verona (ridden by Mr Nicky Henderson) Fontwell, February 27, 1978

Overall European champion Rheingold (joint top-rated at 137 in Racehorses of 1973; champion older horse, champion middle-distance horse)

Prix de l'Arc de Triomphe winner Rheingold (1973)

British Classic winners Enstone Spark (1978 1,000 Guineas), Tap On Wood (1979 2,000 Guineas), Moonax (1994 St Leger), Haafhd (2004 2,000 Guineas), Ghanaati (2009 1,000 Guineas)

Other Classic winners Dibidale (1974 Irish Oaks), Sir Harry Lewis (1987 Irish Derby), Nicer (1993 Irish 1,000 Guineas), Zimzalabim (1993 Osterreichisches Derby, Slovenske Derby), Bolas (1994 Irish Oaks), Moonax (1994 Prix Royal-Oak), Hula Angel (1999 Irish 1,000 Guineas)

Cheltenham Festival winner Nomadic Way (1992 Stayers' Hurdle)

Ascot Gold Cup winner Gildoran (1984, 1985)

Champion two-year-old fillies Durtal (1976 Cheveley Park Stakes), Desirable (1983 Cheveley Park Stakes), Negligent (1989 Rockfel Stakes)

Grade 1 winner in North America Redwood (2010 Northern Dancer Turf Stakes)

Most prolific Group 1 winner Rheingold (4)

Most prolific Pattern winner Further Flight (9, including 5 Jockey Club Cups 1991-95)

Most prolific winners in a season Nagwa (13 in 1975), Duboff (9 in 1975)

Last winner Wardat Dubai, Wolverhampton, October 3, 2015

Runner-up in trainers' championship 1990 (to Henry Cecil)

Group/Grade 1 wins 46 (GB 31, France 9, Ireland 5, Canada 1)

Total Pattern wins 224 (GB 184, Ireland 19, France 15, Germany 3, Italy 1, Canada 1, Qatar 1)

Most wins in a British season 113 in 1990

Total wins in Britain 3,181 (3,171 Flat, 10 jumps)

Main awards HWPA Derby Award for Outstanding Achievement (2009), Cartier Award of Merit (2011)

Compiled by John Randall

◀Memorable moments: from top, Rheingold wins the 1973 Arc; Nomadic Way powers home in the 1992 Stayers' Hurdle; dual Gold Cup winner Gildoran at Ascot in 1984

with the Hamdan Al Maktoum-owned horses in his care, but on his son's death he took out a training licence once more, saddling 17 winners in each of two seasons, including Fadhayyil, who almost gave Hills another Royal Ascot success in 2015, only to be beaten in the Jersey Stakes by Dutch Connection, trained by son Charlie.

This is an edited version of an article that appeared in the Racing Post on June 29

BRASS TACKS

Brass Tacks is a familiar sight to many in the Equestrian world. This long established and reputable company stands for quality in English leather headcollars and brass nameplates.

We take great pride in our customer care.

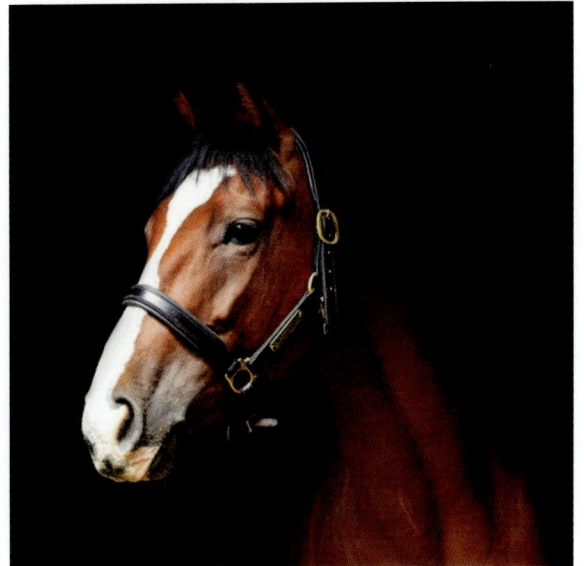

Our Classic padded English leather headcollars combine traditional craftsmanship with modern comfort, featuring complimentary engraved brass nameplates that make each piece uniquely yours. Whether you're preparing for travelling or daily stable use, our leather headcollars deliver the quality and durability that discerning horse owners demand.

www.brasstacksonline.com

The turf Flat season in Britain bursts into life as starter Stuart Turner sends the 17 runners on their way in the Brocklesby Stakes at Doncaster on March 29. Victory goes to 3-1 favourite Norman's Cay (purple, centre)

EDWARD WHITAKER (RACINGPOST.COM/PHOTOS)

IN THE
PICTURE

'It's magic' – special success as Thurles continues to race

THURLES staged an important fixture on October 9 – the first meeting since the bombshell news in August that Ireland's only privately owned racecourse would close with immediate effect.

The announcement from the Molony family caused shock and dismay in racing but a few weeks later a temporary reprieve was agreed between Horse Racing Ireland and the track's owners, which enabled its 11 allocated fixtures to go ahead between October and March.

The County Tipperary track has long been a cornerstone of the jumps scene in Ireland because of its capacity to race through the winter and provide regular schooling. The first recorded race meeting took place there in 1732 and it has been owned by the Molony family since the early 1900s.

Revealing the closure on August 1, Riona Molony cited a challenging financial landscape and increasing industry demands as key factors in the decision.

She said: "It has been an honour and a privilege for our family to have run Thurles racecourse, and I am officially announcing our retirement today. Since my beloved husband Pierce passed away in 2015, with the help of our four daughters Patricia, Helen, Ann Marie and Kate and our wonderful staff, we've managed to keep the show on the road and I know he would be very proud of us for that."

If the closure had gone ahead, Thurles would have been the first racecourse in Ireland to shut since Tralee in 2008. In late August, however, a temporary solution was found, with operational responsibility of the racecourse passing to Horse Racing Ireland.

"Keeping Thurles operational until March of next year affords all interested parties time to consider a longer-term plan for the racecourse," said a joint statement on behalf of HRI and Thurles Race Company.

Among the winners at the October 9 meeting – the track's sole Flat fixture – was local trainer Mark Molloy, who is pictured giving Riona Molony a kiss as she presents the trophy for the Welcome Back To Thurles Handicap. Also in the picture are Molloy's daughter Alex and rider Killian Leonard, who rode 11-4 shot Tickling to victory.

Expressing his joy at the reopening, Molloy said: "It's magic. It means a lot to me as I'm great friends with the Molonys. I felt the family had done an amazing job with the racecourse over the past ten years since Pierce passed away and I felt last winter was very hard for them for so many reasons. This track is hugely important at all levels and I think now there is a realisation of that."

Picture: Caroline Norris (racingpost.com/photos)

GIANT OF THE TURF
WHO CONQUERED FLAT AND JUMPS

By Andrew Dietz
and David Carr

PETER EASTERBY, the hugely successful trainer who founded a Yorkshire dynasty, was hailed "a genius" following his death in the early hours of June 9 at the age of 95.

Easterby, a figurehead of one of racing's most famous families, left an enduring legacy in the sport following his 46 years with a licence. He became Britain's finest dual-purpose trainer by being the first to train 1,000 winners under both codes, including masterminding a then record five Champion Hurdle victories as well as two Cheltenham Gold Cup triumphs.

Easterby was responsible for Sea Pigeon and Night Nurse, two of the sport's biggest stars in the late 1970s and early 1980s and who are both buried in the grounds at Habton Grange, the yard near Malton in North Yorkshire where his son Tim now holds the licence, assisted by grandson William.

Born Miles Henry Easterby – known to everyone as Peter – at Knayton, near Thirsk, in 1929, he assisted his uncle Walter and Frank Hartigan before starting training in 1950, 11 years before his younger brother Mick, who still holds a licence with his own son David.

It might have taken him three years to win a race, but Easterby went on to make his mark on the biggest stage, scoring twice at Royal Ascot with Goldhill in the 1960s and landing a first Champion Hurdle with 720gns purchase Saucy Kit in 1967. Night Nurse and Sea Pigeon won two

Champion Hurdles apiece, while Alverton (1979) and Little Owl (1981) took the Cheltenham Gold Cup.

Easterby was champion jumps trainer for three seasons running, from 1978-79 to 1980-81.

On the Flat, he won a string of big handicaps, including two Lincolns and three Ayr Gold Cups. The remarkably versatile Sea Pigeon collected an Ebor, two Chester Cups and three Vaux Gold Tankards.

Jonjo O'Neill, the leading jockey-turned-trainer, rode Sea Pigeon to victory in his first Champion Hurdle as well as successfully switching codes to win the Ebor with a remarkable weight-carrying performance under 10st. Among many other big winners for Easterby, he was aboard Alverton in the Gold Cup.

Leading the tributes from the racing community, O'Neill said: "He was a genius and I couldn't speak highly enough of him. He was a top man and a great person to ride for. He could train a five-furlong sprinter to a staying chaser – it didn't make any difference. Flat or jumps, he could train them all and was a great all-rounder. He was a relaxed and placid man to work for, which would only give you confidence. He was a great man and a good friend who will be sadly missed."

John Francome, another riding legend who was a seven-time champion jockey, partnered Sea Pigeon to his second Champion Hurdle victory in 1981.

He said: "Peter was a charming man, absolutely lovely. He couldn't have been

▶*Continues page 174*

PETER EASTERBY
1929-2025

easier to ride for. It was an amazing feat to train 1,000 winners, Flat and jumping.

"My favourite story about him was when Jim McGrath sent a friend to buy a horse and he said the horse was £20,000. Jim's friend said he wanted to spend a bit more than that and straight away he said 'that's for a half-share'. That was Peter in a nutshell, he was as sharp as a tack and like that almost right up to the last minute."

Easterby also landed high-quality Flat races with Goldhill (King's Stand Stakes) and Sonnen Gold (Gimcrack) and finished ninth in the Flat trainers' championship in 1979, his best season.

He had sent out a total of 2,513 winners by the time he retired in 1996, scoring with his final runner Balhernoch in a novice hurdle at Sedgefield.

Lifelong friend Jack Berry, the former jockey, trainer and leading fundraiser, has fond memories of a man who left a lasting impression on the sport.

"He was a great old boy. Look at the horses he trained – they were fabulous," he said. "He made the horses and it was before all the big money came on the scene. He was a brilliant trainer. I knew Peter really well and, although he did a lot of bargaining and things like that, you wouldn't get a better man. The Easterbys are a really sporting family and a credit to their profession. He had a good life and helped a lot of people along the way."

Easterby's wife Marjorie, who died in 2012, played a huge supporting role behind the scenes and they had three children, Carolyn, Tim and Leila, with many other members of the family involved in racing.

This is an edited version of an article that appeared in the Racing Post on June 10

Four of the legendary trainer's greatest triumphs

Night Nurse heroically defends Champion Hurdle crown A big brute of a horse, Night Nurse beat his rivals into submission from the front through his relentless galloping, compiling an eight-race winning streak en route to his first Champion Hurdle in 1976.

A year later, though, his crown had slipped following defeats in the Fighting Fifth and Christmas Hurdle and he went into his title defence without a run since Kempton. This was a golden era of hurdling and against the likes of 6-4 favourite Birds Nest, the mighty Monksfield and stablemate Sea Pigeon, and on unsuitably heavy ground, Night Nurse was sent off at 15-2. His trainer had not lost faith and later declared he'd had his biggest-ever bet on his star hurdler. "I backed him three times and then had a bit more on," he said.

Night Nurse was in front at the last, albeit narrowly, and went away from Monksfield to win an epic race – thought by many to be the best-ever Champion Hurdle – by two lengths.

The following month Night Nurse and Monksfield – in receipt of 6lb from his Cheltenham conqueror – met again in the Templegate Hurdle at Aintree and the sequel provided even greater drama, with the pair dead-heating in what has been described as the greatest hurdle race of all time.

Alverton emerges from snowstorm to light up Cheltenham If there was a horse who showed Easterby as a worker of miracles, it was Alverton. Despite having fragile forelegs after breaking down badly as a four-year-old, he became a prolific winner on the Flat and finished runner-up in the Ebor. However, it was over jumps that Alverton really made his name, winning the 1978 Arkle and the Gold Cup the following year.

In the 1979 festival showpiece, Alverton had ground to make up on tearaway leader Tied Cottage as the pair emerged from the engulfing snowstorm turning for home. Inch by inch, Jonjo O'Neill reduced the lead and Tied Cottage was only just in front at the last. The duel came to an abrupt end, however, when Tied Cottage crumpled on landing to allow Alverton to come home alone.

Alverton tragically died in the Grand National 16 days later, but he will be forever remembered for the heights he scaled from such a precarious beginning.

"To win a Gold Cup with a horse from the Flat was a very special piece of training," O'Neill said. "Peter nursed him back from his leg problems, starting on the Flat, then over hurdles and fences. That was Peter really – he got the best out of every horse."

Sea Pigeon's great weight-carrying Ebor success The Ebor has come a long way since 1979 but Sea Pigeon's performance in victory all those years ago is still one in a million.

Sea Pigeon's place in history was already assured thanks to back-to-back Chester Cup victories (1977-78), the latter under 9st 7lb.

Set the seemingly impossible task of carrying 10st in York's historic handicap, the local hero created pandemonium on the Knavesmire when he was announced the short-head winner from Donegal Prince, to whom he conceded 40lb including his rider's allowance, after an agonising wait for the judge's verdict.

Nobody was more relieved than jockey Jonjo O'Neill after he eased up prematurely on Sea Pigeon. "I was confident he'd won but Peter and his head lad Graham Lockerbie thought I'd got him beat," O'Neill said. "When I saw the photo-finish I couldn't believe how close it was."

Through his two Champion Hurdle wins – the second achieved at the age of 11 – Sea Pigeon went on to lay claim to being the greatest dual-purpose horse of all time.

Little Owl leads home stable one-two in Gold Cup Most of Easterby's best horses were bought for a modest sum and Little Owl was no different, having cost a little over 2,000gns at Doncaster sales.

He took to fences like a duck to water and headed for the 1981 Gold Cup undefeated in seven completed chases, with the only blot on his copybook a fall in the previous year's Sun Alliance Chase.

Although the Gold Cup had gone through a spell in the doldrums, it was a strong running with two-time King George winner Silver Buck and famed stablemate Night Nurse among the opposition.

Little Owl, ridden by amateur rider and owner Jim Wilson, was only seven but on just his ninth start over fences he led home the staying-on Night Nurse by a length and a half.

Easterby said he did not feel pressure as a trainer but he admitted to having "a bit of a shake" as his pair came to the last fence.

He needn't have worried as it turned out to be another champagne moment for arguably the finest dual-purpose trainer in British racing history.

This is an edited version of an article by Andrew Dietz that appeared in the Racing Post on August 5, 2019 – Easterby's 90th birthday

▶Fab four: from left, Night Nurse, Alverton, Sea Pigeon and Little Owl

'His achievements were unparalleled'

By Andrew Dietz

LEADING racing figures from around Britain descended in their hundreds on the quiet North Yorkshire market town of Helmsley for a service of thanksgiving at All Saints Church in memory of Peter Easterby.

In a family tribute, Tim Easterby spoke of his father's many interests, including hunting, shooting, nights out and dancing, but racing was always his main passion.

"Dad was a man of few words, but the words he said usually meant a lot to people," he said. "He wouldn't say much, unless he was trying to sell a horse, of course – something he was a master at.

"I was very fortunate that we spent so many hours watching horses on the gallops. Dad was forthcoming and quick-witted about all the horses and how they were going. Often we had to send videos to owners, especially over Covid, without sound because he would say things like, 'That grey horse is useless'. We'll miss the quips that definitely can't be repeated in church."

Recalling his father's many Cheltenham triumphs, Easterby said: "Our parents had a great time down at Cheltenham; on one particular occasion after a Champion Hurdle victory, my uncle Philip complained the next morning that his fingers were sore from opening bottles of champagne."

A strong contingent from the north included Jack Berry, Kevin Darley, Richard Fahey and Michael Dods, while Jonjo O'Neill, who rode Sea Pigeon to victory in the Champion Hurdle and Ebor, and David Elsworth, another training great, were among those who came from further afield to pay their respects.

"Our operations were far apart with me in the south and him in the north, but we always shared some mutual respect – usually he beat me," Elsworth said. "In the early days I had Sea Pigeon quarantined with me when he first came over from America.

"Peter and I always passed the time of day and I was a great admirer of his – he was always great value and a great character. He has the respect of everybody as his achievements were unparalleled."

Jockey-turned-trainer Alan Brown, who rode two Arkle winners for Easterby, was among the many past and present riders at the service.

"He was a brilliant trainer and a fantastic man who would always give someone a chance if you worked hard enough," he said. "He was life-changing for me because I got the job there and went from stable lad to jockey. He was a great man to ride for and knew his horses inside out. I couldn't speak highly enough of him."

Russ Garritty, who rode for Easterby over jumps in the mid-1990s, said: "He was a great man and a legend. He gave anybody a chance to achieve something. He was very fair and straight down the middle with no airs and graces.

"With his record of training more than 1,000 winners under both codes, there's nobody better than him, no matter what people say. In my eyes, he was the best."

This is an edited version of an article that appeared in the Racing Post on June 28

Great success from Cheltenham to Chester

Full name Miles Henry Easterby

Born Knayton, near Thirsk, North Yorkshire, August 5, 1929

Family Father: William Easterby (farmer & amateur rider). Uncle: Walter Easterby (trainer). Brother: Mick Easterby. Wife: Marjorie. Children: Carolyn, Tim, Leila

Stables Habton Grange, Great Habton, near Malton, North Yorkshire 1950-96

First winner Double Rose, Market Rasen, March 7, 1953

First Flat winner King's Coup, Thirsk, April 15, 1955

First big-race winner King's Coup (1957, 1958 & 1959 Thirsk Hunt Cup, 1959 Rose of York Handicap)

Champion Hurdle winners Saucy Kit (1967), Night Nurse (1976, 1977), Sea Pigeon (1980, 1981)

Cheltenham Gold Cup winners Alverton (1979), Little Owl (1981)

Lloyds Bank (Stayers') Hurdle winner Town Ship (1977)

Other Cheltenham Festival winners Alverton (1978 Arkle Chase), King Weasel (1980 Cathcart Chase), Clayside (1981 Arkle Chase), Ryeman (1983 Arkle Chase), Jobroke (1986 County Hurdle)

Night Nurse's other big-race wins 1975 Fighting Fifth Hurdle, Sweeps Hurdle, 1976 Scottish Champion Hurdle, Welsh Champion Hurdle, 1977 Templegate (Aintree) Hurdle (dead-heat), Welsh Champion Hurdle, 1979 Sean Graham Trophy (Mildmay Novices') Chase, Buchanan Whisky Gold Cup Chase

Sea Pigeon's other big-race wins 1977 Scottish Champion Hurdle, Chester Cup, Vaux Gold Tankard, 1978 Scottish Champion Hurdle, Chester Cup, Vaux Breweries' Gold Tankard, Fighting Fifth Hurdle, 1979 Ebor Handicap, 1980 Welsh Champion Hurdle, Vaux Breweries' Gold Tankard, Fighting Fifth Hurdle

Tingle Creek Chase winner Easby Abbey (1975)

Other big-race wins over jumps Prominent King (1979 Ascot Long-Distance Hurdle), Father Delaney (1980 Tote Pattern Chase), Pay Related (1982 H&T Walker Goddess Chase), Sula Bula (1984 Oteley Hurdle), Cybrandian (1984 H&T Walker Goddess Chase), Nohalmdun (1986 Christmas Hurdle, 1990 Aintree Chase), Young Benz (1989 Top Novices' Hurdle, 1991 Perrier Jouet (Maghull) Novices' Chase)

Other big-race wins on Flat Goldhill (1963 Windsor Castle Stakes), Able Albert (1983 City of York Stakes), Jamarj (1988 Sceptre Stakes), Norton Challenger (1991 City of York Stakes, 1992 John of Gaunt Stakes)

Last winner & runner Balhernoch, Sedgefield, January 24, 1996

Champion jumps trainer 3 times: 1978-79, 1979-80, 1980-81

Total wins 2,513 (Flat 1,511, jumps 1,002 including 1 in Ireland)

Compiled by John Randall

▼ The order of service for the funeral of Peter Easterby at All Saints Church in Helmsley on June 27

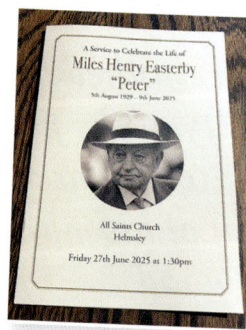

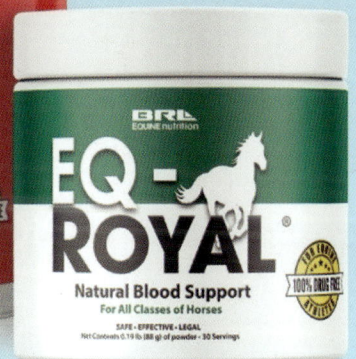

THE
BIGGER
PICTURE

A glorious summer scene at the Newmarket
July meeting as Zavateri and Charlie Bishop
arrive in the winner's enclosure, accompanied
by trainer Eve Johnson Houghton (blue dress),
after the Group 2 July Stakes
EDWARD WHITAKER (RACINGPOST.COM/PHOTOS)

Bardwell back from heart attack to land Leger Legends win

GARY BARDWELL caused something of a surprise when he won the Leger Legends charity race at Doncaster in September on 40-1 shot Shazani. Yet the 57-year-old was lucky to be there at all, let alone land the much-loved race for a second time.

As Bardwell related after his two-length victory, he had returned from a brush with death to get back in the saddle. "A year and a half ago I had a heart attack riding out," he said. "I got laid off by Godolphin and I was riding out for a friend of mine and I had a heart attack on a horse.

"I was very lucky. The ambulance came, they put an ECG on me and said, 'We've got to get you to Papworth Hospital straight away.' I had a stent put in and ever since then I've been fitter than anything."

The dual champion apprentice now rides out for John and Thady Gosden – "they're great people and I really enjoy it," he said – and that put him in shape to partner the Roy Bowring-trained Shazani in the mile race restricted to former professional jockeys.

Bardwell was back in the line-up after missing the 2024 race, having until then taken part in every edition since it started in 2010. After many years of trying he finally won in 2021 on Godolphin's Natural Colour, describing that success as "up with the best of all my big winners".

Shazani was stepping up to a mile for the first time and Bardwell said: "I rang the trainer and he said, 'Do what you want, he won't get a mile in a horsebox because he's only been running over six furlongs'.

"So I didn't disappoint him. I was waiting for them all to come past me. I gave him a little squeeze at the three pole and he picked up and galloped all the way to the line. It's amazing."

Bardwell, who won the Chester Cup on Bangalore in 2000, has always been one of the veterans in the race, having retired from the professional ranks in 2003. This time he was followed home in second by Franny Norton, who is two years his junior and had been retired only 12 months. In fifth was Adam Kirby, who won the Derby on Adayar in 2021 but had called time on his career in April at the age of 36 after years of battling with his weight.

In all, 14 ex-professionals took part on a day that raises funds for the National Horseracing College and the Injured Jockeys Fund's Jack Berry House.

Reporting: David Carr and Nick Pulford
Picture: John Grossick (racingpost.com/photos)

Trawlerman landed the
Gold Cup at Royal Ascot
with great authority
to take over as the
dominant force
in the staying
division

PRIZE CATCH

By Lewis Porteous

WHO needs speed when you have a stayer as strong as Trawlerman? After dominating the first two days of Royal Ascot courtesy of the devastating change of pace shown by Field Of Gold in the St James's Palace Stakes and Ombudsman in the Prince of Wales's, John and Thady Gosden turned to an old friend with a very different arsenal to conquer the Gold Cup.

Trawlerman may lack the breathtaking brilliance and stunning acceleration of his two exalted stablemates, but they could never match his bottomless reserves of stamina or his deep well of bravery. Combined, those qualities enable him to maintain a remorseless gallop over marathon distances.

Trawlerman has never been a slouch in the staying division.

He was, after all, the last horse to beat Kyprios, who is widely regarded as the best stayer of recent years. But, at the age of seven, success in the Gold Cup lifted him to an altogether higher plane.

Having felt they had failed to make the race enough of a test of stamina when he was beaten a length by Kyprios in the 2024 Gold Cup, the team behind Trawlerman were hell bent on taking the fight to their rivals from the off on an afternoon when the heat was better suited to relaxing by the pool than pounding your rivals into submission over two and a half miles. The Godolphin homebred was in his element.

There was no Kyprios to contend with but there was Illinois. Ballydoyle's new challenger was bringing middle-distance quality to the staying ranks in his first Gold Cup. It was not enough. Trawlerman was far too

relentless for his main rival and the other six, the majority of whom had never been asked to gallop so strongly for so long.

For a few moments after the stalls opened it looked as if the pace could be a false one, but by the time the field swept by the winning post for the first time, Trawlerman and William Buick were already out in front and moving up the gears, leaving their rivals strung out with the daunting prospect of a full lap of Ascot still to go.

Illinois appeared to be travelling ominously well for Ryan Moore, but closing to within a couple of lengths of Trawlerman early in the home straight was the closest he came. Buick threw on more coal and his partner steamed away.

The gap between the pair started to extend. Initially it was a gradual process but the closer Trawlerman got to the winning post, the quicker Illinois dropped out of the

rear-view mirror. At the line the gap between first and second was seven lengths, with the same distance to Dubai Future in third. It was a rout.

"It was very clear when we ran him last year in the Gold Cup that he went a bit steady," said John Gosden after the race. "William said, 'From four out, I'm going to notch it up, notch it up, notch it up. If they stay, they're going to have to stay every inch'. He's an out-and-out galloper and William judged it perfectly, which isn't easy over two and a half miles."

★★★★

GOSDEN snr had joined Saeed bin Suroor and Sir Henry Cecil as a winner of five Gold Cups, second only to Aidan O'Brien's nine in the post-war period, and spoke effervescently about the staying division and his latest winner, who is willing to mine to the

▸Continues page 184

bottom of his capabilities every time he steps on to a racecourse.

"This week we've had two real class horses with a turn of foot and now one of the most relentless gallopers," he said. "I love the Cup races and always have done. The Gold Cup is more important than anything else and, once you've won it, you want to see if you can win it again."

Detractors will be minded to point out there was no Kyprios by which to judge Trawlerman's tour de force, but there was no arguing with the fact he lowered Rite Of Passage's 2010 track record by the thick end of two seconds. It was enough to achieve a career-high Racing Post Rating (123) and official rating (121). Kyprios did not reach the same level on RPRs in either of his two Gold Cup wins, although he went much higher to 128 in his astonishing 2022 Prix du Cadran.

We might have seen one of the all-time great clashes had Kyprios not succumbed to a career-ending injury a few weeks before Royal Ascot. Instead Trawlerman completely dominated under a masterclass from Buick.

"It's all about rhythm," replied the winning jockey when asked what it was like riding a front-runner over two and a half miles. "You've got to get them into a rhythm. You've got to make sure they're breathing properly at every stage of the race, keeping it all as smooth as possible. It's a rhythm thing and he was so smooth throughout the race. It's in the last half-mile where you separate horses. That's where you find out whether they stay or whether they don't. That's where this guy comes into his own."

★★★★

THE Gold Cup was the second leg of an unbeaten four-race season in Britain for Trawlerman, who made the staying crown his own in the absence of Kyprios.

He set out his stall by making all in the Group 3 Henry II Stakes in May, which proved the perfect dress rehearsal for the big

one and no doubt gave Buick the confidence to go out hard at the royal meeting.

Warming to the task in front, Trawlerman slowly began to turn the screw down the back at Sandown but it wasn't until the home straight that his rivals truly felt the burn of the leader's relentless gallop. There were only four runners, yet 25 lengths separated first and last.

Back from a nine-week break following the Gold Cup, Trawlerman had to shoulder a Group 1 penalty in the Lonsdale Cup at York and, unlike at Sandown and Ascot, never established a lead over his rivals in the opening mile.

Instead he had to wrestle the advantage from Shackleton early in the straight, a move that could have easily left him susceptible to those waiting in his slipstream. The challengers soon came, with Sweet William closing to his left and Al Nayyir bearing down to his right, but Trawlerman, in his trademark hood, was merely waiting to turn them away.

Showing a willing desire to battle, he first resisted Al Nayyir's challenge and then fended off the persistent charge of his stablemate Sweet William to cement his status as the number one stayer in Europe.

"You always feel like you're in control," said Buick. "You can see them in the corner of your eye or

▲ Big fish: previous pages, Trawlerman runs away with the Gold Cup; above, William Buick salutes the Royal Ascot crowd; below, the leading stayer of the year adds the Lonsdale Cup at York and the Long Distance Cup at Ascot to his haul

under your arm, and he always gives you more."

Back at Ascot on Champions Day, Trawlerman still had more to give. Once again Sweet William was his main challenger in the Long Distance Cup and Trawlerman repelled him by a length and a half, virtually the same distance that had separated them at York.

A second Group 1 victory of the season took Trawlerman's career earnings past £1.9 million. "He's a superstar and I'm delighted for him that he's capped his year off in such style," Buick said. "He wears his heart on his sleeve and he's a proper horse. He's a joy to ride."

The race between the two stablemates was a joy to watch too. "The crowd made a hell of a roar because they saw the pink colours and thought Sweet William was going to get Trawlerman," said John Gosden, who added: "Trawlerman was at his imperious best in the Gold Cup, but today he might not have been totally."

It may not have been as clear cut as Royal Ascot but then again it was over four furlongs shorter. And that's what makes Trawlerman such an absorbing athlete. The further he goes the stronger he becomes, which is exactly why in 2025 he towered over the division where courage conquers all.

Oisin Murphy is given a guard of honour by his weighing-room colleagues on Champions Day at Ascot after becoming British Flat champion jockey for the fifth time
EDWARD WHITAKER (RACINGPOST.COM/PHOTOS)

IN THE PICTURE

Buick reaches elite landmark of 2,000 winners

WILLIAM BUICK reached another milestone in his glittering career in July when he joined an elite group of Flat jockeys to ride 2,000 winners in Britain.

The landmark victory came on El Cordobes for Godolphin and trainer Charlie Appleby in the Group 2 Princess of Wales's Stakes at the Newmarket July meeting. He became the seventh current jockey to reach the 2,000-winner mark in Britain, alongside Frankie Dettori, Joe Fanning, Ryan Moore, Jamie Spencer, Luke Morris and Jim Crowley.

"It means a lot," said Buick, who turned 37 this year. "When you get to 2,000 winners it makes you realise you've been doing this for quite a long time. For it to happen here at the July course, which is my home track, and for it to be for Charlie and Godolphin in the feature race, it couldn't have worked out any better. My family are my biggest supporters, so thank you to them and to all the owners and stable staff who have made this happen. It's a big team effort and we know how much it takes to get horses to the races."

The Norwegian-born rider, who is the son of multiple Scandinavian champion jockey Walter Buick, was British Flat champion in 2022 and 2023. He had his first ride in Britain in 2006 when he was an apprentice for Andrew Balding and had his first winner in September of that year.

He was joint-champion apprentice in 2008 when tying with David Probert and had his first top-level win on the Mick Channon-trained Lahaleeb in the 2009 EP Taylor Stakes in Canada, before he became number one jockey to John Gosden a year later. He had his first Classic success in 2010 aboard the Gosden-trained Arctic Cosmos in the St Leger.

Buick was appointed retained rider to Godolphin in 2015 and has enjoyed a host of memorable successes in the royal blue silks. He had double Classic glory for Godolphin and Appleby this year on Ruling Court and Desert Flower in the 2,000 and 1,000 Guineas, while his sole Derby success came in 2018 on Masar. He has won seven British Classics and the Oaks is the only one missing from his CV.

Appleby said: "Masar winning the Derby is the one that stands out just because of the whole occasion. We're very lucky to have William as part of our team and huge congratulations to him and his family. It's a huge achievement and long may it continue."

Reporting: David Milnes
Picture: Edward Whitaker (racingpost.com/photos)

ICE COLD

Dylan Browne McMonagle landed his first Classic with a supremely confident ride on Al Riffa in the Irish St Leger

COOL and confident. That was how Joseph O'Brien described Dylan Browne McMonagle's winning ride on Al Riffa in the Irish St Leger. He could just as well have been talking about the 22-year-old's rise to the summit of the Irish Flat jockeys' championship in pursuit of a first title.

The final Classic at the Curragh was a distilled version of McMonagle's season. He was nerveless, assured and brilliant. Just as he had been all year. Every move he made had the hallmark of rare quality.

Al Riffa had only recently moved up to the staying trip of a mile and three-quarters, landing the previous month's Curragh Cup by five lengths, but McMonagle rode him with the utmost confidence off a solid pace in the Classic. With 300 yards to run, when many riders might have been tempted

to strike for home on the strong-travelling Al Riffa, the ice-cool youngster took another pull. He knew the right time to strike.

Finally, he urged his willing mount to the front just inside the final furlong. Amiloc, winner of the King Edward VII Stakes at Royal Ascot on his previous start, was quickly passed and reduced from potential winner to toiling runner-up. Al Riffa was four lengths clear at the line, once again showing the extra gear that most stayers lack.

"We knew that the horses who were guaranteed stayers were probably going to try to expose the stamina of some of those that weren't so guaranteed," O'Brien said. "The pace was really strong and Dylan was cool and confident."

★★★★

IT WAS fitting that McMonagle's first Classic triumph should come on Al Riffa, who has carried him to a string of landmark moments. O'Brien's stable star gave him his first Group 1 in the 2022 National Stakes and then his first overseas success at the top level in the 2024 Grosser Preis von Berlin. "He deserved to get his Classic," said the rider after the Irish St Leger. "He's one of my favourites. He's an improving horse and will only get better with age. Stepping up to a mile and six furlongs was always going to be a big help and conditions were perfect."

Before this new-found staying prowess, there was a sense that Al Riffa had not quite lived up to the early promise of his Group 1 win as a juvenile. McMonagle, however, had launched a strong defence of his old pal in a Racing Post interview just before the Irish Champions Festival. "Look at the horses who have beaten him – they're superstars," he said. "The likes of City Of Troy and Rebel's Romance. City Of Troy was horse of the year last year and Rebel's Romance is a worldwide superstar."

'Superstar' might very soon be a tag that is attached to McMonagle, such has been his rapid ascent from pony racing prodigy to Classic-winning rider. The boy from Letterkenny, County Donegal, who rode more than 200 winners in pony racing is now a leading man in the professional ranks. In just six years since his first ride on the Flat, he was fast approaching 400 winners by the time of his Irish St Leger triumph.

"When I start off every year, I want to beat last year's number," he told David Jennings in that Racing Post interview. "Thankfully, I've been doing that every year since I started. Hopefully I can keep on growing and the numbers keep going up and the quality gets better. I just need to keep on improving."

★★★★

O'BRIEN'S Owning stable has been the perfect place for McMonagle's drive towards the top. The stable jockey's admiration for his boss, who is only ten years older, knows no bounds. "He does everything right, the way it should be done," McMonagle said. "He expects 100 per cent from everyone, because he gives 100 per cent himself.

"No stone is ever left unturned. He's the same as me and everyone else in there in that he just wants to see the whole thing getting better all the time. He wants to get the best out of everything – his staff and his horses. Every day you go racing, he expects the best."

Many now expect the best from McMonagle. Invariably he delivers.

Reporting by David Jennings, Conor Fennelly and Nick Pulford

◀Classic combination: Dylan Browne McMonagle celebrates his Irish St Leger triumph on trusted partner Al Riffa

By Lee Mottershead

THE person remains indistinguishable from the persona. As he prepares to call the opening race at Catterick, Derek Thompson is still very much Tommo. The laughter, enthusiasm and catchphrases are there in abundance. He continues to be a workaholic, notoriously careful with money and happy to embrace his reputation for being a real-life homage to Alan Partridge. He is what he has always been, yet although we thought he would never change, he has, if only a little.

With his 75th birthday approaching, Thompson has admitted to himself that he cannot do all he used to do, certainly not to the same standard. Some things are harder than they used to be, which explains why the end of his 60-year commentary career in Britain is now nigh. When he signs off for the final time at Wolverhampton on Tuesday it will also mark the end of Tommo on the telly. The story is not over but important chapters are coming to an end.

Thompson was for 28 years an integral part of Channel 4 Racing, a popular member of an ensemble that continues to inspire affection among those who adored its blend of expertise and lightness. As a BBC Radio employee he became a Grand National commentator at the age of 22, when handing over to Peter Bromley in 1973, the year Red Rum chased down the valiant Crisp. He has worked for Sheikh Mohammed in Dubai and defeated the future King Charles III in a Plumpton charity race while wearing split breeches. He has been the voice of judo and synchronised swimming at the Olympic Games and assumed the unlikely role of negotiator following the IRA's kidnapping of Shergar.

More recently, there have

▸Continues page 194

'It left me in tears and I need to stop – I don't want to be thought of as the old guy who made mistakes'

Legendary presenter Derek Thompson gave this honest and entertaining Racing Post interview in July shortly before his final shift in a British commentary box

BOX

Fire door
Keep shut

been unexpected resurgences of fame thanks to Radio 1 DJ Greg James picking up the line, "Are you well? I thought you were," used by Thompson in a now iconic advertisement for the Crown Hotel, Bawtry, while Graham Norton's BBC1 primetime show ensured millions of people savoured the moment when the At The Races studio-based Thompson handed over to Robert Cooper and "a beautiful lady" at Hereford. "It's a man actually, Derek," replied Cooper, sealing a piece of television gold.

It was a gaffe that has done no harm to Thompson, whose enduring popularity remains evident at Catterick, in whose far from luxurious commentary box he is preparing for the opening race, initially by twiddling a few knobs in an attempt to make contact with the on-course production team.

"Hello guys, it's Tommo upstairs; is there anybody there?" asks Thompson, who then hears a voice through his headphones. "Sean, are you well? I thought you were," he continues. A little later there is a "ho, ho, ho" and an "I love it", which is followed by some banter with stewards' secretary Adie Smith. "Good to see you, Big Fella," replies Thompson, who then runs his eyes down the list of runners for the Pinker's Pond Apprentice Handicap. "Golden Prosperity, Pinjara, Going Underground, John Kirkup," he whispers before declaring: "So, John Kirkup used to be a mate of mine, a long time ago. He used to live just up the road. A nice lad. Was he a vet? I don't know if he's still alive."

★★★★

BACK in 1968 Thompson risked an impromptu meeting with his maker when riding in a Catterick novice chase for his father Stanley, a steel stockholder and permit holder whose five-year-old gelding Grand Corton first collided with a corrugated iron fence behind the start and then galloped into a big, black birch

▸Continues page 196

'He's down to earth and so nice. His great enthusiasm really comes through in his commentary'

Derek Thompson's final stint as a commentator came on a Tuesday night at Wolverhampton

He is signed in as 'Delboy' on the check sheet and as he walks to the weighing room to check the jockeys' colours – "Michael O'Hehir taught me to do that" – it is as though David Jason himself is walking among the racegoers, *writes David Carr.*

Derek Thompson is hugely popular with the public, spreading smiles as he goes and dispensing the odd "big fella" and "Are you well? I thought you were" on his way.

Some big names are here. Derek is particularly chuffed that William Derby has made the three-hour trip down for the evening.

But there is nowhere else the York chief executive would rather be, saying: "I grew up with Tommo in his Channel 4 days. He's part of my childhood."

The feeling is just as heartfelt from the racegoers who stop the man of the hour and ask for autographs.

People like Barbara McKenna from Bridgnorth, who marvels: "He's down to earth and so nice. His great enthusiasm really comes through in his commentary."

Or Chris Bennett from Cannock, who says: "I'm sorry he's going, it's been lovely to see him here over the years."

Our hero has got through plenty of autographs by now, having started the evening signing his way through a pile of racecards so huge that you feel the true value on Antiques Roadshow in 2125 will be a copy he hasn't signed.

He is a thorough professional in these things, smiling perfectly on cue when asked to pose for a photo on a bench proclaiming Arena Racing Company's £1 million bonus – and maintaining that grin even when someone suggests the caption should be "Tommo's taking a pay cut!" He is in his element on his last visits to the commentary box, as he points out that Frankie Dettori – one of hundreds to send good-luck messages through the day – used to stand with him there to watch the races as a young and eager-to-learn apprentice.

There is no last shout of "Photo!" as all his three races have clear-cut winners, two of them ridden by Luke Morris, who says of Tommo: "He's a real credit to the sport and to himself. I grew up with Channel 4 and The Morning Line and he was very much the face of it. I grew up admiring his work and luckily enough he's been around me when I've had some great days. He should be tremendously proud of what he's achieved."

Not too proud to relay some of his early gaffes, including the day he was calling a local point. Tommo recalls: "I was 17 and my brother came to challenge at the last and I shouted, 'Come on Howard!' The stewards weren't pleased."

But, like Delboy, this is someone whose mistakes tended to be laughed off by a public who took him to their hearts.

This is an edited version of an article that appeared in the Racing Post on July 24

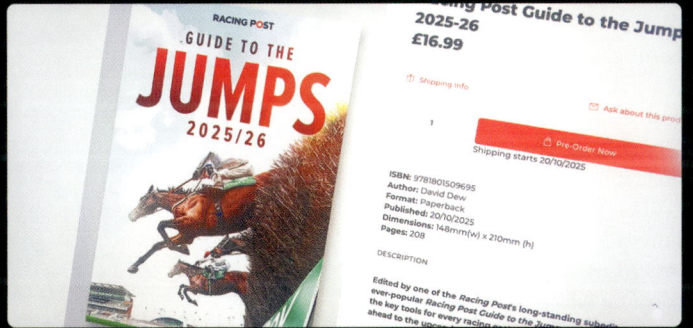

fence. The horse was fine but his jockey was knocked unconscious. Grand Corton may have been suffering from failing eyesight, an affliction that also befell Stanley Thompson when the part-time broadcaster was commentating at the Eyton point-to-point in 1966.

"Halfway through a race he turned off the microphone and told me he couldn't see the horses," recalls Thompson. "He handed me the microphone and I carried on the commentary. I loved it. The first time I did the Grand National my heart was beating so fast I couldn't hold the binoculars. I was 15 when Dad gave me the microphone. That's 60 years ago. I'm so lucky to have done it for so long."

These days he does it aided by Lucozade but no binoculars, instead relying on a piece of paper on which he has drawn the colours of each runner in draw order.

"If you took that away, I couldn't remember any of the horses," admits Thompson. "There are two or three commentators who can get to a 30-runner race, look at the racecard and then call them home. It's incredible. I used to be able to do that but I can't now."

The reality is Thompson has always done the job his own way, turning each commentary into a performance.

"Photo! Wow!" he screams at the end of the second and third races, following each of which he does what he has always done and heads to the weighing room to check that the colours worn by the jockeys resemble those inked on to his aide memoire.

"It was Michael O'Hehir who taught me to come to the weighing room all those years ago when I did the commentary on the 1973 Grand National, the youngest person ever to do it," he says, his mind then heading elsewhere when spotting one of the raceday officials.

"The judge here is the spitting image of the manager at the Wolverhampton Holiday Inn,"

reveals Thompson. "I always say to him, 'Can you book me in next week for my usual room?' It's a joke. Hey, I love it. And, do you know what, the manager of the hotel where I stay in Jersey is the same guy who opened the door for me as a 15-year-old doorman at the hotel in Belfast where we were doing the Shergar story. Incredible."

To be fair, so, too, is Thompson, who will continue seeing the Jersey hotel manager during his regular trips to commentate, host and do a bit of everything – something he has always been very good at doing – on the Channel Island. There will be other ways to earn and keep busy, but not at Catterick, where he receives a congratulatory bottle of champagne after the fourth contest.

Two races later he heads out through the main exit, passing a lady who wishes him a happy retirement. A minute or two after that there are shouts of, "See you, Derek" and "Ta'ra, Derek" from two gentlemen in a minibus who spot Thompson driving out of the car park in a vehicle branded with the words, 'Derek (Tommo)

▲Curtain call: Derek Thompson on his final day as a commentator in Britain at Wolverhampton on July 22

Thompson, Sponsored by Acklam Car Centre'. The great man places his right hand and arm through the driver's window and acknowledges their friendliness.

★★★★

THE next greeting comes from Thompson's wife Caroline, who welcomes him back to their home in Carlton-in-Cleveland. It is a beautiful cottage and one that contains two cats and a surprise, for on a wall behind the sofa are blue neon lights that spell out, "Are you well? I thought you were!" Mrs Tommo, who describes herself as a wife and full-time carer, explains they were a present to her husband. "I wanted it to be as tacky as possible," she stresses as we head out to the garden, where the conversation gradually becomes more serious.

The change of direction kicks in when conversation turns to the subject of health. Thompson named his autobiography Too Busy To Die as a nod to the fact he survived cancer in 2012. There have, thankfully, been no relapses but there was a scare of a different kind four years ago.

▶Continues page 198

Step up your hay game.

The Sanderson Hay Steamer
Fast, Easy, Automatic & Reliable

Using **Pulse Steam Technology™** to provide a hassle-free solution that is controlled with ease.

Steaming: 80%

Discover more

haysteamers.co.uk

Go on, your phone is right there

SANDERSON

"At about 3am I leaned over to Caroline and said, 'Darling, you had better get me to hospital'," recalls Thompson, whose wife responded immediately. Doctors diagnosed a mini-stroke. It was likely not his first.

"The way I saw it, old people suffered from strokes and I was still young, although the truth is I was 70 years of age," says Thompson. "The doctors said there was evidence it had happened before. A few weeks earlier I'd been interviewing someone on the Newmarket gallops when I nearly fell over. That could have been another mini-stroke."

There was a further visit to hospital at the start of this year. Two days after going under general anaesthetic he made the four-hour car journey from North Yorkshire to Ayr. By then, and following encouragement from son James, Thompson had already announced he would be retiring from Britain's commentary boxes at the end of this year. The Ayr bumper on January 6 caused him to bring forward that retirement to midsummer.

Try as he might, Thompson, described by one press-room colleague as looking terrible through the day, was unable to identify the name of clear winner Out Of The Woods until close to the line. It was the sort of experience commentators dread.

"I felt awful about it," says Thompson. "In the end I called the first, second and third right, but I knew I had made a complete hash of it. At the two-furlong marker I thought, 'What's happening?' It should have been a simple race, and I had the colours in front of me, but I was looking down, thinking, 'What is that horse? Who is he?' There were three horses in red but I couldn't work out which one was in front. When something like that happens, you feel fear.

"I made sure I apologised to Lucinda Russell because she had trained the winner but, aside

from that, all I wanted to do was get in the car and drive the four hours back home. I tried to be positive, as I always do, but the social media abuse was awful; it left me in tears. What happened at Ayr made me think hard about stopping sooner than I'd originally planned, without a doubt. It was a hard thing for me to accept but I'd made a mistake in a race that should have been easy."

Devastated for her husband, Caroline Thompson encouraged him to post a message on social media the following day. That proved helpful, as did the intervention of former police superintendent Sean Memory, who made direct contact with some of those who had been most abusive. There is agreement in the garden that there might have been nothing to fire up the vile trolls had Thompson been prepared to fork out for a hotel in Ayr.

"Totally," says Caroline, who points out that although her husband is sometimes guilty of "tightness", he can also be "astonishingly generous". Regrettably, he was unwilling to spend money on himself the night before the fateful bumper.

"It's crazy, I know," he says. "I think about money all the time. I went to a betting shop today to pick up some winnings because I wanted that money in my pocket. I've got to keep on earning. If I do stay in a hotel, I'll go for a bacon sarnie in Greggs rather than pay for something at the hotel."

★★★★

THE honesty is admirable. Interrupted only by the occasional sip from a glass of wine, the frankness keeps on coming.

"I still love commentating, but since Ayr I've found it quite hard and quite worrying," he says. "I've been wondering how many runners I'm going to get in races. I'm all right with nine, ten, 11 or 12, but I would possibly struggle with a 25-runner race. I know I

can still do the job but other people seem to be doing it better. I've always worked hard to try to ensure I stayed up with the leaders; now I'm struggling to stay in touch.

"I need to stop. I don't want to be thought of as the old guy who made mistakes. I want to be thought of as a guy who was pretty good at commentating and retired at the right time. I've commentated on Red Rum and Crisp, Dubai Millennium in the Dubai World Cup and Frankel winning maybe the best maiden ever run. I've been so lucky. I saw those horses and described them. Wow! I'll have that for the rest of my life."

The passion and the pleasure are impossible to hide.

"I don't commentate on the Derby or the King George but that doesn't matter to me," adds Thompson. "I loved doing Catterick today. The reaction I get at the races is amazing. A husband and wife from Canada came up to me and thanked me for everything I had done. They said they had a runner at Catterick a few years ago and that I had been the commentator. They told me they would never forget it. People come up to me and ask for a selfie or an autograph. That's an honour for me."

Almost all those people will have fond recollections of Thompson's marathon innings as a face and voice in their homes. Such was his fame, he was once the subject of a 'Gotcha' set-up by Noel Edmonds on his Saturday night primetime television show. He took that in good humour. He takes practically everything in good humour.

"When I covered judo at the Olympics, I used the immortal phrase, 'He's got him by the lapels!'" says Thompson, breaking into a laugh, of which there were many when he worked for Channel 4, most notably as presenter of The Morning Line.

"It was like playing for the best football team in the world," he

says. "I think you could switch to one of our programmes and even if you had no interest in racing you wouldn't turn us off. The Morning Line was like the comedy programme Friends. We were the original Friends. None of us tried to say we were better than anyone else. We trusted each other."

★★★★

THAT trust has undoubtedly been felt by those producers, directors and editors who have worked with a broadcaster who so often tells us he loves it because he really does.

"You use recognition on the telly to get other work but I suppose I've done enough over the years for people to know who I am," says Thompson, who has no intention of stopping work altogether, particularly as he and his wife now have shares in five horses and own two others outright, including this year's 66-1 Redcar winner Cheerleader.

Perhaps that is another reason why he sounds horrified at the idea of taking time off for an occasional holiday, although the head comes out of the hands when a cruise around the Norwegian fjords is suggested.

"I've got a lot of time for the Norwegians, so I'd like to go back to Norway, but there's no way I could spend time lying on a beach," he reveals. "I've had one holiday in the last ten years because, to me, working in racing is like a holiday. People go to the racecourse for a day out. I'm paid to go for a day out. Aren't I lucky?"

Rest assured, his luck is not about to run out. The work diary might not be as full as it used to be, but Thompson remains on the books of a number of racecourses for raceday presenting, while he also looks after customers of the Racing Breaks travel company. Moreover, he has no plans to stop being the face and voice of racing in Jersey,

▲ Calling time: Derek Thompson at home in Carlton-in-Cleveland; opposite page top to bottom, being interviewed by Sky Sports on his final day of commentating at Wolverhampton; with his wife Caroline; behind the microphone at Catterick and meeting racegoers

where small fields make calling the horses an entirely pleasurable experience. Yet for those who fancy one last British encore of "Photo!", "Who's gonna get there?" or "That's one for the judge", there is just one more opportunity to enjoy a bit of Tommo commentary magic.

"I now realise it's definitely time to call it a day, so I'm looking forward to Wolverhampton," says Thompson. "I never thought I would say I'm looking forward to my final day, but I really am. I've reached the stage where I'm pleased to be hanging up my proverbial binoculars. Now is the right time, without a doubt."

What, then, has he got planned for his last hurrah?

"Tune in and find out," he declares, his face beaming.

We really should. It's the very least the big fella deserves.

This is an edited version of an article that appeared in the Racing Post on July 20

British racing called off for a day in protest over tax

BRITISH racing went on strike on September 10 with all fixtures rescheduled, creating an unprecedented blank day in protest against proposed tax increases.

The action was part of an 'Axe The Racing Tax' campaign in opposition to Treasury plans to replace the existing three-tax structure of online gambling duties with a single remote betting and gaming duty. Modelling by the BHA showed that a rise in the tax rate applied to sports betting from 15 per cent to 21 per cent could result in an annual loss of £66 million in income for British racing.

The four scheduled meetings on September 10 – at Carlisle, Lingfield, Uttoxeter and Kempton – did not take place as a result of agreements involving the BHA and the owners of the four tracks. It was thought to be the first voluntary blackout in British racing's modern history. One report put the loss in income to the sport at about £200,000.

The Racing Post front page went dark to mark the day of protest, carrying a short message on a black background that read: "For the first time ever, racing has voluntarily cancelled all the meetings scheduled for today, in protest at government tax proposals that would be catastrophic for the sport. To understand why this matters – and why racing is important for Britain – read on."

Inside, editor Tom Kerr described the racing industry as "impressive and important – but fragile. It is something that should be protected and nurtured, not just because it is part of our national fabric, but because it is a productive and valuable component of the British economy."

With no action on the tracks, a number of high-profile trainers and jockeys turned out in Westminster to carry racing's message to the heart of government. The protest began with a group of jockeys posing in front of Big Ben, wearing white silks carrying the messages 'axe the racing tax' and 'Back British racing'. Multiple Flat champion jockey Oisin Murphy was among them, along with jumping's retired champion Richard Johnson and the glamour couple of Tom Marquand and Hollie Doyle.

Flat trainer Hugo Palmer made the journey from his Cheshire yard. "I think we're definitely doing the right thing by being here," he said. "Everyone here must have hope. If you don't, you give up."

Warwickshire-based Dan Skelton, Britain's leading jumps trainer, was also there. "Things like this bring people together," he said. "At the end of the day, if government wants to make this decision, we want it to at least be a hard decision to make."

Picture: Edward Whitaker (racingpost.com/photos)

ENDPIECE

Bank holiday crowds flocked to Epsom's stables in National Racehorse Week

'We love all these horses. I could tell you all of their names, all their backstories, and it's nice to be able to show the public how much the horses mean to us'

By James Milton

THE weather in Epsom is Group 1 standard as inquisitive visitors start to arrive at George Baker's magnificent Downs House Stables. Baker, along with fellow Epsom trainers Pat Phelan and Jim Boyle, is welcoming the public into his yard as part of National Racehorse Week. The event is billed as "a nationwide annual celebration of the racehorse" and a sunny bank holiday morning seems the ideal way to kick off the week.

"We're expecting 150 people, so I won't be leading them round like a tour guide," grins Baker, who, on top of his hosting duties, is sending out four runners that day. "I've warned the punters that horses do bite but, other than that, they're free to roam around the place."

There is a similarly no-nonsense approach to health and safety at Ermyn Lodge, where dual-purpose trainer Phelan informs visitors: "There's one stable we've put red tape around –
▶ *Continues page 206*

▲Access all areas: Georgia Dingle, head of PR at Great British Racing, at Downs House Stables in Epsom at the start of National Racehorse Week
▶Visitors to Pat Phelan's Ermyn Lodge Stables, where the attractions include Delilah the Shetland pony and a demonstration by Tom the farrier

that means stay away. She's small but she'll bite you!" Racing fans, of course, are a hardy bunch. The threat of a nip or a chomp won't dissuade them from getting up close and personal with the horses.

Despite the political and financial pressures on the racing industry, there is no sense of siege mentality at the yards of Baker, Phelan and Boyle. Instead, there's a feeling that National Racehorse Week is an opportunity to showcase the sport's deep well of love for the horses in their care. Those horses may not be conscious of the vital PR role they are playing this week but, barring the odd petulant snort and toss of the head, they appear to relish the extra attention.

Every day is a 'Day' of some sort and every week is a 'Week'. As well as being the Epsom leg of National Racehorse Week, this is also National Kiss And Make Up Day, National Banana Split Day and the start of Belgian Beer Week.

It's a little early for a Stella Artois – or, indeed, a banana split – at Downs House but those arriving at 8am are invited to make themselves tea or coffee. Georgia Dingle, head of PR at Great British Racing, is hanging up a banner at the front gates, with a view over the famous racecourse where a seven-race card takes place in the afternoon.

"We've moved National Racehorse Week to the summer holidays for the first time and the interest has been huge," says Dingle. "We have around 14,500 spaces at events and we're almost fully booked at the start of the week." One of the most sought-after tickets is for a tour of Nicky Henderson's Seven Barrows base. And you'll have more chance of getting into Lady Gaga's London gigs than the seven sold-out sessions at Charlie Johnston's Kingsley Park yard.

The big-hearted support of high-profile trainers certainly makes Dingle's task easier. "Everyone's behind it, everyone gets what we're trying to do," she says. "It's such a joy for the team planning the week because whenever we ask people to do something they say yes! Olly Murphy has got 800 people coming on Thursday – his yard kept getting booked up but he just told us to keep adding more spaces."

The switch to the school holidays is designed to attract more young families to the events and it has aligned perfectly with Epsom's racing calendar. As Dingle explains: "Today works brilliantly because Epsom are having their family fun day, so people can look round the yards in the morning and then go racing in the afternoon."

★★★★

AMONG the early birds at Downs House are Liz King, her husband John and their ten-year-old granddaughter Ivy. Liz and John, who live in Wokingham, are regulars at Windsor's summer evening meetings and Ivy gained some exotic riding experience on a beach holiday to Cape Verde. "Usually we just see the horses at the racecourse or on television, so it's lovely to meet them up close," says Liz.

Andrea Oakley and her mother Wendy have spent their lifetimes working in racing but they too are thrilled to get a glimpse behind the scenes at the revamped Downs House. "I used to work in Epsom, so I'm just being nosy really," says Andrea, who also spent time working for Lady Herries in Arundel and now retrains racehorses.

"All of them have different characters and they make us laugh," beams Wendy, adding: "I'm 83 but I'm still riding as often as I can."

Just starting out on his racing journey is three-year-old Rupert, who is enjoying the view from his father James Secker's shoulders. "We live locally and often walk past here, so it's nice to have a look inside," says Secker. He comes from a family of racing fans and Rupert, who has a Shetland pony called Pablo at home, may soon be in the market for a bit more horsepower. "He nibbled my knee!" he cries delightedly, pointing at one of the horses.

▸ Continues page 208

'There's nothing quite like this in any other sport'

By David Carr

RACING took over the centre of Chester in National Racehorse Week when the public had the chance to meet two retired racehorses.

Great British Racing brought its 'urban racing yard' to Northgate Street in the heart of the city with TV stars and racing enthusiasts Chris Hughes, who is a National Racehorse Week ambassador, Sam Quek and Rachel Lugo (from The Real Housewives of Cheshire).

Jockey Lilly Pinchin was on hand to give riding tips as people rode a mechanical horse while wearing a virtual reality headset.

Passers-by could also watch farrier and physio demonstrations, with the chance to ask the experts about caring for racehorses and see jockey demonstrations.

Hughes, who is an owner, said: "I have loved being part of the event in Chester. Getting to experience these magical horses up close cannot be underestimated and to be able to share that with so many people is so rewarding.

"It's been brilliant to be able to show people just how much care goes into looking after racehorses. Everyone working in the sport is passionate about providing the best possible care we can to the horses we all adore and I'm really proud of the fact that so many members of the public have been able to see that.

"There's nothing quite like this in any other sport. It's fantastic that the events during the week are free to attend with everyone welcome to join. You don't get the opportunity to go behind the scenes like this in other sports."

Quek said: "It was fantastic to be able to share my love for horses and the sport with so many families. Thoroughbreds are amazing, empathetic animals and to be able to have them here in Chester and give the public the chance to meet them up close has been wonderful."

This is an edited version of an article that appeared on the Racing Post website on August 27

Another Shetland pony, named Delilah, is delighting the crowd at Phelan's yard, although her arrival for a grooming session provokes some growls of displeasure from the thoroughbreds accustomed to taking centre stage.

Delilah is soon surrounded by young admirers. "Keep away from the back end, Ronaldinho!" Phelan advises a boy in a Brazil football shirt. Another mischievous member of the Ermyn Lodge team tells a kid: "Ask Mum and Dad to buy you one – they're not that expensive . . ."

Phelan discusses Epsom's decline as a training centre from the glory days of Geoff Lewis, Reg Akehurst and Terry Mills, citing the property prices in Surrey compared with Newmarket as the main factor.

He breaks off to answer a question from a visitor – "What does it mean if the horses are nodding their heads?" "They're just a bit anxious, that's all."

To a certain extent, the organisers of National Racehorse Week are bound to be preaching to the choir. However, not everybody is a seasoned racing fan or industry professional. Kevin Sze is originally from Hong Kong but now lives near Epsom. "I didn't go racing at Happy Valley or Sha Tin because I'm not a gambler," he says. "But this is a nice thing to do on a bank holiday."

Has he stroked the

▶ Jim Boyle: "Days like this are really important"

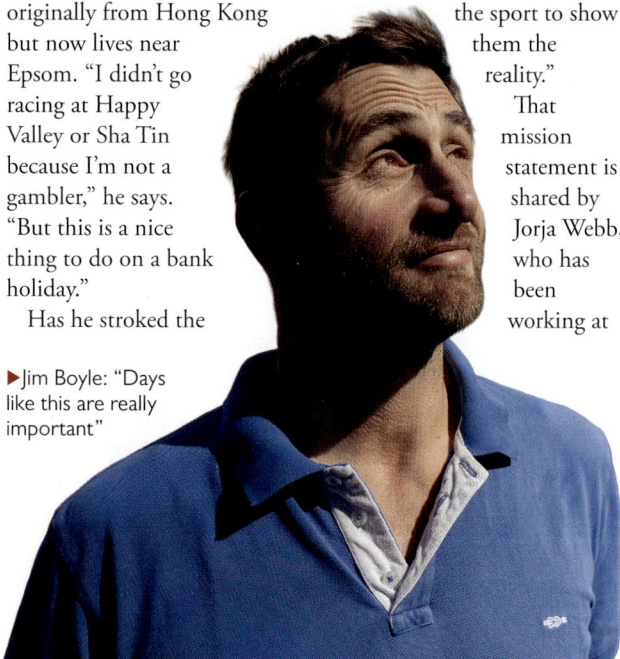

horses? "Yes," Sze says, motioning gently with his hand. Still got all his fingers? "Yes, they're all still there!"

Dingle emphasises that the remit of National Racehorse Week goes beyond traditional training yards, studs and aftercare centres. "We also have 55 community events including one in Chester where we're setting up a mini-racing stable in the city centre," she says. "It's great to take horses to urban areas where people may not have seen or touched a racehorse. We've got a lovely group of racehorses, some retired and some still active, and we take them to meet community groups and youth groups. The horses love it – they're just like big Labradors!"

★★★★

DEMYSTIFYING the sport for newcomers is one important objective of the week. Recalling the early days of her husband George's training career, Candida Baker says: "I grew up with horses but I'm not from a racing background and I found that people could be a bit snooty. I always say that there's no such thing as a stupid question about racing. If someone thinks it's cruel, it's our duty to the sport to show them the reality."

That mission statement is shared by Jorja Webb, who has been working at

Phelan's yard for two years in her first job in racing. She wears a long pair of socks bearing the words 'Totally Knackered' and admits: "It's a very busy day for us staff but I love talking to people about what we do here.

"We want to show them that racing isn't a cruel game. We love all these horses. I could tell you all of their names, all their backstories, and it's nice to be able to show the public how much the horses mean to us."

At 10am at Ermyn Lodge there is a demonstration by Tom the farrier, who fits new shoes on a good-natured filly as Phelan provides a running commentary. "It's amazing that we can go to the moon but we're still nailing shoes to horses' feet in this day and age," the trainer muses. "It's still the most secure way to do it and if you don't have four feet, you've got nothing."

While Phelan delivers this stark verdict to a rapt audience, two members of his staff are checking on one of their more bashful charges: "Charlie's hiding!" "Oh, why? Darling, what's wrong?" Their affection for this shy chap is impossible to feign.

Children arriving at the week's events are offered a 'Learning Pack for Young Curious Minds' but it's an educational experience for those of all ages. At Phelan's yard we learn that rubbing a potato on a horse's cheek will clear up any warts. And, according to one of the 'Did You Know?' cards stuck on the wall at Jim Boyle's South Hatch Stables, horses have the largest eyes of any land animal.

Each box at Boyle's yard is also decorated with a pen portrait of its resident, including their name, age, nickname, groom and an irreverent profile. Buy The Dip (Dippy) and Irezumi (Zumi) are notorious for parting company with their work-

riders ("Such fun!"). Son Of Man (Sunny) confesses that "I love snacks" and "my mum says I can be a proper pain to ride sometimes".

★★★★

BOYLE is receiving almost as much attention as his puckish horses. He patiently debates the handicapping system with one man, poses for a selfie with another, and is shown sepia photographs of the South Hatch site from the 1970s, when it was briefly used as a riding school. A couple who have lived in Epsom for 35 years congratulate him on the development of this slick, modern yard which is taking shape before our eyes.

"Just wait for this lorry," a staff member in the car park instructs us, adding ruefully: "It's delivering 11 new stables – a day earlier than expected . . ."

The locals are clearly grateful for Boyle's commitment to maintaining Epsom's training traditions. Like Baker and Phelan, he appreciates the heritage and history of the town while keeping a keen eye on the future. "Our old yard was horrendous," he grimaces. "Especially in January when it was cold and wet and the horses were sick but now I'm happy to come to work. It's only taken 18 years of blood, sweat and tears!"

Boyle is aware of the impact that National Racehorse Week can have on the sport. "Days like this are really important because they help us engage with the local community, which we haven't always done as well as we should," he says.

And when it comes to community engagement, there are fewer better ambassadors than a racehorse – preferably one with four securely shod feet, two large eyes and bags of character. Warts and all.

This is an edited version of an article that appeared in the Racing Post on August 28